RSPB

GARDEN BIRDS

giving
nature
a home

RSPB
GARDEN
BIRDS

Marianne Taylor

BLOOMSBURY WILDLIFE
LONDON · OXFORD · NEW YORK · NEW DELHI · SYDNEY

BLOOMSBURY WILDLIFE
Bloomsbury Publishing Plc
50 Bedford Square, London, WC1B 3DP, UK
29 Earlsfort Terrace, Dublin 2, Ireland

BLOOMSBURY, BLOOMSBURY WILDLIFE and the Diana logo are trademarks of
Bloomsbury Publishing Plc

First published in Great Britain 2019

A catalogue record for this book is available from the British Library

Library of Congress Cataloguing-in-Publication data has been applied for

ISBN: HB: 978-1-4729-5591-3; ePDF: 978-1-4729-5592-0; ePub: 978-1-4729-5590-6

2 4 6 8 10 9 7 5 3

Design by Lee-May Lim
Printed and bound in Great Britain by Bell and Bain Ltd, Glasgow

To find out more about our authors and books visit www.bloomsbury.com and sign up for our newsletters

Published under licence from RSPB Sales Limited to raise awareness of the RSPB (charity registration in England
and Wales no 207076 and Scotland no SC037654).

For all licensed products sold by Bloomsbury Publishing Limited, Bloomsbury Publishing Limited will donate a
minimum of 2% from all sales to RSPB Sales Ltd, which gives all its distributable profits through Gift Aid
to the RSPB.

Contents

Introduction

Nature is in trouble around the world, including right here in the UK. You only need to check the newspapers or the TV, and a scientist or a celebrity with wildlife-related credentials will be telling you as much. Once in a while, we'll have a good-news story of a species fighting back from the edge of extinction with the help of committed conservationists, but those are spotlights in a darkening landscape that is losing its wildlife and wild spaces hand over fist.

Do you believe it, though, if you glance up from the newspaper or screen, to look out on a garden loud and vibrant with birdlife? Where Goldfinches and Blue Tits decorate the branches of the acer on which your bird feeders hang? Where Blackbirds uproot worms from a vivid green lawn and a Pied Wagtail struts along the shore of your pond, while Robins ferociously chase other Robins away over the wall to next door's garden? Where a dazzling Great Spotted Woodpecker taps away at a low bough of the Apple tree at the back of the garden, or House Martins dip and turn as they zoom into the row of mud nests cemented neatly under the eaves of your house?

It's hard to take on board the sorry state of our natural world if you're lucky enough to have a garden in which birds are thriving. Few sights give more of a joyous impression of natural abundance than a set of bird feeders attended by an endless pageant of beautiful wild birds, all furiously active on a cold-weather day as they gather for the easy pickings on offer. The householder can enjoy the spectacle and feel glad for being able to help these birds survive the rigours of winter, so that they can bring forth a healthy new generation when spring arrives. Watching garden birds is good for the soul – their energy and beauty foster a positivity that inspires us on every level. For those living in towns and cities, garden birds allow a dose of life-enhancing nature to filter through the concrete and brighten every day, and for country dwellers, they provide an immediate connection with the wider and wilder world beyond the fence.

THE VALUE OF GARDENS

Gardens and their wildlife are much more than just a pleasant diversion for humankind. A useful tool for looking at how much wildlife loss has occurred is the Biodiversity Intactness Index. This measure was developed in around 2005 by a team of environmental researchers, to quantify species loss in modern times. The UK's score of 81 per cent biodiversity intactness in the index is a dismally low figure, which is below the global average of 85 per cent, and also below that recorded for 189 other countries around the world. Our natural, wild places are being lost to farmland and to development, and species are lost along with their habitats. The issues surrounding this are linked to politics and to economics. They are complex, not to say daunting. It is in our gardens, though, that we ordinary people can take control, exert our influence and make a difference.

In 1985, the European Commission initiated the Coordination of Information on the Environment (CORINE) to look in detail at land use in the UK, and this has been updated ever since. Today, the data from the Corine Land Cover Inventory is available online and it makes for interesting, if rather depressing, reading. Of the available land in the UK, 56.7 per cent is used for farming of one kind or another. We have built houses and other buildings, as well as roads, on 5.9 per cent of the available land, so just 34.9 per cent of land is in a reasonably natural state (though most of this land is also modified or managed to some extent). That leaves 2.5 per cent, which is described, intriguingly, as 'green urban'.

The Goldfinch population has increased considerably in the UK over the last few decades, in part because of garden bird feeding.

The breakdown by country within the UK reveals a stark difference between England (72.9 per cent farmland, 14.5 per cent natural, 8.8 per cent built on and 3.8 per cent green urban) and Scotland (26.4 per cent farmland, 70.7 per cent natural, 2.1 per cent built on and 0.9 per cent green urban). Northern Ireland's stats are pretty close to those for England, while those for Wales correspond fairly closely to the national average.

So, what is 'green urban'? It is the smallest category for every country but it still makes up a significant amount of land cover – 6,062km² in the UK overall, and 4,950km² in England. It includes parks, sports fields and the like, but more than two-thirds of it is made up of private gardens. Added together, our individual patches of outdoor space comprise an estimated 4,330km² and every single garden has the potential to support plenty of wildlife – or almost none – depending on what we choose to do with it. If we reflect that our gardens would once have been woodland or meadow, long ago, then surely we can rise to the challenge to make them a genuinely valuable wildlife habitat in their own right.

Birds are the most visible indicator of whether a garden is a good place for wildlife. However, they need more than just well-stocked bird feeders to settle down and raise their families in a garden environment. Understanding that birds are just part of a much wider and more complex web of life is key to making yours a better garden for them, and to help make the UK's tapestry of gardens a functional and joined-up ecosystem that supports and encourages as much wildlife as possible.

WHAT MAKES A BIRD A GARDEN BIRD?

There are some 300 bird species that breed or overwinter in the UK or migrate through every year – some are very common, others much less so. If we add on all scarce and rare visitors that have been recorded here at least once, the list grows to more than 600. A very high proportion of these birds have been observed, at one time or another, in people's gardens – even the most extreme rarities. However, some gardens are really exceptional in their location, their make-up, their function, or all three, so will always attract an eclectic and unusual assemblage of birds. Leaving all the random oddities aside, there are only a few dozen species that regularly visit gardens of all sizes, but they are a pretty mixed bunch.

Starlings have been declining in the UK since the mid-1980s, and their numbers are also falling in mainland Europe.

SPECIAL GUESTS

Very rare birds could potentially show up in any garden, including yours. Those most likely to turn up are songbirds, which may be attracted to flocks of other birds that are clearly coming to a food source – many rare thrushes, buntings and finches have been found in private gardens, feeding alongside our own familiar thrushes, buntings and finches. If you find a 'rare' and have confidently identified it (with or without help from other birdwatchers), you should inform your county bird recorder, but it is up to you whether or not to 'put out the news' more widely. Many birders will travel some distance to see a rare bird, and you may not fancy the idea of hundreds of them peering over your garden wall. However, some householders have made the best of such situations by allowing access in exchange for a donation to a charity such as the RSPB.

Sometimes a bird shows up in the garden that you cannot find in a field guide at all. Such oddities could be 'mega-rarities' that aren't covered by your book, but there are two other possibilities. The first is that it is a common and familiar bird species with unusual plumage. Birds can have genetic quirks that make their plumage paler than usual or white-patched (leucistic) or darker (melanistic). Watch the bird carefully – its shape and behaviour can help you identify the species even if its colours are all wrong.

The other possibility is you have a caged bird that has escaped. Canaries, which are not necessarily yellow but can be green, red, grey or white, are common escapees, as are various exotic finches and parrots, quails, doves, pheasants and fancy breeds of domestic pigeons. If possible, catch the bird and pass it to the RSPCA or other rescue charity, as most domestic escapees are unlikely to survive well in the wild (the fully established Ring-necked Parakeet *Psittacula krameri* is a notable exception).

Most of what we think of as classic garden birds are, by their evolutionary history, adapted to live in woodlands – particularly deciduous woodlands, with some open areas and scrubland. You will still find them in woodlands like this today – and quite commonly – but they are adaptable enough that they can live in the garden environment too. They also tend to be the species with adaptability built into their feeding behaviour. Many are insect-eaters in spring and summer, then switch to a vegetarian diet of berries and seeds in winter. Their methods for finding food are varied, so they have the natural curiosity and experimental flair needed to work out how to access a bird feeder.

The RSPB's Big Garden Birdwatch collates bird sightings from thousands of households recorded during one hour of garden-watching. The participants choose which hour, but all the counts are done during three days in January. In 2019, 472,758 participants logged a total of 7,669,138 birds, of 80 species, but the top 10 remain almost unchanged from previous years. From the top, they are House Sparrow, Starling, Blue Tit, Blackbird, Woodpigeon, Goldfinch, Great Tit, Robin, Chaffinch and Magpie. All can be regarded as true woodland birds except the top two, which have, over millennia, become associated with humankind; they live alongside us, make use of our resources, clean up the food we waste, nest in our homes and are, in short, associated more with people and houses than with trees and woods. The next 30 species include many related to the top 10 birds – other types of tits, finches, thrushes, crows and pigeons – as well as gulls and a handful of waterbirds.

For birdwatchers keen on keeping lists, there is a perennial dilemma about what 'counts' as a bird seen. For the real purists, only birds that land in your garden (or land in or on a tree or other plant that's growing there) can be ticked off on your garden list. More relaxed birdwatchers will also count 'flyovers', so each and every bird seen from your garden counts as seen, even if a bird is just passing over and would not, for any reason, ever land. This accounts for the vast garden lists assembled by some birdwatchers who live on the coast and can tick off various seabirds without leaving their patio – birders on

Garden bird feeding is of most benefit to woodland birds like the Blue Tit.

particularly exposed east-facing stretches of coastline may also record an array of scarce and rare birds dropping into their gardens during migration season.

The Big Garden Birdwatch's rules insist only birds that land in the garden can be counted, and so its results focus on species that depend, to at least some extent, on gardens as foraging habitat. This means some pretty common urban-dwelling birds, such as gulls, are recorded less regularly than you might expect. It also means that one particular trio of birds strongly associated with houses and towns go entirely unrecorded by the Big Garden Birdwatch – they are the Swallow, House Martin and Swift (see Aerial feeders, pages 192–205). These three birds, specialists at catching insects on the wing, are far more likely to fly over a garden than make landfall in it – and they are also absent in January, being long-distance migrants that spend the winter in Africa.

When bad weather strikes, gardens can offer a refuge and feeding opportunities for bird species that, in normal circumstances, would not ever need to leave their usual habitats. Snow and ice bring open-country species like Skylarks and Meadow Pipits, Snipes *Gallinago gallinago* and Woodcocks into rural and even suburban gardens, while in a heatwave you might observe birds of the wider countryside, such as warblers, coming to drink from a topped-up garden pond.

HOW TO MAKE THE PERFECT BIRD AND NATURE GARDEN

The principal thing that will attract birds to your garden is food. Birds are highly mobile and (in winter particularly) many species will roam a fair distance through the day in their search for sustenance. Put out food consistently and your garden will soon be mapped as part of the daily 'rounds' of bird flocks that forage in your local area. The market for different kinds of bird food and ways to dispense it is large and thriving, and we look at this below.

Putting out bird food, however, is not necessarily going to encourage birds to linger or to nest in your garden. It's the equivalent of having a garden full of nectar-rich exotic flowers to attract butterflies. Some of the more nomadic-natured butterflies may well visit, but if they can't find the native plant on which they lay their eggs, they will not stay, and other kinds of butterflies probably won't turn up at all.

So, in addition to food, you need to meet the birds' other needs if you would like them to stick around longer and perhaps to nest in your garden or nearby. They will require a source of fresh water for drinking and bathing; somewhere safe to rest, to sleep and to take cover from predators; and places to forage for natural food (very few birds can survive just on the food we offer them, and arguably we shouldn't encourage them to do so anyway). Offer all of this, along with good nest sites, and at least some birds are likely to nest in your garden.

Bird foods and feeders

Feeding garden birds is most important in winter and early spring, when natural food is at its scarcest. Their struggle at this time is fuelling their rapid metabolism enough to keep warm, so high calories are needed. Fats provide calories in the most efficient way possible – many small birds would naturally eat mostly high-fat seeds through winter, but fats of animal origin can be useful too.

Commercial bird foods

Sunflower seeds and **peanuts** are classic high-fat bird foods. The former are available with or without their husks – not all birds can de-husk them, so the shelled seeds (sunflower hearts) are more attractive. If you are offering intact sunflower seeds, you'll find the ones with black husks are more popular than the striped ones, as their kernels have a higher fat content. Peanuts should not be offered whole in the breeding season as they can choke chicks.

Nyjer seeds are sometimes marketed as the 'Goldfinch magnet'. These tiny black seeds (you'll need a special feeder as they will spill out of ordinary ones) are high in oils and are popular with thinner-billed finches like Goldfinches and Siskins. However, some people find their Goldfinches prefer sunflower hearts and the nyjer seed goes uneaten.

Mixed birdseed can be a bit of a mixed bag. Some mixes contain a high proportion of wheat, which most small birds will not eat (House Sparrows are an exception) – pigeons and gamebirds will take these feeds, though. A better mix for all-round feeding will contain small seeds like millet and

nyjer, as well as crushed peanuts, pinhead oatmeal and sunflower seeds. Some mixes are marketed as 'no mess', meaning all the ingredients are free of husks and other inedible bits, while others are 'no grow', meaning there is nothing in them that will germinate if they fall or are placed directly on the ground.

Suet-based bird foods are extremely popular and successful, and come in various shapes and sizes. **Suet pellets** are little sausages of slightly crumbly suet, sometimes mixed with other ingredients such as dried fruit or dried mealworms. They can be placed in the same sort of mesh feeders you would use for peanuts. Other suet-based foods include **fat balls** and **suet cakes**, both of which are also typically combined with other ingredients such as crushed peanuts and small-grade birdseed. They can be offered whole or crumbled, or placed in suitable feeders. These foods are very high in fat and appeal to almost all garden birds, sometimes even attracting species that don't usually visit feeders, such as Goldcrests. *A word of warning – commercial fat balls are sometimes packaged in plastic mesh bags. These should be removed before you put the fat balls out, as birds can get their toes and tongues tangled in the mesh.*

Mealworms are the larvae of a type of beetle. They can be reared in captivity, and are of a suitable size and softness for many birds. They are very appealing to a large number of species, especially the insectivores – many a garden Robin has been lured onto a human hand with the bribe of a palmful of wriggling mealworms. You can buy mealworms dead and dried (and then rehydrate them), and also alive, in various sizes. If you buy live mealworms, you can begin to propagate your own at home, though this is not particularly easy (see box, page 13). When feeding live mealworms, discard any that are dead or discoloured. **Waxworms** are also available commercially as live bird food. Note that maggots are not suitable for garden birds.

With hollow trees and other natural crevices hard to find, most Barn Owls in Britain nest in old buildings.

REAR YOUR OWN MEALWORMS

Here is the RSPB's advice on setting up your own live mealworm production line at home.

Prepare a large tin, plastic container or glass fish tank as follows.

1. Punch small holes in the lid for ventilation.
2. Place a layer of old hessian sacking in the bottom and sprinkle this fairly thickly with bran.
3. Add a slice or two of bread and raw potato, followed by another two layers of sacking/bran/bread/potato, like a three-decker sandwich. Adding a raw cabbage leaf on top will provide extra food and help prevent the mealworms from dehydrating.
4. Place the container in a safe place at room temperature, not in hot sun.
5. Introduce 200–300 live mealworms into the prepared container.
6. After a few weeks the mealworms will turn into creamy-coloured pupae, then into little black beetles.
7. The beetles will lay eggs, which hatch into mealworms and so on. Take out some mealworms as necessary to manage the colony size to your requirements. Replace the bread, potato and cabbage as necessary.
8. If you want to start new colonies, prepare another container and transfer some bits of dry bread (these will carry beetle eggs) from the flourishing colony.

Home-made bird foods

It is very easy to make foods at home that will appeal to garden birds, and doing so can save you a lot of money if you have many hungry bills to feed. Base your home-made recipes around fat, and follow a few common-sense rules to ensure what you offer will be good for them.

Home-made fat balls and **suet cakes** are simple to make. You can buy packets of suet in pellet form – and this is perfectly good to offer to the birds as it is. To make fat balls, melt the suet and mix it with dry ingredients. The ratio can be up to 1:2 (one part suet, two parts dry ingredients). Too much weight of dry ingredients will mean your mixture doesn't hold together well, but you can just re-melt it and add more fat. The dry ingredients can include ground peanuts, pinhead oatmeal, small mixed seeds, grated Cheddar cheese and dried fruits. Do not use dried vine fruits (such as raisins, currants and sultanas) in areas that dogs and cats can access, as dried fruits can be very harmful to them if eaten. The mix can then be pressed into moulds of whatever kind you like, or into the empty shell of a coconut threaded onto a string for hanging. Or you can allow it to cool and firm up, and then shape it into balls.

A very useful standby that costs pennies is **home-made bird pastry**. For this, combine one part lard (by weight) with two parts plain flour. Mix well, bind it all together with a little water, and you'll end up with a pastry dough that is easy to shape into balls and sausages for feeders; you can also just smear handfuls of it into a tree branch fork. As with the fat balls above, you can add additional dry ingredients such as grated cheese, crushed dried mealworms or dried fruit if you wish.

Some **household scraps** and various foods you may have in the cupboard or fridge can be offered almost as they are – this can be useful if you run out of regular bird food. They include bacon rind (chopped up small), grated cheese, soaked dog or cat biscuits, raisins and other dried fruit, cut-up apples and pears, and cooked rice.

Foods to avoid

Don't put out the following things for birds to eat:

- Bread, as it lacks nutritional value and may swell in birds' stomachs. Granary bread soaked in water is not too bad but there are better options.
- Uncooked rice, wheat and other grains – most birds cannot digest these foods and will avoid them.
- Any food with added salt – most birds cannot easily filter out any excessive salt they consume.

Suet cakes like this are easy to make, and are life-savers for small birds such as tits in cold weather.

SQUIRREL TROUBLE

When we feed the birds, we often soon find we are also feeding the squirrels. Across most of the UK, the Grey Squirrel *Sciurus carolinensis* is very common and a regular garden visitor. It is clever and agile, and if there is any way it can get at a bird feeder or bird table, it will quickly learn to do so, whether this involves a huge leap from the ground, a shimmy along a washing line or scaling a vertical pole. Those lucky enough to live in areas where Red Squirrels *S. vulgaris* occur will find that these lovely mammals are no less skilled at getting to even the most hard-to-reach bird feeders.

Some feeders are marketed as squirrel-proof, though not all are. A sturdy cage structure around the feeders should keep out adult squirrels, but a small young squirrel could get through or, much worse, get stuck while trying. The RSPB's Squirrel Buster feeder works very well, with a clever solution to the problem: 'An adjustable weight-activated mechanism inside this ingenious high-quality feeder instantly closes the feeding ports when "someone" too heavy arrives'.

Alternatively, you could decide to use distraction rather than cunning, and purchase a special feeder just for the squirrels. These are typically box-shaped, resembling a bird nest box but with a bottom shelf on which the squirrel

sits, and a hinged lid allowing the squirrel to access the peanuts or whatever other food you've placed inside.

Brown Rats *Rattus norvegicus* are also sometimes problematic in the garden. If you keep food off the ground you should escape their attentions. They are quite capable climbers and may be able to scramble up to a pole-mounted bird table, but hanging feeders usually defeat them. Other small rodents like Wood Mice *Apodemus sylvaticus* and Bank Voles *Myodes glareolus* may also manage to access some feeders, though most people are so enchanted by these appealing little rodents that they don't feel the need to take any steps to discourage them.

- Any kind of oil or soft fat (such as cooking juices from a roast) – this can get onto birds' plumage and will destroy its waterproofing capabilities. Melted hard fat (with no added salt) can be given once you've put it in a mould (perhaps with dry ingredients) and allowed it to set firm.

Feeder types

The classic bird feeder is a tube with a closed dome-shaped top, a closed or mesh bottom, and open sides (either mesh, or solid metal or plastic with openings through which birds can get at the food). Feeders designed for tiny food items such as nyjer seed usually have solid sides with tiny openings, while those intended to hold fat balls have an open cage-like shape. Others are designed to hold peanuts or sunflower seeds and have a fine mesh, or they have solid plastic sides with a series of half-roofed round holes or ports, through which birds can poke their heads. They come in a wide range of sizes, with a loop at the top for hanging, and they may or may not have some perches (but almost all birds manage well without perches). Feeders made especially for bird cakes are oblong rather than tubular, and various other, more fancy designs are available. Some work very well, others not at all.

Bird tables offer a flat surface on which you can place all kinds of foods. They are usually made of wood, and either come on a stand or have a hanging hook. Most have a peaked roof to keep rain off the food and drainage holes on the table itself in case rain gets on there anyway. Some come with

hooks underneath to hang tubular feeders on. Some have a cage that fits over or around the feeding surface, to keep out larger birds and also squirrels. And some are for ground-feeding birds.

Setting up a feeder or a whole feeding station takes a little thought. Many feeders go ignored because their position is too exposed. While small birds like to see all around so they can spot danger coming, they also need some cover into which they can dive if a Sparrowhawk appears. So ideally your feeding station will be next to some kind of quite dense shrubbery, but with an open view on the other sides. Try to think like a small bird and avoid placing your feeder close to a wall, hedge or other longitudinal feature, which a hunting Sparrowhawk could use to hide behind as it picks up speed on its approach flight. Sparrowhawks are among our most spectacular garden birds and, although they prey on smaller species, they will occur in an ecosystem only with a healthy population of smaller birds to support them. So, their presence is a very good sign that your local wildlife is doing well.

Sometimes, feeding stations very near the house aren't successful at first as birds are wary, but they will usually become more confident over time. Keep in mind, though, that birds are not good at coping with windows – if your window reflects trees and sky, they will try to fly through them, with painful and sometimes deadly consequences. If you are having problems with window-strikes, there are various ways to prevent this. The RSPB recommends stick-on bird silhouettes fixed to the glass. It also suggests you try vertical blinds which can be angled so that you can observe your garden while reducing dramatically the appearance of the windows as a flight path.

Water

Birds need fresh water to drink, and also to bathe in. The water has to be reasonably clean and accessible from dry land – for bathing, the bird must be able to stand safely in it belly-deep. These rules don't apply to Swifts, Swallows and House Martins, which can drink and bathe in flight by skimming low over water and sipping from the surface, or very briefly splashing in for a high-speed on-the-wing bath – if you have a swimming pool or a very big pond, you may see them doing exactly that.

For our less agile birds, shallow water in a pond or container with gently sloping sides is needed. There are plenty of suitable bird baths on the market, or you can make your own with an inverted dustbin lid or similar shallow, watertight and dish-shaped object. If it is possible to elevate the bath, so much the better – birds are aware they are vulnerable when bathing in particular, and will

Fresh water for drinking and bathing is important and also makes for some amusing scenes, like this Robin enjoying a splash.

A SHORT HISTORY OF GARDEN BIRD FEEDING

In the UK, gardens of one kind or another have been around for millennia, ever since we began to have permanent homes and to keep livestock and grow produce. They were mostly practical through medieval times and into the Tudor, Elizabethan and Stuart years, though larger parks increasingly had formal, ornamental elements. Later on, through Georgian and Victorian times, private gardens became highly ornamental and new, exotic plants arrived – also non-native animals, which needed to be fed. There is no doubt that some wild birds would have taken advantage of all the new opportunities this provided.

In 1890/91, an unusually cold winter gripped the UK, and newspapers ran stories encouraging people to put out scraps for the birds. People enjoyed seeing birds at closer quarters and the feel-good factor of helping them to survive the winter. By 1910, feeding garden birds was reported to be a popular hobby. Gradually, people began to buy and prepare food especially for birds rather than putting out kitchen scraps, and by the 1970s you could buy a variety of bird tables and feeders, as well as bags of peanuts and birdseed marketed as specifically for garden birds.

As more people began to feed birds, so the number and variety of birds coming to exploit the bounty grew. Peanuts attracted Siskins as regular visitors to UK gardens while visiting Blue and Great Tits learned how to peck through the foil tops of milk bottles to drink the cream. Towards the end of the 20th century, Blackcaps from eastern Europe began to overwinter in the UK rather than Iberia and North Africa, a novel behaviour made possible by widespread garden bird feeding. By the turn of the century, there was a healthy and fast-growing market for all manner of garden bird food and feeders, and also for nest boxes. In a 2012 survey, about 64 per cent of UK households reported feeding garden birds at least some of the time. Today, the RSPB is spearheading a movement to encourage people to give nature a home in their garden, highlighting the importance of green spaces for wildlife.

appreciate being out of reach of wandering cats. If not, place the bath somewhere with a good all-round field of view but close to some kind of cover. You can use stones to create a more varied sloping 'shoreline', so birds of all sizes can find a spot where the water is the right depth for them to bathe.

If space permits, a pond is just about the best thing you can add to your garden to improve its attractiveness to wildlife, including birds. Its waters will encourage a whole new range of insects with aquatic larval life stages – they form the foundation of a thriving underwater ecosystem, and when the winged adults emerge, non-aquatic birds eat them. Native water-loving plants attract even more insects, and if your pond is fish-free it should attract frogs, toads or newts (or perhaps all three), all of which can be food for various wild birds as well as delightful to observe in their own right. And, of course, a pond is a permanent source of drinking and bathing water for birds, provided its shores are accessible and slope gently at least in places, or the pond has some very shallow parts. Bigger is better with ponds, but even the smallest permanent pool delivers lots of benefits for birds and other wildlife. The RSPB offers advice on building garden ponds large and small (see Further reading, page 220).

Plants for a wildlife garden

When deciding which plants to grow in a wildlife garden, you should aim for a good variety of species, and most should be native to the UK. Native plants are important because they have, over many millennia, co-evolved with our native insects. Many common native plants are vital food for a number of insect species – the Stinging Nettle *Urtica dioica*, for example, supports more than 40 species of insects, while for oak trees it's nearly 300. However, there are some native plants that have evolved a strong resistance to foliage-eating insects, and there are also non-native plants that provide an excellent source of nectar for bees, butterflies, moths, hoverflies and the like. Some popular non-native garden plants are native to Europe and are utilised by insect species that also occur here. So, there is room in a wildlife garden for well-chosen non-native plants too.

Most of our small birds eat insects – so if you want plenty of birds in the garden you need plenty of insects, and for the insects you need native plants, of as wide a variety as you can manage. In some cases the birds will be eating the plant too – or more likely its seeds or fruit – so plants with edible seeds or fruit are also good to have in the garden. Plants are also important from a structural point of view, offering shelter in which birds can rest, hide and nest.

How you plan out your garden plants depends on many factors, including size, shape, slope, orientation, soil type, personal taste and budget, but here are a few ideas to keep in mind.

Trees are very useful in any wildlife garden. If you have trees already, hang on to them if possible, especially if any are native species. If you'd like to plant a tree but have limited space, something like a Rowan *Sorbus aucuparia*, Holly *Ilex aquifolium* or Crab-apple *Malvus sylvestris* tree would fit the bill – these all produce fruits that birds will appreciate.

Bushes and shrubs provide shelter and nesting sites for birds like Blackbirds and Robins. Many kinds also produce flowers that are valuable nectar sources, and later on a crop of berries that will help sustain thrushes and Blackcaps through winter. As always, native species are best – consider Hawthorn *Crataegus monogyna*, Spindle *Euonymus europaeus*, Alder Buckthorn *Frangula alnus* and Blackberry *Rubus fruticosus*.

A properly planned and managed **hedgerow** is much more than just a row or double row of identikit trimmed bushes. It should contain a variety of plants, ideally native species. The woody component can be provided by the likes of Hazel *Corylus avellana*, Beech *Fagus sylvatica*, Dog-rose *Rosa canina*, Blackthorn *Prunus spinosa* and Hawthorn, with perennial herbaceous plants like Cow Parsley *Anthriscus sylvestris*, Stinging Nettles and the like being allowed to grow around the bases once the woody plants are fully established. Not every garden has the space for a hedge, of course. You also may already have one that is made from less ideal non-native plants, but it can still be useful to nesting birds if it is reasonably dense.

Many **climbing plants** are valuable additions to the wildlife garden, with Ivy *Hedera helix* a particular star. Its flowers offer late-autumn nectar for insects, and when it is allowed to grow thickly on a wall it provides nest sites for birds – especially our beleaguered House Sparrows. Honeysuckle *Lonicera periclymenum* and jasmines are climbers whose night-scented flowers draw in plenty of moths, as well as providing a delightful fragrance.

Natural grassland is vanishingly rare in the UK today, with 99 per cent of it lost since the 1930s, so creating your own **wildflower meadow** is a wonderful act of conservation as well as a great way to add more biodiversity to the garden. In some ways, meadow management is an exact science, but you may also enjoy great results just from throwing a few packets of native wildflower seed at an area of bare ground and then letting it grow at will until the end of summer, when you give it its one mow of the year. If you'd like to try a more structured approach, the RSPB offers a step-by-step guide (see Further reading, page 220).

A bird table should be out of reach of cats, with nearby cover for birds to escape Sparrowhawk attacks.

Bug hotels can create a great focal point in gardens and they offer homes for all kinds of invertebrates.

If you have a garden pond, you can try your hand at growing aquatic and water-loving plants. You can also use similar methods to create a **bog garden** – a patch of permanently wet ground in which native plants that favour soggy soils, such as Cuckoo-flower *Cardamine pratensis* and Yellow Flag Iris *Iris pseudacorus*, can be planted.

HOMES FOR WILDLIFE

Your garden's appeal may be enhanced even more by adding a few structural details that can harbour and shelter wildlife. Compost heaps, log piles, leaf piles and drystone walls all offer habitats for insects and other invertebrates. Decaying plant matter is food for beetle larvae, while drystone walls encourage moss and lichen to grow and also offer crevices where insects can shelter – even perhaps potential bird nest sites. A bank of bare earth may encourage mining bees and their associated parasitoids, such as bee-flies. The 'bug hotels' or 'bee houses' you can buy or make for yourself are also worthwhile. A good one includes holes and spaces of a wide range of sizes, and is stacked vertically to save space.

Nest boxes

In nature, Blue and Great Tits and many other woodland birds nest in different kinds of cavities. These might be crevices in rock faces or among tree roots, or even occasionally the burrows of small mammals, but they are most often holes in trees. These holes are formed either through natural decay at a site where the tree lost a branch, or are made by woodpeckers (which excavate a new nest-hole each year). Suitable sites have a small entrance aperture leading to a good-sized chamber, and are sheltered from rain and out of reach of most predators. They are, predictably enough, in short supply in natural conditions, but happily they are easy to replicate artificially.

Wooden nest boxes are perfect replacements for natural tree holes, and help boost numbers of hole-nesting birds like Tree Sparrows in gardens.

A classic nest box for a Blue Tit or Great Tit is a tallish rectangular wooden box, about 25 × 20 × 15cm, with a sloping roof that hinges for easy cleaning, a couple of drainage holes in the floor, and a

CATS AND GARDEN BIRDS

Debate rages over whether Britain's 10 million or so pet and feral domestic cats have a significant impact on wild bird populations. Most small birds vastly 'overproduce' through the breeding season, having 10 or more young per pair in one or more broods, because they 'know' most of the youngsters will be lost to predators in their first year. But predation by pet cats is different to that by wild predators – the cats' survival does not depend on healthy prey populations, as they will be fed anyway. So although it's natural for cats to hunt birds, cat predation cannot be treated as a natural part of a wild ecosystem.

Whatever your stance on this, no one wants to see cats kill garden birds. If the cats in question are yours, the best thing you can do is keep them indoors overnight, between dusk and dawn. These are the times when birds are most vulnerable, especially in summer when young fledglings are out and about. It will also help protect your cats from dangers like crossing roads in the dark and fighting with other cats. A quick-release collar with two bells on it can also help reduce predation.

If you have a problem with neighbours' cats entering your garden, there are various deterrents you can try. Pellets of dried lion dung, available from garden centres, can discourage them, and there are various scarers that work to a greater or lesser extent. If you have a dog, its part-time presence in your garden can also help keep cats away. Hitting the cat with a well-timed squirt from a water pistol is also often effective, especially if the cat doesn't see you doing it.

round entrance hole in the front or side, quite near the top of the box. The hole only needs to be big enough for the adult bird to squeeze through, though smaller holes will limit the range of species that can use them. For example, a 25mm hole will admit a Blue Tit but not the slightly bigger Great Tit, which needs 28mm, while the House Sparrow will need a 32mm entrance hole. Too big a hole will allow easy access for predators to get at the nest contents.

If your nest box comes with a stick perch below the hole, it's best to remove it. Tits and other songbirds are very good at clinging to vertical surfaces and don't need a perch; in fact, it may make the box more accessible to predators. Squirrels and Great Spotted Woodpeckers can get into a nest box quickly by enlarging the entrance hole – you can prevent this by choosing a box with a steel plate around the hole. The woodpecker may also attack the box by drilling at the sides – prevent this by pinning some fine-grade chicken wire to the box sides, or by choosing boxes constructed from Woodcrete, a very hard (but still insulating and breathable) material made of sawdust mixed with resin.

Ideally, a nest box will be fixed to a tree trunk in a spot where it gets some shade, quite high up (at least 2m ideally). Don't place two nest boxes too close together, as the birds are territorial when nesting and the first pair to move in might not allow another pair to become their close neighbour. The exception is nest boxes for House Sparrows (and, if you are lucky enough to have them, Tree

Sparrows). These species form loose colonies, so their nest boxes can be positioned just a few metres apart. The same goes for House Martin nest boxes, which go under the eaves.

Nest boxes along these general lines will work for quite a few other bird species too, including the Nuthatch and (if scaled up appropriately) the Starling, Kestrel and various others. Some birds prefer a slightly different, 'open-fronted' style of box, where the front panel comes only halfway up to the height of the box, in the style of stable doors. Boxes like this attract Robins and Spotted Flycatchers, particularly if placed within some cover (an Ivy-clad wall is ideal).

Depending on what birds are found in your local area, you could consider various other box types. Special nest boxes are available for House Martins, Swifts and Tawny Owls, for example. If you are handy with woodwork, you can build your own – ideally use pieces of hardwood that are at least 15mm thick (for insulation). They can be treated with a non-toxic preservative. Detailed guides can be found online – for example, from the British Trust for Ornithology (BTO) website (see Further reading, page 220).

THE GARDEN THROUGH THE YEAR

Every garden is different, but natural cycles are reasonably consistent across the UK. The guide below takes a month-by-month look at life in a typical wildlife-friendly garden, in terms of bird activity, and which tasks should be carried out each month in order to support garden birds throughout the year.

January

Activity This time of year is mostly just about survival, but some birds will already be singing and establishing territories. Look out for unusual visitors, especially in freezing weather.

Garden tasks Keep feeders topped up, especially with fat balls and other high-calorie foods. Make sure fresh water is available, particularly when temperatures drop below freezing. This is the last chance to put up new nest boxes for tits. Take part in the RSPB Big Garden Birdwatch this month.

February

Activity Many resident bird species are now singing. Listen for Chaffinches and Dunnocks joining the chorus this month. If you are not already familiar with the songs of commoner species, this is a good time to learn them, in readiness for the summer visitors arriving from next month. Tits will be prospecting nest boxes, and you may see territorial chases.

Garden tasks Continue to offer plenty of food and water, especially in cold weather. Prepare soil in beds for sowing some native wildflower seeds, which will attract insects – their seeds will provide more food for birds later in the year. This is also a good time to start planting native trees and shrubs.

March

Activity Many birds are courting and nest-building, with much song and activity. The very first summer visitors appear towards the end of the month.

Garden tasks Natural food remains in short supply this month so continue to keep feeders stocked. Sow wildflower seeds and consider planting evergreen hedges. Avoid cutting back shrubs and hedges between now and autumn, to prevent disturbing any nesting birds. Put up bug hotels to attract solitary bees and other invertebrates. You could put out nesting material for birds – short, soft pet hair is good (avoid using pet hair if your pet has recently had any external flea treatments), or very short pieces of wool; chicks can get tangled in long strands of tough material.

April

Activity Look out for birds carrying food for newly hatched chicks. Activity at bird feeders will dwindle as insect numbers increase. Listen for unfamiliar birdsong as our summer visitors return, and say goodbye to the last winter visitors.

Garden tasks Make a note of which nest boxes have been used. This is a good time to plant summer-blooming wildflowers to attract nectar-feeding insects, and to trim lavender, Rosemary *Rosmarinus officinalis* and other perennial herbs so they produce more flowers later on. Maintain some muddy patches in dry weather – Swallows and House Martins will use the mud as nesting material.

A garden pond is a great source of small flying insects for aerial hunters like the House Martin.

May

Activity Many baby birds will leave their nests this month – look for them out and about, being fed by parents. Migrants are still on their way in, with the chance of an unusual visitor.

Garden tasks This is a good time to offer live mealworms in addition to other food. Wildflower seeds can still be sown. Keep an eye on your pond and remove duckweed and blanketweed (leaving it at the pond edge, so any aquatic animals that came up with it can return to the pond). It's particularly important to keep cats indoors from dusk until dawn for the next few months as baby birds are most vulnerable at these times.

June

Activity Many young birds will be around, with new fledglings appearing and older ones starting to become independent, and beginning to moult into adult-like plumage. Some adults will be starting on their second broods.

Garden tasks Deadheading flowers will encourage more growth, which in turn will attract more insects. Make sure you continue to supply fresh water if there are prolonged dry spells. Look out for young birds in trouble – they are more likely to fly into windows or suffer other misadventures than are adult birds. Use natural pest control, or rely on birds and other wild predators to deal with problematic insects.

July

Activity Later broods of chicks start to fledge. Birds in general can start to seem scarcer as the moult begins and they become more secretive. Swifts are very active catching flies for their well-grown young, but will mostly have left breeding areas by the end of this month.

Garden tasks Provide fresh water for birds, and keep ponds topped up with rainwater from the water butt. Continue to deadhead flowers.

If you have fruit trees, leave a few windfalls around in autumn to attract Blackbirds and other thrushes.

August

Activity This is a quiet time for birds, as breeding activity is mostly over and many birds are in full moult. Larger birds like crows often look conspicuously tatty, with many missing flight feathers; young birds born this year can be distinguished by their intact flight feathers, as these are not moulted until the bird is a year old. The young birds do, however, moult their body plumage soon after fledging, and are likely to be in confusing 'halfway' plumages.

Garden tasks Cut back grass in meadow areas a little bit at a time so butterflies and other insects have refuges. Continue to ensure that fresh water is available for birds, and that ponds are kept free of excessive weed growth as well as falling leaves. This is a good month to make drystone walls and log piles to provide winter shelter for insects, and foraging grounds for birds like Wrens.

September

Activity Birds are finishing their moult and migratory species are preparing to depart. Look out for unusual visitors over the next couple of months. Some species begin to form flocks, which will persist through winter. Dispersing young birds may boost numbers in your garden.

Garden tasks Leave some windfall fruit for birds, especially thrushes, and leave seedheads of plants like sunflowers. Consider planting new trees, shrubs and perennials for next year.

October

Activity As winter approaches and natural food dwindles, garden birds visit feeding stations more often. Migration is in full flow – watch the skies for birds going overhead. Stormy weather may ground migrants.

Garden tasks Take down and clean out nest boxes; make any necessary repairs before replacing them. Consider moving any that were not used, or adding new ones (including for larger species such as Kestrels or owls). Collect some fallen leaves for a compost heap, which will provide shelter and habitat for worms and other invertebrates; leave others in piles for Blackbirds to search through.

November

Activity Look out for winter visitors like Redwings, Fieldfares and Bramblings; the former in particular can arrive suddenly, mob-handed, and strip berry bushes very quickly. Some birds will be caching food for the colder days ahead.

Garden tasks This is a good time to plant berry-bearing native shrubs. Make sure feeders are well topped up with a variety of high-calorie foods, including nuts, seeds, suet-based foods and perhaps bird pastry (see page 13 for recipe).

December

Activity Feeding stations will be very busy as birds spend the short days fuelling up, but the very first signs of breeding behaviour may also be seen this month. Look out for unusual winter visitors in freezing weather.

Garden tasks Offer plenty of fatty foods to sustain the birds through colder weather; make sure bird baths and other water sources stay topped up and unfrozen. Keep feeders clean with regular disinfection – this should be done frequently throughout the year, whenever you are using bird feeders.

WATCHING GARDEN BIRDS

Much of the joy of encouraging birds into your garden comes from watching their behaviour and interactions. It's also wonderful, of course, to find a new and unusual species, but simply observing the everyday birds coming and going reveals all kinds of details. You'll see how the Great Tits bully the Blue Tits, which in turn bully the Coal Tits – the latter often dart in at top speed, grab a nut or seed, and fly off to another part of the garden to store their prize for later. You may see 'your' Robin facing off against the one that lives next door – fences and hedges are often adopted as territorial boundaries, along which much posturing takes place. You'll notice how some birds, like Long-tailed Tits and Goldfinches, usually turn up and leave in busy, constantly conversing flocks, while others are strictly solitary and drive off others of their own kind on sight. You might see a Song Thrush industriously tackling your garden snail problem by smacking the molluscs to bits on a big stone, or a Goldcrest hovering around the tips of a conifer twig to pick tiny insects from between the needles. Then there is the heart-stopping moment when a Sparrowhawk races in from nowhere, scattering the little birds and perhaps making off with an unlucky victim in its talons. Every single species has its own wonderful array of quirks and habits, its own particular character and beauty, and you will soon become familiar with, and fond of, each one.

Put a comfy seat close to a window with a good view into your garden and keep a pair of binoculars nearby, and you'll soon wonder why you bother watching TV at all. To take things up a level, you could turn the garden shed into a birdwatching or photography hide, or if you spend enough time in the garden, the birds will soon grow very relaxed in your company. For a more intimate look into their lives, a nest box with an inbuilt camera connected to a screen indoors can provide remarkable viewing of the breeding process (though if you are watching with your children, be warned that things can get upsetting – even in perfect conditions not every chick will survive to adulthood, and sometimes broods fail completely for no apparent reason).

There are many ways your observations can help further our knowledge of bird behaviour, distribution and population trends. The easiest is to participate in the RSPB's Big Garden Birdwatch each January. This large-scale national survey provides an insight into the changing fortunes of our garden birds, and requires just one hour's commitment each year – see the RSPB website (page 220) to find out what's involved.

If you find you catch the survey bug, there are many more you can contribute to – a lot of them are organised by the BTO. The Garden BirdWatch survey, which has been running since 1994, asks volunteers to count garden birds all year round – find out more at the BTO website (page 220). The BTO is also currently running surveys on garden birds with plumage colour abnormalities and bill deformities, and on the general health of birds and other wildlife in the garden – for details of these and more, see Further reading (page 220). New projects are started regularly. To log sightings of birds at any time, you can use the BTO's BirdTrack website (see page 220) or app. For birds and also other wildlife, use iRecord (see page 220).

Nest boxes with inbuilt cameras provide a wonderful opportunity to observe the intimate details of the family lives of wild birds, such as the Great Tit family seen above.

Many people who go birdwatching regularly would report that their hobby first began after they started taking an interest in their garden birds. Being an RSPB member gives you access to nature reserves in wonderful wild places throughout the UK, and going further afield to find and watch the kinds of birds and other wildlife you probably won't encounter in your garden is a wonderful thing indeed. Volunteering at a local nature reserve will enable you to put your wildlife gardening skills to good use and learn new skills too. However, at home is where you can exert the most influence and do the most to help birds and other wildlife.

ABOUT THIS BOOK

This book presents detailed 'biographies' of 47 common garden birds. It looks at how to identify them, their distribution, their beak-to-tail length in centimetres and their weight in grams, their conservation status in the UK (red, amber or green), their preferred habitat and their abundance in the UK and abroad, and then goes on to explore their biology and general behaviour in detail. Each account ends with some guidance on how to attract the species to your garden and encourage it to breed. Finally, Other garden birds (pages 206–219) looks at a range of more unusual garden visitors.

The sections are ordered and themed by the birds' general appearance and lifestyle, rather than in the taxonomic order used in bird field guides. This approach means that some families (such as tits and finches) are grouped together but others are not. The species selection includes representatives from a wide range of bird families, reflecting how important gardens are to a great range of birds.

There is no more comfortable way to enjoy wildlife than to watch the birds attracted to your garden, including House Sparrows.

Tits

With their colourful plumage, adventurous natures and agile antics, these little birds are particularly popular. The Blue Tit and Great Tit are some of the easiest species to attract to your garden, both to feed and to breed. Tits belong to the songbird family Paridae, though here the more distantly related Long-tailed Tit is also included.

Blue Tit
Cyanistes caeruleus

12cm
10.5–11.5g

GREEN

This familiar and much-loved little bird is one of the most reliable visitors to gardens big and small throughout the British Isles. It is common in all kinds of woodland and other habitats with some trees. The Blue Tit is extremely active, agile and inventive, and is invariably one of the first bird species to discover new feeding opportunities in its local area.

INTRODUCTION

The Blue Tit is a small, compact bird with a relatively large head, and large, powerful feet and legs. The bill is short and quite stout. The colourful pattern of yellow underside (with a faint dark belly-stripe), white cheeks narrowly outlined in dark blue, a dark eye-stripe, a blue crown-patch circled with white, and the green back and bluish wings with a single whitish wing-bar is unique among British birds. The intensity of colour is quite variable (see 'Ultra-special' box). In juvenile plumage the colours are much drabber, and the cheeks are yellow rather than white. The Blue Tit gives a variety of bright ringing or buzzing calls. The song is a very variable short series of chattering notes, with the start usually higher pitched.

The Blue Tit holds down larger food items with its feet, and pecks off and swallows small bits at a time.

The African Blue Tit occurs in the Canary Islands and northern Africa. It is darker-headed than our Blue Tit.

DISTRIBUTION, POPULATION AND HABITAT

Blue Tits occur throughout Britain and Ireland, being absent from only the most open mountainous regions of north Scotland and some of the most northerly Scottish islands. Those found in the British Isles are of the subspecies *C. c. obscurus*, which occurs nowhere else. Blue Tits on mainland Europe are classified as *C. c. caeruleus*, and there are at least seven other subspecies elsewhere across the species' range, which covers most of mainland Europe and extends into western Russia and south-east through the Middle East. The very similar African Blue Tit *C. teneriffae* occurs in North Africa and the Canary Islands, while in north and east Eurasia its other close relative, the larger, whiter and fluffier Azure Tit *C. cyanus*, can be found. Where Azure and Blue Tits both occur, they hybridise, producing an intermediate form known as Pleske's Tit *C. pleskei*.

There are an estimated 15 million Blue Tits in the UK in winter, but not all of those will still be around to breed the following spring – many will die and some may be visitors from mainland Europe. Britain's breeding population is about 3.6 million pairs. The Blue Tit's breeding population has been on a gradual upward trend over the last few decades, with a 29 per cent increase between 1967 and 2015 overall, but there has been a moderate decline since 2005.

Blue Tits are woodland birds, and they fare especially well in oak woodland. However, they can also thrive in mixed and even coniferous woodland, and will visit more open habitats close to wooded areas, such as reed beds and heathland. They are common in parks and gardens of all kinds provided there are trees, including in city centres. However, they are most likely to breed successfully in parks and gardens with native deciduous trees that support a thriving population of small invertebrates.

ULTRA-SPECIAL

To our eyes, Blue Tits are fairly colourful birds. To the birds themselves, though, there's an extra dimension to that colour, thanks to their ability to perceive wavelengths within the ultraviolet spectrum. The blue crown-patch strongly reflects ultraviolet light, especially in males. It's been found that females choose their mates partly on the basis of how bright the crown-patch appears to them, and brightness seems to be an indication of how good a father a male Blue Tit will be, because males with fewer parasites tend to have brighter heads. Not only this, but females themselves invest more time and energy in rearing their broods when paired with a brighter male.

BEHAVIOUR

Blue Tits are generalists and omnivores, feeding on insects, spiders and other invertebrates, and also seeds, berries and nuts – in addition, they will try almost any kind of food left out at garden bird-feeding stations. In the breeding season, for the weeks they are feeding their chicks, Blue Tits become something of a specialist, and are heavily dependent on small, soft-bodied invertebrates, especially caterpillars and aphids.

Blue Tits are innovative foragers. They mainly search for food in trees, exploring bark and foliage for insects and other invertebrates, but they will also forage on the ground, in reed beds and on the

Blue Tits are usually the first birds to discover and use a newly installed bird-feeding station.

walls of buildings. They can dismantle leaf buds to search for invertebrates within, and will eat some of the plant matter, too. They can easily be enticed to fly to a human hand for food, and do so in various city parks, such as Kensington Gardens in central London. They are adept at clinging, climbing and hovering, so very few foraging spots are out of their reach – they are also fast and bold, and can take food from under the noses of larger and more aggressive species. This adaptability and ability to innovate serves them well for surviving in varied conditions. It is not even that unusual to see Blue Tits managing to feed successfully despite being burdened with grotesque bill abnormalities (when the two mandibles do not meet perfectly, perhaps due to injury, so one or both continue to grow to a remarkable length).

Male Blue Tits may be heard singing all year round, but singing intensifies in late winter as the male seeks a partner. Once he has attracted an interested female, he performs a circling 'moth' display flight on rather stiff wings, around the treetops. He then settles near her and 'dances', with the body held horizontally, the tail fanned out and the crest raised.

The pair seeks out and inspects possible nest sites. These need to be cavities with small entrance holes that are sheltered from rain and have a clear flight path. They will use natural holes, such as old woodpecker nests, or spaces where a tree trunk or bough has partly decayed, but are also quick to move into suitable nest boxes. The female builds a nest inside, forming the main structure from moss and shaping the nest cup with vigorous wiggling. She lines the cup with feathers (including those shed from her own belly as she develops her brood patch). She lays a clutch of eight to 12 (occasionally up to 16) finely speckled white eggs and incubates them from the day the last or second-to-last egg is laid. The incubation period is about 14 days, during which she sits tight, leaving only briefly to feed (the male also brings her food). Males are sometimes polygynous,

MILK MONITOR

The first recorded incidence of tits attacking doorstep milk bottles was in 1921. Having milk delivered to your home is much less common today than it was through most of the 20th century, but many will recall the glass bottles left by your friendly local milkman at the crack of dawn, each full of whole milk with a layer of particularly fatty, creamy milk at the top. The bottles were sealed – initially with waxed board and later with a foil cap, but these proved no obstacle to hungry and enterprising Blue Tits, who pecked at the bottle tops until they accessed the cream. This occurred regularly, and the habit spread across the UK and through bird culture – like most intelligent animals, birds are good at learning by example. Other tits would watch those who'd discovered the trick, and copy them.

Today, most people buy milk in plastic bottles with screw-on lids and get it from the supermarket. So this feeding opportunity is no longer widely available to the birds, but should there be a shift in human culture back to milk deliveries to the doorstep, it's almost certain that our garden Blue Tits would be back to their milk-thieving ways in short order.

Fledgling and juvenile Blue Tits have yellow faces, and greyish-blue rather than bright blue caps and wings.

pairing with and provisioning two females and their chicks, though one nest gets a disproportionate amount of their effort.

The eggs hatch at about the same time, and the parents must now keep busy, bringing small, soft-bodied invertebrates to feed the chicks. The young birds grow rapidly, and all fledge at about the same time, at around two weeks old. In fact, the chicks in most nests in any given area will fledge at about the same time, in the first half of June (later further north). The fledglings can fly (weakly) from the day they fledge, and will associate with their parents for the next few weeks, gradually gaining independence. Blue Tits almost invariably have just one brood each year, though they may try again if they lose their clutch or chicks at an early stage.

British Blue Tits are rather sedentary. Ringing recoveries have revealed a few British-ringed birds travelling to France, Belgium and Germany, while we in turn have been visited by Blue Tits ringed in the same countries, and also the Netherlands, Norway and Lithuania – this last bird travelled 1,389km to turn up in Kent in spring 2016. Unlike our own birds, some Blue Tits in eastern and northern Europe are habitual migrants, heading south-west for the winter (though typically over much shorter distances). The numbers that migrate vary according to population (increased travel after a successful breeding season results in a higher-than-usual population) and food supplies (failure of the beechmast crop triggers a larger migration).

The most adventurous UK bird was a juvenile ringed in Essex, which travelled to the Scottish Highlands (717km). More typical movement was demonstrated by the oldest recorded British Blue Tit, which was ringed as a first-winter in Eversholt, Bedfordshire, in December 1986, and was recaptured in the same village exactly 10 years later, then again another three months and 10 days later. The oldest Blue Tit on record in Europe was a ringed bird in the Czech Republic, which lived to at least 11 years and seven months old. However, most Blue Tits only survive about three years.

IN THE GARDEN

It is a rare garden that won't draw in a Blue Tit or two, especially if you offer suitable food in winter. Blue Tits are attracted to peanuts, sunflower seeds (hearts and whole), mixed birdseed, and all kinds of fat-based bird foods, including suet cake and fat balls. Traditionally they came to feed from halved coconuts and kitchen scraps like raw bacon fat. They will also feed on mealworms, with live mealworms useful in the breeding season. They can access hanging bird feeders of all kinds.

Nest boxes for Blue Tits should be about 25 × 20 × 15cm, with a sloping roof and a 25mm entrance hole (no perch is needed). Hang the box at least 2m above ground level, out of full sunshine, on a tree trunk or wall in a spot with a clear flight path in front. A metal plate around the entrance hole and fine chicken wire pinned to the sides can help discourage woodpeckers and squirrels from attacking the box.

Great Tit
Parus major

14cm
18–19g
GREEN

This is the largest member of the tit family in the British Isles, and is almost as familiar and common a garden visitor as the Blue Tit. Great Tits are bold and conspicuous garden birds, and are easily attracted to bird-feeding stations, where they will dominate other smaller birds such as Blue Tits through aggressive posturing and outright attacks.

INTRODUCTION

This is the largest and most assertive of the British tit species, dominating most other small birds at garden feeders.

The Great Tit has a black head with white cheek-patches that are entirely encircled with black, this continuing as a stripe down the breast and belly. In males, the stripe flares out and becomes very broad between the legs, while in females it narrows and becomes patchy. The underside is otherwise yellow. The back is greenish, the wings are blue-green with a short, conspicuous whitish wing-bar, and the tail is bluish with white outer feathers. Birds have a stout, shortish bill and sturdy blue-grey legs. Females are on average less bright than males, and juveniles much less so, with greyish rather than black heads, and this dark coloration not completely encircling the yellowish cheek-patches. Juveniles also show a prominent pale white nape patch, which can cause confusion with Coal Tits. The Great Tit's song is a persistent two- or three-note seesawing phrase, sometimes written as *tea-cher, tea-cher, tea-cher*, and recalling a squeaking gate. It has a large repertoire of other calls, including a ringing Chaffinch-like *twink* and various dry scolding notes.

MELANISM

Pigment abnormalities in garden birds are quite common, with unusual white or pale feathers (leucism) the most often seen form of aberration. Melanism, where there is excess dark pigment, is relatively rare, but the BTO conducts a survey on plumage aberrations in garden birds and has recorded melanism more often in Great Tits than in any other species – the species has accounted for about 40 per cent of all sightings of melanistic birds.

Melanistic Great Tits typically have solid black heads and undersides that are duskier than usual; they also lack a white wing-bar. A similar aberration occurs in Blue Tits (as seen in this photo) – identification is then only possible by ignoring colour and pattern, and concentrating instead on the bird's size, shape and behaviour. This aberration is caused by a genetic mutation, so runs in family lines – therefore, cases tend to concentrate in particular geographic regions.

DISTRIBUTION, POPULATION AND HABITAT

The Great Tit occurs almost everywhere in the British Isles, except a few open mountainous parts of the Scottish uplands and some of the most northerly Scottish islands. The subspecies occurring in Britain is *P. m. newtoni* – it is replaced by *P. m. major* on mainland Europe. Beyond our shores, the species is very widespread, occurring across almost all of Europe and through central and northern Asia to China. It is also present in north-west Africa and the northern Arabian peninsula. It has three close relatives in eastern Asia, all of which look very similar – the Japanese Tit *P. minor*, the Cinereous Tit *P. cinereous* and the Green-backed Tit *P. monticolus*.

There are about 2.5 million breeding pairs of Great Tits in the UK. The population has grown strongly and steadily through the last few decades, with a 99 per cent increase between 1967 and 2015, but there was a slight (6 per cent) decline between 2010 and 2015.

Great Tits are woodland birds, and occur anywhere where there are some trees in which to forage. Their preference is deciduous woodland but they also occur in coniferous forest, and they are common in parkland and gardens.

BEHAVIOUR

Like other tits, Great Tits mainly eat insects and other invertebrates in the warmer months, and change to a more vegetarian diet (up to 90 per cent) in winter. They feed their chicks mainly on caterpillars, and on other soft-bodied invertebrates, including spiders. In autumn they take a large amount of beechmast. When dealing with a large or tough food item, they grip it between both feet while pecking at it.

Great Tits are not as agile as the smaller tits, but they are great climbers and clingers, and their aggression enables them to displace their smaller cousins easily from a food source. They are very adaptable and quick to explore new opportunities – along with Blue Tits, they are usually the first birds to find a new garden bird-feeding station. They will feed on carrion, and there are reports of Great Tits using pine needles to winkle insect larvae from holes in tree bark – a rare example of tool use in a small songbird. They are keen observers of other birds' activity and fully exploit this – they

often track down and steal food cached by Coal Tits and Marsh Tits. There is also evidence that paired Great Tits can learn to act cooperatively to access food.

Studies show that Great Tits display high individual variation in personality traits such as speed of exploratory behaviour and levels of aggressiveness, and that these are largely inherited from the parents. In some years, depending on food supplies, being a fast and aggressive explorer is a more successful strategy. In others, it's better to be slower and more methodical. So a range of personality types persists in the Great Tit population, and overall those with intermediate personalities survive best.

Male Great Tits become territorial and begin to sing in January, if not even earlier. Their courtship includes the slow-circling 'moth flight' and posturing to display the broad black belly stripe. Once paired up, a male Great Tit confines his singing mainly to dawn, and spends the rest of the day closely attending his mate to ensure no other males can approach her. Studies have shown that mate-guarding takes precedence even over feeding for male Great Tits during the weeks between courtship and egg-laying, and unlike in the Blue Tit, it is very rare for males to attempt to support more than one female and nest (although casual extra-pair copulation is still frequent).

Great Tits nest in cavities of various kinds, including old woodpecker nests, natural hollows in tree trunks or boughs, crevices in rock piles and the like. They also readily use nest boxes and other artificial structures not intended to accommodate them, such as inside post boxes or pipework.

The female builds the nest on her own, out of moss with a soft feather lining. In it she lays seven to nine eggs and incubates them alone for about 14 days. The eggs hatch at the

The juvenile Great Tit is a drabber version of the adult, and its black cheek surround and chest stripe is often incomplete.

same time, as incubation does not begin until the last or penultimate egg is laid. Both parents feed the chicks, which fledge at 18–21 days old. By fledging time, the parents often look very careworn, sometimes almost bald from their weeks of squeezing through the nest-hole, but they continue to feed the fledglings for another couple of weeks. It is rare but not unknown for parents to have a second brood (although young from second broods are in poorer condition, with lower survival rates). After breeding and moulting, adult and young Great Tits roam more widely and join flocks of other tits to search for food.

SONGBIRDS OF PREY

It is rather shocking to contemplate a small songbird preying on another vertebrate animal, but the Great Tit is not a bird to pass up a feeding opportunity, however unconventional. At a certain cave in Hungary, Great Tits regularly hunt, kill and eat hibernating Common Pipistrelles *Pipistrellus pipistrellus* in the winter. Studies have shown that the tits are attracted by the calls the bats make when approaching the end of their hibernation period. When they find a bat, they pull it from the cave wall and carry it down to eat, feeding mainly on its brain. There are also documented cases of Great Tits catching and killing other, smaller birds such as redpolls, and even in one case a Yellowhammer, a significantly heavier bird. These predatory ways seem to come to the fore only in the coldest winter weather.

ADOPTING A HABIT

If Blue Tits are already occupying a suitable cavity, Great Tits will often evict and sometimes kill their smaller cousins, even if eggs have already been laid. They may then end up incubating a couple of Blue Tit eggs and rearing the young alongside their own. They do not recognise the Blue Tit chicks as alien, but the cross-fostered youngsters grow up with an identity crisis, responding to Great Tit song rather than that of Blue Tits. However, the effect seems to wear off quite quickly, with the young birds somehow 'realising' they are a different species. This is a good thing, as a Blue Tit trying to compete directly with Great Tits for food and mates will not fare well. However, being reared by Great Tits may be beneficial to the young Blue Tits in various ways, including giving them access to a wider range of foraging opportunities and exposing them to more varied types of song.

Perhaps this explains why the cross-fostering is sometimes done on purpose. Blue Tits cannot displace Great Tits from a nest but they have been known to sneakily lay an egg or two in Great Tits' nests. In some woodlands, up to 7 per cent of nests contain young of both species. In nature, Great Tits don't lay their eggs in Blue Tits' nests unless they are going to take over the nest completely, but cross-fostering studies in captivity show that Great Tits reared by Blue Tits never grow out of their conviction that they are Blue Tits.

Great Tits in Britain are not typically migratory, and many young birds will disperse only a few kilometres from their birthplace. However, ringing records have shown that the species is capable of lengthy journeys. Several Great Tits ringed in the UK have been found in mainland Europe, with records from Belgium, Germany, Denmark and Lithuania. The furthest travelled was 1,447km, by a year-old female. As these birds were mostly ringed in the UK in winter, it is likely that they were born abroad and migrated to Britain – Great Tits in northern and eastern Europe are more migratory than our 'own' birds. Coming from the other direction, a Latvia-ringed female Great Tit found in Kent had travelled 1,407km, while another female from Russia had covered 1,397km.

A Great Tit exits a nest box carrying a fecal pellet – a sure sign that a brood of chicks has hatched.

The longest movement within Britain was 711km – a bird that moved from Hertfordshire to the Highlands (and was just over five years old when recaptured there). The oldest UK Great Tit reached 13 years, 11 months and three days – this bird had travelled a more typical 48km over its lifetime. The European record is held by a German bird, aged 15 years and five months.

IN THE GARDEN

Most gardens will already be visited by Great Tits on their 'rounds'. Offering peanuts, sunflower seeds (hearts and whole), mixed birdseed, suet cakes and fat balls will entice them to linger. They will also take mealworms to feed their chicks in the breeding season. Great Tits are bold and inquisitive, and can readily learn to feed from the hand, given a little patience.

Great Tits need a nest box with an entrance hole at least 28mm across. If you wish to encourage the smaller tit species instead, choose boxes with a 25mm entrance hole – while the smaller species will use a box with a Great Tit-sized hole, they probably won't get the chance if there are any Great Tits around. The box should be placed 1–5m up on a tree trunk or wall with some shade, and with a clear flight path to the front of the box.

Coal Tit
Periparus ater

12cm
9g
GREEN

The most lightweight of our tit species, the Coal Tit is a furtive little bird that tends not to linger long on the feeder, so good views are hard to come by. The reason for this is apparent if you watch a little longer – the other tit species drive it away when they get the chance, so the Coal Tit is a grab-and-dash merchant at the bird table. However, it has some clever tricks up its sleeve to help it survive, despite its underdog status.

The strikingly top-heavy, big-headed silhouette of the Coal Tit is distinctive, as is the bird's rather long, slim bill.

INTRODUCTION

This is a very small bird with a rather top-heavy look, thanks to its relatively big head and longish bill, on a compact and rather short-tailed body. It has a black crown and a large black bib that reaches onto the breast and flares out at the sides – sometimes there are dark patches further down on its front. The cheeks are white and the back of the head bears a wide white stripe, outlined with black. Its upperside is a rather drab olive-grey, with a prominent double white wing-bar, the front of which takes the form of a row of spots rather than a continuous white line. The underside is pale with a subtle peachy wash, strongest on the flanks. It has greyish feet and legs, with large, strong toes and claws. In juvenile plumage, the pattern is the same but the black parts are duller grey, and the cheeks and underside have a yellow tint. The song is like a high-pitched, speeded-up Great Tit's song – a clear, bright, two- or three-note refrain that is repeated several times in each burst. Coal Tits have various simple high-pitched calls.

DISTRIBUTION, POPULATION AND HABITAT

Coal Tits occur almost throughout the British Isles, including most of the Highlands and parts of the Hebrides and Orkneys. They are absent from very open areas such as the mountainous Highlands and around the Wash. Their population density is highest in Scotland. The subspecies present in Britain is *P. a. brittanicus*, while Ireland has its own subspecies, the yellow-cheeked *P. a. hibernicus*. The larger and greyer *P. a. ater* of mainland Europe is a regular visitor to southern and eastern Britain, though it is often overlooked. The world range beyond Britain encompasses most of Europe, parts of north-west Africa and the Middle East, and a broad swathe of north-central Asia across to Japan; the species also occurs in mountainous parts of southern Asia. Two closely related and similar-looking species, the Rufous-naped Tit *P. rufonuchalis* and Rufous-vented Tit *P. rubidiventris*, occur in Asia.

In the UK, there are about 680,000 breeding pairs of Coal Tits. Overall, the species increased by 49 per cent between 1967 and 2015, but most of that increase took place before 1980. The trend since then has been generally stable, but there was a 16 per cent decline between 2010 and 2015. In Scotland, the decline over the same period was 22 per cent.

Coal Tits occur in all kinds of woodland but are generally outcompeted by Great and Blue Tits in most areas, and excluded from the best nest sites. They have an advantage over their cousins in coniferous forest, though, being able to exploit fully resources that the other species find difficult to access. They are fairly common in parks and gardens, even in some city centres.

Fledgling Coal Tits look pristine but soon become scruffy as they begin their post-juvenile moult.

CACHING IN

If you watch a Coal Tit coming to a feeder, you may notice that it takes out a single seed or nut and flies away with it. If you watch what happens next, you may see it find a quiet spot to eat its trophy, or you might instead see it stash the food to eat later. The tit will carefully place the seed under some loose moss or wedge it in tree bark. Each item is stored separately – this is known as 'scatter-hoarding', and reduces the chance of the bird losing its entire store-cupboard to a thief. Great and Blue Tits often notice Coal Tits storing food and promptly pinch it, but they are unlikely to track down every item. Coal Tits have been shown to have a distinctly better memory for food locations than do Great Tits, thanks to a larger hippocampus (the brain region responsible for long-term memory). However, a Coal Tit is unlikely to remember the whereabouts of everything it has stored. If you offer whole sunflower seeds to your garden birds and you have visiting Coal Tits, don't be surprised if you find an unexpected sunflower growing out of your lawn one day.

Pet hair, collected from a brush and placed outside in bundles, makes ideal nesting material for garden birds like Coal Tits.

BEHAVIOUR

Coal Tits are omnivores and, like other tits, are adaptable and opportunistic. They are both very active and very agile. Their relatively long, slim bills are well suited to extracting insects from between pine needles; they can also access seeds from larch, Sitka Spruce *Pichea sitchensis* and fir cones, and will feed on Alder *Alnus glutinosa* and Beech catkins. Their small size and light weight makes it easier for them to access food items at the tips of the smallest twigs. Coal Tits consume a large amount of beechmast, and like other tits, they need a large supply of small, soft-bodied invertebrate prey when rearing chicks.

In the Caledonian forests of the Scottish Highlands, Coal Tits greatly outnumber Blue and Great Tits, and when these tougher rivals are away, they will linger at feeding stations much longer. If you watch the bird feeders at the Osprey Centre at RSPB Abernethy Forest, you'll see dozens of Coal Tits visiting at the same time. Like other tits, they can also quite easily be persuaded to take food from the hand.

Male Coal Tits begin to sing in late winter, finding a very high point within their territory from which to deliver their monotonous but far-carrying song. When a female approaches a male, he sings more intensely, with wings fluttering and tail fanned.

Like other tits, Coal Tits are cavity-nesters, but Great and Blue Tits often exclude them from optimum nest sites, such as nest boxes and old woodpecker nest holes. Their creative solutions to this problem include nesting in old rodent burrows, and in spaces between exposed tree roots; other potential sites include holes in drystone walls. They are much more willing to nest at low levels than the other species; their inconspicuous appearance helps them to avoid attracting the attention of ground predators as they visit the nest, but many broods are taken by weasels and other mammalian predators.

The female Coal Tit usually lays nine or 10 eggs, and incubates them for up to 16 days. The chicks fledge after about 17 days in the nest. The parents care for them for another couple of weeks. In winter, adults and youngsters form flocks, often with other tits and small birds, sometimes including finches like Siskins.

WHO'S THE DADDY?

Most songbirds are socially monogamous, meaning they pair with one partner and the two birds work cooperatively to raise one or more broods of chicks. However, most are also very quick to take advantage of the chance of a sneaky mating with a neighbour. The result of these extra-pair copulations is a brood of chicks with mixed parentage. This is particularly common in Coal Tits, with up to 25 per cent of all nestlings being raised by a male that is not their father.

It is easy to see why a male would indulge in extra-pair copulation – the chance to father a few extra chicks and spread his genes a little further. But for a female the motivation is less apparent; she will produce only one clutch of nine or 10 eggs regardless of their parentage, and there might be consequences if her partner 'knows' she has mated with another male, or males. He has no interest in investing energy in caring for another male's offspring, so if he has cause to 'suspect' this, he may abandon the nest. So why does she take the risk? The logical answer is that chicks from extra-pair copulations have a survival advantage over those from within-pair copulations (perhaps because the female would choose to have extra-pair copulations only with males that are 'better' genetically than her own mate). But studies on survival rates of extra-pair and within-pair chicks show that there is no significant difference, so this behaviour remains a mystery for now.

Coal Tits in the UK are not very migratory, though they make short-distance movements in response to food shortages. Those living in more unforgiving parts of mainland Europe, further north and east, are much more prone to these 'irruptive' movements. Continental Coal Tits arrive in Britain each year – they are most often found on the south and east coasts, and are most likely to be detected by bird ringers, as the size and colour differences between them and 'our' Coal Tits are quite subtle.

Coal Tits ringed in Belgium, Germany, France and the Netherlands have turned up in the UK on occasion, and British-ringed birds have been recovered from Belgium and Germany. Within Britain, the longest journey was 636km, made by a juvenile ringed in the Highlands that turned up three years later in Herefordshire. The longevity record in the UK and Europe is held by a Scottish bird, which was recaptured by a ringer nine years, two months and 25 days after it was ringed as a first-winter (in other words, in the first winter of its life; so, not yet a year old) at the same location.

IN THE GARDEN

Larger gardens with a few trees, especially conifers, are very likely to attract some Coal Tits, as will smaller gardens if they are near suitable habitat. These tits visit gardens much more often in winter when there is a poor crop of Beech, Sitka Spruce and other tree seed. They will come to hanging feeders stocked with peanuts, seed and suet foods – they particularly appreciate food items that are big enough to be worth caching (although you should never offer whole peanuts during the breeding season). Large hanging feeders with plenty of space for many birds will appeal to them most, and they will also visit open bird tables if they can easily grab a nut or seed and beat a hasty retreat.

A nest box with a 25mm entrance hole will suit Coal Tits, although unless you live in an area where they are the most abundant species, it will probably be Blue Tits that move in, as Coal Tits are not able to hold their own against a Blue Tit pair intent on stealing their nest site. Placing the nest box lower down (below 1m) and partly hidden might improve the chances of Coal Tits moving in, and offering plenty of boxes may help too; if all the local Blue Tits are comfortably accommodated, then Coal Tits will be free to investigate the spare boxes.

In late May or early June you should see the first fledgling tits in the garden, with their parents in close attendance.

Long-tailed Tit
Aegithalos caudatus

14cm
9g

GREEN

This delightful little bird often descends in small flocks on a garden bird-feeding station, taking over the feeders for a few minutes before moving on. It is, despite its name, not a true tit, but belongs to a different family and is technically described as a 'bushtit'. Recent genetic studies have now shown that the tit family (Paridae) and the bushtits (Aegithalidae) are not even very closely related. However, in many aspects of its behaviour and ecology, the Long-tailed Tit is very like the true tits.

INTRODUCTION

Its delightful black, white and pink colour scheme and distinctive outline make the Long-tailed Tit unique among British songbirds.

The Long-tailed Tit's tail is slightly longer than its body, making this a very small bird in terms of body size. It is rotund, with a tiny, blunt black bill, giving the overall impression of a ball on a stick, or a lollipop. It has a pale head and body, and a black back, wings and tail, with a pinkish-orange flush across the flanks and shoulders, and broad black 'eyebrows' that extend into fine blackish streaks on the cheeks. The eyes look rather small, and have prominent eyelids forming a ring of pinkish or yellowish skin. The legs and feet are black, and daintier than those of the true tits. The tail has a graduated shape, the central feathers longest, and both tail and wing feathers have white edges (this is obvious when the tail is viewed from below). Juvenile Long-tailed Tits have dusky cheeks contrasting with a whitish forehead. They lack the pink tones of adults but have brighter pink eye-rings. Their tail is a little shorter than that of adults when they are newly fledged but they quickly grow to adult proportions. Flocks keep in touch with constant short *see* notes and dry trilling calls.

FLUSHED WITH FURY

The eyelid colour of Long-tailed Tits changes with age, becoming less deeply red as juveniles go into their first winter. But studies also indicate that the colour can be influenced by other factors, including body condition – birds with darker eyelids tend to be heavier than pale-lidded individuals. Eyelid colour can be an indicator of mood as well. The skin is highly vascularised here and additional blood flow (for example, when the bird is agitated) will cause it to redden.

DISTRIBUTION, POPULATION AND HABITAT

Long-tailed Tits occur over nearly all of the British Isles, being absent only from open upland parts of north and west Scotland, parts of the far western Irish coast, and most of the more northerly Scottish islands. Beyond Britain, their range spans Europe and parts of south-western Asia, and extends broadly eastwards through central Asia to Japan and much of eastern China. There are many subspecies – in the British Isles we have *A. c. roseus*, and occasionally the pure white-headed *A. c. caudatus* from northern Europe and Asia turns up, especially on the east coast. The Long-tailed Tit is the only member of the family Aegithalidae to occur in Europe, but there are another five to eight species of bushtits (biologists' opinions differ on their classification). All occur in southern Asia except for a single species in North America.

There are an estimated 340,000 Long-tailed Tit breeding territories in the UK, though this may represent more than 680,000 birds as there are often non-breeding helpers assisting breeding pairs at the nest. The population trend has fluctuated, with a sharp peak followed by a sharp fall through the 1970s, but since about 1990 the trend has been generally upwards. For the UK as a whole, numbers rose by 17 per cent between 1995 and 2015, with a remarkable 63 per cent increase in Scotland over that period. Like many very small, non-migratory birds, the Long-tailed Tit suffers heavy mortality in severe winters, although the year following such a winter is likely to bring a corresponding boost to breeding success for the survivors, as competition is reduced.

Good habitat for Long-tailed Tits includes plenty of scrubland, as well as trees. They prefer deciduous woodland with a well-developed shrub layer, but they also live in more open scrubby or heathy habitats. They are common in parks and gardens.

BEHAVIOUR

This little bird is naturally almost exclusively insectivorous. Its size, agility and light weight enable it to explore twigs, bark and foliage thoroughly, and locate well-camouflaged foods like moth eggs and larvae; it also takes many spiders, and a little plant matter in autumn and winter. Visiting bird feeders and tables does not fit as naturally into its foraging style as with the true tits, but it will visit and, while it is not especially keen on seeds and nuts, it greatly enjoys suet products such as suet cakes.

Long-tailed Tits habitually forage in flocks and communicate constantly with their buzzing contact calls. They move from twig to twig, working their way quickly along and dangling upside down as frequently as they are the right way up. When one bird flies, in conspicuously undulating flight, to a new tree or bush, the rest of the group soon do the same, one at a time in a follow-the-leader manner.

Travelling in family groups, Long-tailed Tits descend upon feeders in gangs and usually feed together in relative harmony.

The only time you are likely to see Long-tailed Tits alone or in pairs, rather than in little (or large) gangs, is during the breeding season (starting in March) but even breeding pairs are often joined later on by relatives that offer help at the nest, bringing extra food for the chicks (see 'We are family' box).

Unlike the true tits, Long-tailed Tits are not cavity-nesters. Instead, they build a fully developed nest in a dense bush or the fork of a tree. The pair works together to build it, and what they produce is a true work of art. The outer structure is a combination of pieces of moss, woven together with spider silk taken from egg cocoons or webs. The resultant springy, stretchy, bag-shaped structure is lined inside with a huge number of tiny feathers (more than 2,000 in some cases), and the birds cover its exterior with flakes of lichen for camouflage. The nest is otherwise quite unprotected, and studies show that fewer than 20 per cent of nests avoid attack by predators.

The female lays six to eight lightly speckled, pale pinkish eggs, which she incubates on her own for 15–18 days. The time she spends in the cramped quarters of the nest can often result in conspicuously bent tail feathers by the time the eggs hatch and she begins to go out foraging for food for the chicks, alongside her mate and any helpers that may have joined them.

The chicks leave the nest at about 17 days old, and spend the first few days of their outside life sticking together in a tightly packed group, waiting for an adult to bring food to them. After this they begin to make tentative explorations on their own and to forage for themselves, but the group will remain together until the following spring. Other small birds often team up with Long-tailed Tit flocks – you may well find other tit species moving around with them, and also perhaps Goldcrests and overwintering Chiffchaffs.

Long-tailed Tits are largely sedentary in the UK. The longest recorded movement within the British Isles is just 336km, an adult that travelled from Norfolk to Dorset (though it did make the journey in an impressive 15 days). As with other very small birds that struggle badly in cold weather, Long-tailed Tits will undertake short-range movements to try to find warmer conditions with better feeding opportunities.

Recoveries between Britain and Europe are very few, and involve birds moving to and from Belgium and eastern England. However, the Continental subspecies *A. c. caudatus*, distinctive for its pure white head, is a partial migrant occurring in boreal Scandinavia, and individuals of this form turn up in Britain on occasion (often in small parties) – a straight-line journey of more than 500km.

Fledgling Long-tailed Tits lack obvious pink tones and have dark masks and scarlet eyelids, giving them a roguish look.

WE ARE FAMILY

Long-tailed Tits show a level of sociality that sets them apart from the true tits. It is rare to encounter them alone outside the breeding season, and flocks are usually of family groups comprising parents and chicks, along with any non-breeding assistants at the nest. The groups form in summer when the chicks fledge, and stay together through winter.

Two or more family parties will generally team up to form larger flocks, which forage and roost together. The latter is of great importance through winter, when huddling together for warmth can mean the difference between life and death.

Come spring, birds pair up within their flocks if they can, and the groups break up somewhat, though they will re-form on cold nights in early spring for roosting. Those individuals (of both sexes) that fail to find partners, or whose nests fail at an early stage (a common occurrence in this species), will seek out a local male relative with an active nest and provide assistance with feeding the young. This way, they invest some energy into the continuation of their genes. About half of all successful nests have benefited from having at least one extra adult helping out, and chicks from these nests survive better than those reared by their parents alone. The year-round social and cooperative side of Long-tailed Tit life explains why this species does not really go in for territorial behaviour, or perform an elaborate courtship.

The oldest British-ringed Long-tailed Tit was first caught and ringed as an adult at a site in Surrey in October 1999. Ringers then recaptured the bird at the same site no fewer than nine times, the last occasion being eight years, 10 months and 25 days after the first. There are records of older birds from Denmark – 11 years and one month, and at least 10 years and nine months.

IN THE GARDEN

Visits by Long-tailed Tits to garden bird feeders tend to be sporadic – a party may turn up once a day and feed frantically for two minutes, before moving on and not returning. Offering a fatty suet cake or suet nibbles (ideally ones that include something of insect origin) is most likely to work for them, and they prefer a large feeder so the whole group can eat together. Flocks on the move are highly vocal and announce their arrival with constant short purring calls – often they will be accompanied by a few other tits and perhaps a Goldcrest or Chiffchaff.

Persuading Long-tailed Tits to nest in the garden is more difficult. They prefer thick, thorny bushes (and are most successful in this kind of spot), so planting bushes like Hawthorn and Blackthorn may do the trick. Putting out small feathers for birds to take as nesting material is a tactic that can attract many species, but especially Long-tailed Tits, as they use feathers in such vast numbers when completing the inner lining of their nests.

Marsh Tit
Poecile palustris

12cm
12g
RED

This tit is quite a frequent visitor to larger gardens in some parts of the UK, but has undergone a dramatic decline over the last few decades. It is distinctive and easy to tell from the more common tit species given a decent view, but distinguishing it from its rarer relative, the Willow Tit, is one of the most tricky challenges for UK birdwatchers.

INTRODUCTION

The Marsh Tit is about the same size as a Blue Tit, but with a sleeker silhouette and a more balanced, less top-heavy shape than a Coal Tit. It has a plain, dull brown upperside with no wing-bars, and a paler buffish underside. The cheeks are white, and it has a neat black cap and small black bib under the chin. Juveniles are very similar but their black head markings are slightly duller brownish black. The call is a sneezing two-note *pit-choo*. The song is variable but always a rapid series of ringing or explosive notes – the species' voice is the surest way to distinguish it from the Willow Tit.

DISTRIBUTION, POPULATION AND HABITAT

Marsh Tits are fairly widespread in England and Wales, and just reach south-east Scotland. They are not present in Ireland or on the various islands off the Welsh and English coasts. The range continues through most of Europe and into western Asia, and then there is a separate large population in Mongolia, south-eastern Russia and north-eastern China. The subspecies in Britain (and western France) is *P. p. dresseri*.

There are about 41,000 breeding pairs in the UK. The population has declined severely over the last few decades, with a 79 per cent fall across the UK as a whole between 1967 and 2015, and a 23 per cent decline recorded between 2010 and 2015. Its decline appears to be driven largely by lower annual survival rates rather than reduced breeding success, and is associated with a fall in woodland quality – particularly the loss of a good understorey layer.

Although less colourful than other tit species, the Marsh Tit is still a rather striking and dapper little bird.

NAME-CHANGING

If you have an older field guide, it may give the scientific name for the Marsh Tit as *Parus palustris*. Not so long ago, all of our six true tit species belonged to the genus *Parus*, but today only the Great Tit does – the other five are in four different genera.

Scientists don't just do this to make books go out of date. Studies of the mitochondrial DNA of animals helps reveal how closely related different species really are, and in the case of the tit family, it showed that not all species placed in the genus *Parus* were close relatives, and that the genus should be broken up into multiple genera. One new genus is *Poecile*, which includes the Marsh and Willow Tits. It is one of the few groups

of true tits with representatives in America. The American *Poecile* species are the chickadees – some of the USA's most well-known and much-loved wild bird species.

This species is misleadingly named, as it prefers drier woodland and is not a marshland species at all. It occurs in and around the edges of Beech and other deciduous woodland with a scrubby understorey, including in larger gardens and parkland.

BEHAVIOUR

The Marsh Tit has a typical tit diet of mainly insects with some seeds and fruit in autumn and winter. It takes a large quantity of beechmast in autumn and winter. Like the Coal Tit, it makes caches of food to tide it over in the colder months, and has a very good memory for where it has placed items.

It forages in a typical tit manner, searching tree bark, foliage as well as the ground for food, moving rapidly and with agility. It will join mixed feeding flocks of tits that pass through its territory, but it does not stay with the flock when it moves past the territory boundary.

Like the other true tits, this bird nests in natural tree holes and other cavities, sometimes near or even in the ground. Pairs stay together year round and long term, often using the same nest site year-on-year if they breed successfully. The female lays five to nine eggs and incubates them for about 15 days, and the chicks fledge at about 20 days old.

This is a highly sedentary species. No Marsh Tits ringed outside the British Isles have ever been recovered here, nor have any British-ringed individuals ever been found overseas. The oldest UK bird was ringed as a juvenile in 1984 and caught again by a ringer in the same area 11 years and three months later – a ringed Swedish bird just beats this record, surviving to 11 years and 11 months.

IN THE GARDEN

Marsh Tits will come to bird tables and feeders for seeds, peanuts and suet-based foods. They tend to make fleeting, furtive visits, and you are unlikely to see more than one or two at a time, so they are easily overlooked.

A nest box suitable for Blue Tits (see page 33) will work for Marsh Tits, but they will invariably be displaced by their more dominant relatives if there is any shortage of nest sites. If you have Marsh Tits in the garden, offer lots of nest boxes in a variety of settings and you may be lucky.

You'll usually see Marsh Tits in pairs or singly, though they may briefly join roaming flocks of other tit species.

Willow Tit
Poecile montanus

12cm
12g
RED

This little bird is extremely difficult to tell from the Marsh Tit. It is much rarer, though, having suffered one of the worst population crashes of any British bird since the 1970s. However, where its numbers remain healthy, it will readily come to gardens.

INTRODUCTION

The Willow Tit looks very like the Marsh Tit, with a black cap and small black bib, pale cheeks, dull brown upperside and paler buff-tinged underside. It often looks thicker-necked than the Marsh, with the body and head making a smooth egg shape. Juveniles are a little drabber, with brownish-black rather than pure black head markings. A good view is needed to tell the species from a Marsh Tit by appearance. Its voice is quite different, though – the call is a rather harsh, down-slurred *djerr* note, and its song (though variable) is often a series of sweet-toned long notes, lacking the 'sneezy' quality of the Marsh Tit's song.

DISTRIBUTION, POPULATION AND HABITAT

Willow Tits occur very patchily in England, Wales and south Scotland, with many gaps in their distribution, especially in the south. They are absent from Ireland. The world range extends right across northern and central Eurasia to Japan. Subspecies *P. m. kleinshmidti* occurs in the UK. This subspecies is much more like the Marsh Tit in appearance than most others – in Sweden, for example, separating Marsh Tits from the markedly paler and greyer Scandinavian *P. m. montanus* is quite straightforward.

The Scandinavian subspecies of Willow Tit is a distinctly frostier-plumaged version of our own rather ginger-toned subspecies.

An estimated 3,400 pairs of Willow Tits breed in Britain. The population crashed by 91 per cent between 1967 and 2015 – the cause is not clear but is probably related to large-scale changes in woodland quality. The Willow Tit's distribution has also become very fragmented, which is a big problem for such a sedentary species – small, isolated populations are at risk of inbreeding.

AN ID HEADACHE

In recent years, experts have provided various reliable new ways to tell Marsh and Willow Tits apart visually, but seeing the identifiers on a fast-moving bird is difficult – whereas they are often easy to see in photos.

Marsh Tit   *Willow Tit*

Bill spot Marsh Tits have a white spot on the lower mandible, near the base on the cutting edge. In Willow Tits, the bill is all black.

Cheek pattern Marsh Tits' cheeks are white at the front and brown-tinted at the rear, with a clear demarcation. Willow Tits' cheeks are uniform off-white.

Wing-panel Marsh Tits' wings are plain brown. Willow Tits show a vague pale panel in the secondary feathers.

Flank colour Marsh Tits' flanks are drab grey-brown. Willow Tits have a brighter orange tint to the flanks.

Other much-cited identification features, such as bib size and shininess of cap, are less reliable.

In the UK, the Willow Tit prefers damp and scrubby woodland with a thick understorey and some standing deadwood; it does not need a large number of mature trees and often fares better in young woodland. Some sites that support it are former industrial areas now reverting to early-stage woodland. It is subject to a Biodiversity Action Plan at present and also an RSPB/Wildlife Trust 'Back from the Brink' project in the Dearne Valley in Yorkshire, one of its strongholds. Conservation measures being carried out to help it include thinning out mature trees to encourage the understorey, and leaving 1m stumps when felling trees to provide nest sites. We also need to understand its ecology more thoroughly, through surveys and observations.

BEHAVIOUR

Willow Tits feed mainly on insects and other invertebrates in the warmer months, and take more seeds and fruit in winter. They will chip at dead, rotting wood to find invertebrate prey. They are not usually seen among mixed feeding flocks.

This species is monogamous. It nests in cavities, like other tits, but rather than relying on existing holes it often creates its own, digging out a hole in a rotting tree stump. Females lay one clutch of six to eight eggs and incubate them for 14 days, then both parents feed the young in the nest for about 19 days. The chicks are fed for another couple of weeks after fledging.

Like the Marsh Tit, the Willow Tit is highly sedentary – none ringed outside of the British Isles has ever been recovered here, and no British-ringed individuals have ever been found overseas. The UK longevity record is 11 years and four months; another ringed bird in Finland has equalled this record.

IN THE GARDEN

Marsh Tits outnumber Willow Tits by about 11:1 in the UK, but if you live in a good area for Willow Tits, they may well come to the garden. They are quick visitors, so you'll need patience to get a good view.

Because Willow Tits excavate their own nest cavities, they prefer a nest box partly filled with sawdust, and they also seem to prefer taller, deeper nest boxes that blend in well with their surroundings. Try covering the outside of the box with bark from the same kind of tree as the one you fix the box to. If this species does nest in your garden, or if you see any evidence of breeding behaviour, you should inform the Rare Breeding Birds Panel (see Further reading, page 220).

Willow Tits can struggle to find nest sites in heavily managed woodlands where damaged trees are removed rather than left in place.

Finches

Most of the finches that live in or regularly visit the British Isles can be classed as 'garden birds', and through winter some species will spend time in even the smallest garden as long as food (natural or in feeders) is on offer. These seed-eating species belong to the songbird family Fringillidae, and many are noted for both their colourful plumage and sweet song.

Chaffinch
Fringilla coelebs

14cm
24g

GREEN

This distinctive finch is a very common bird in Britain and a regular garden visitor in most areas. Males in breeding plumage are among the most colourful of British birds, and their exuberant song is an uplifting sign that spring is on its way.

INTRODUCTION

The Chaffinch is about the same size as the House Sparrow but looks slimmer and slighter. Males in spring are boldly marked and colourful, with an ash-blue crown, rose-pink face and underside, reddish-brown back, green rump and black wings with two white bars – a broad, short one near the bend of the wing (though this is often hidden by ruffled back or breast feathers) and, further down, a narrower, T-shaped band. The tail is also black with white outer feathers. In fresh autumn plumage, the male is drabber, as the newly grown feathers have pale brown fringes. Through winter, these wear away, revealing more of the brighter parts of the feathers. The female is light fawn brown, a little darker above than below, with the same white wing-bars and white outer-tail feathers; juveniles are similar. The male's bill is blue-grey, while females and juveniles have duller pinky-grey bills. In flight, the white wing and tail markings are striking.

The song is a bright and emphatic chattering phrase lasting about 2.5 seconds, which descends the scale and ends with a little flourish of spluttering notes. Its calls include a ringing *pink* or *vink* note and

The female Chaffinch is plain in colour but has a sleek elegance that readily distinguishes her from the female House Sparrow.

A DIALECTICAL DIALOGUE

Birds, like people, can develop distinctly different 'accents' in different regions, and this phenomenon has been studied in Chaffinches. Young male Chaffinches learn the basics of song from hearing their fathers and other local males, so the songs of two male Chaffinches that live close to one another are likely to be more similar than those of two males from different parts of Britain. The 'rain' call has also been shown to exhibit dialectical variation across a region, as demonstrated by a study of Chaffinches living on various islands in a Finnish archipelago – birds from different parts of the archipelago had their own definite call types and there was almost no crossover.

Studying the minutiae of bird vocalisations is made easier if you use your recordings to make sonograms – graphs that plot sound frequency against time. This visual representation of a sound can reveal the small but consistent differences in song and call structure that ensue when dialects develop.

a flatter-sounding *chwee* note, often repeated at regular intervals over several minutes. This *chwee* call is given by males only during the breeding season, and it is probably used as a sort of song substitute. It is known as the 'rain' call, as it was traditionally believed to be associated with bad weather. Some biologists suggest that it may be used instead of full song when the Chaffinch needs to proclaim his territory, but also to conserve energy, which would tie in with its being heard more frequently in poor weather.

DISTRIBUTION, POPULATION AND HABITAT

In the British Isles, Chaffinches are common almost everywhere, including virtually all islands – they are absent only from the most open and remote mountainous parts of northern Scotland. The world range extends throughout Europe and to North Africa, north-western Asia and parts of the Middle East; the species is also present on some Atlantic islands. There is a small introduced population in the Cape area of South Africa, and introduced Chaffinches have spread throughout New Zealand to become one of the commonest bird species on both the North and South Islands. The subspecies that breeds in the British Isles is *F. c. gengleri*.

In the UK, the breeding population is about 6.2 million pairs strong. Variable numbers from mainland Europe join our breeding birds in winter, while some breeding birds move south. The breeding population has fluctuated since detailed recording began in the late 1960s – overall there was a modest increase of 13 per cent between 1967 and 2015, but this masks a strong general increase up until about 2006, followed by a rather sharp downturn, probably due to the outbreak of trichomonosis, a disease common in some garden birds that badly affects this species.

Chaffinches are woodland birds, doing well in both deciduous and coniferous forest, and also in more open countryside with scrub or hedgerows. They will forage on arable farmland, and visit parks and gardens of all kinds – given a ready food supply and some bushes for nesting, they can form large populations even in city centres, and often exploit areas in the countryside where people gather to eat, such as picnic areas at country parks. At places like this they readily become bold enough to take food from people's hands.

BEHAVIOUR

The Chaffinch is a versatile feeder with a medium-sized conical bill, suitable for cracking smaller seeds but also for dealing with insect prey. In the breeding season it is mostly insectivorous and feeds its chicks exclusively on small, soft-bodied invertebrates. It finds these by gleaning foliage (it takes many caterpillars from tree and bush leaves) and it is also a competent flycatcher. Outside the breeding season it eats seeds and berries; it also eats tree leaf buds in early spring. Non-breeding flocks spend much time foraging on the ground.

Chaffinches can form very large feeding flocks in wintertime. It is always worth checking such gatherings for scarcer species, particularly Bramblings, which often associate with Chaffinches. You may also see Chaffinches in mixed flocks of sparrows and buntings. Flocks tend to forage on the ground – you may see odd birds using hanging feeders but they rarely 'swamp' the feeders in the way that Goldfinches and Greenfinches do.

Male Chaffinches begin to establish territories and sing in late winter – mostly in February but occasionally earlier. Sometimes a pair that breeds successfully will reunite the following year. Females otherwise choose a potential mate on the basis of his song and territory quality. The male will join a female that enters his territory, and continues to sing while hopping rather mechanically to and fro on the branch beside her, holding his wings low to display his green rump patch. Territorial males sometimes aggressively attack their own reflections in house windows.

The nest site is often the fork of a tree or bush, and the deep cup-shaped nest, built by the female, is a beautiful though well-camouflaged structure. It combines moss, fine roots and spiderwebs with a lining of various soft materials, including feathers and animal hair, and the outside is decorated with lichen for camouflage. Inside, the female lays and incubates her clutch of four or five eggs for 12 days, and then both parents feed the chicks in the nest until they fledge at about 15 days old. Both parents feed the chicks for a couple more weeks after fledging. Chaffinches usually have only one brood a year but occasionally produce two. The first-year survival rate of young Chaffinches is relatively high, as small songbirds go.

Chaffinch ringing recoveries show that there is considerable movement between the UK and north-west Europe, notably Belgium, the Netherlands, Denmark, Sweden and Norway. Some birds ringed in the UK have been recovered in Finland and vice versa, and a few moved between the UK and Russia. The longest journey was by a young female caught overwintering in Scotland and recaptured in Russia, 2,362km away. Nearly all ringed birds moving long distances between the UK and north-west Europe have been females, as might be predicted (see 'Bachelor birds' box).

By contrast, numbers moving between the UK and more southerly countries are much lower – a few in northern France, and one extreme outlier – an adult male ringed in Oxfordshire, which travelled 1,572km to Portugal.

BACHELOR BIRDS

Carl Linnaeus, the 18th-century Swedish naturalist who came up with the binomial (two-name – genus and species) scientific naming system for living things, called the Chaffinch *Fringilla coelebs* – it is one of rather few Linnean names that is still used unchanged. *Fringilla* is a Latin word for a small bird. The species name *coelebs* means 'unmarried' and reflects Linnaeus's observation that, in winter, nearly all of the Chaffinches he saw in Sweden were males.

Chaffinches are partial migrants in the northern and eastern parts of their range, with a proportion of the population moving south in winter. When food becomes scarce, the more dominant birds are most likely to stay put, as they aggressively drive away the competition. Chaffinch males are a little larger than females and can oust them from feeding grounds. Come spring, the males lose their hostile attitude towards females, instead becoming deferential and more likely to flee from their mate than attack her.

WARTS AND ALL

If you keep a close eye on your garden Chaffinches, you may spot one or two that appear to have a scaly, spiky encrustation on their feet and legs. In severe cases the affected feet and legs appear grossly enlarged and whitened. The cause of this is a virus called *Fringilla papillomavirus* – it is not dissimilar to the virus that causes warts and verrucas in humans. Affected birds may appear very uncomfortable, though can survive long term with the condition. If you notice cases appearing in the garden, it may help to take down and sterilise all your feeders.

The UK longevity record is held by a female caught and ringed as an adult in Fife, Scotland, in 1997, and observed alive and well at the same site 13 years, 11 months and nine days later. In Switzerland, a Chaffinch was re-caught by a ringer 15 years and six months after it was ringed.

IN THE GARDEN

Chaffinches are so widespread that your garden is probably already on their radar even if they are not yet visiting. They will come to hanging feeders, but as they are not the most agile of birds they prefer the kind that has a perch of some description under the feeding ports. They are very fond of sunflower hearts and most wild birdseed mix, and will also enjoy suet pellets and fat balls. They are habitual ground-foragers, so if it's possible to offer seed on the ground then this is likely to attract them (but be aware that putting seed directly on the ground can attract rats – a ground-feeding tray that you can easily remove is a good compromise).

Unless you have trees or well-established bushes in the garden, Chaffinches are unlikely to nest, but you can support any local breeding birds by maintaining an insect-rich, wildlife-friendly garden with plenty of native plants on which moths and butterflies can lay their eggs.

In many UK public parks, Chaffinches have become habituated enough to people that they will happily come to the hand to feed.

Goldfinch
Carduelis carduelis

12cm
17g
GREEN

This beautiful small finch, with its unique colour scheme, pleasant voice and habit of travelling in large hungry gangs, is a much-coveted garden bird. It is also one of the wildlife winners of recent decades, with a very strong population increase that is at least partly down to the growing numbers of people who feed their garden birds.

INTRODUCTION

There can be few UK gardens that do not have the potential to attract this unmistakable and lively finch.

The Goldfinch is a slim, dainty finch with beautiful and distinctive plumage. It has a bright orange-red face patch, with black around the eyes. The cheeks, upper breast, belly and rump are white, and the crown and neck black. The back and flanks are light pinky buff, and the black wings are marked with a broad, bright yellow wing-stripe. The latter forms a broad and very conspicuous yellow band down the centre of the wing when the bird is in flight. The tail is also black, and the flight feathers and longest tail feathers are tipped with white spots. It has a relatively long and slim bill, horn-coloured with a dark tip, and the legs are a dull pinkish colour. Juvenile Goldfinches have the same wing and tail pattern and colours as adults, but the head and body plumage is uniform streaky pale brown.

The call is a bright, liquid, laughing twitter, and the male's song an extended sequence of similar notes. Flocks are highly vocal and draw attention with their non-stop calls as they move around.

GOLDEN BOYS AND GIRLS

Most of our finches show quite definite sexual dimorphism, with males more brightly coloured than females. The Goldfinch is the exception – telling males from females is very difficult, and (for the average birdwatcher at least) usually impossible. Differences include:

- the size and shade of the red mask (it is redder and extends beyond the eye in males, and is more yellowish and less extensive in females);
- the colour of the feathers on the wing at its bend (solid black in males, mixed with brown in females);
- the colour of the fine, hair-like feathers around the nostril (black in males, grey in females); and
- the slight size variation, males being slightly larger and longer-billed.

However, there is lots of variation within the sexes in all of these criteria, and none of them is easy to see and evaluate. Even for bird ringers, who get to have a much closer and more controlled look at wild birds than the rest of us, many Goldfinches have to go unsexed.

DISTRIBUTION, POPULATION AND HABITAT

This finch is found throughout the British Isles, except for open and mountainous parts of north Scotland, and parts of the northern Scottish island groups. Its world range includes most of Europe to southern Scandinavia, North Africa, the northern Middle East, and into north-western and central-western Asia. It has also been introduced to Australia, New Zealand and parts of South America. The subspecies *C. c. britannica* occurs in the British Isles and also from north-western France across to the western Netherlands.

In the UK we have about 1.2 million pairs of Goldfinches. The species declined sharply in the 1970s and 1980s, a reaction to reduced winter survival as farming methods intensified and there were fewer weed seeds available for the birds to eat. However, the population then increased dramatically through the late 20th and early 21st centuries, rising by 167 per cent between 1990 and 2015. This increase is largely attributable to improved winter survival as more and more Goldfinches visit garden feeding stations – the species has also probably benefited from a decline in Greenfinches (which dominate them at bird feeders) over the same period. It is also increasing elsewhere in Europe, which may be partly due to the decline of the wild-caught cage bird industry (however, it is still targeted for trapping – legally and illegally – over many parts of its range).

The Goldfinch is found in scrubby open countryside with scattered trees, woodland edges, fen and marshland, heathland, parks and gardens – any habitat with a few trees, some bushes and plenty of seed-bearing plants may attract it.

BEHAVIOUR

Goldfinches feed on seeds for much of the year, and are adapted to reach seeds that are difficult for finches with shorter, stouter bills to access. It is widely stated that only the males, with their fractionally longer bills, can get at the seeds hidden between the long spines of Wild Teasel *Dipsacum fullonum* seedheads, although (given the difficulty of telling the sexes apart) this is a difficult claim to verify. Goldfinches in the wider countryside are very reliant on meadows, field

AN ARTISTIC AND SAINTLY BIRD

Because of its red face, and perhaps also its fondness for thistles, the Goldfinch is associated with the crucifixion of Jesus – staining its own face with blood as it attempts to free him of the crown of thorns, in some imagery. It is also often included in representations of the Madonna and child, as a foreshadowing of what is to come.

Poets and artists alike include Goldfinches in their works that celebrate the beauty of nature, and the bird's song is celebrated in Vivaldi's flute concerto in D Major. The famous 1654 work *The Goldfinch,* by Carel Fabritius, depicts a pet Goldfinch chained to a perch – it is a very spontaneous and lifelike representation. The painting plays a key part in the plot of the Pulitzer prize-winning 2013 novel of the same name, by Donna Tartt.

It takes a long bill to extract seeds from the hedgehog-like teasel head without getting spiked in the eye.

margins and other grassy habitats where thistles, Wild Teasels, ragworts and other similar plants are left to stand throughout winter. Modern farming methods have reduced this habitat, but Goldfinches today have more than compensated for the loss by moving, en masse, into towns and villages to visit garden feeding stations throughout winter.

During the breeding season, Goldfinches also take a certain number of small insects, and these are particularly important for small chicks, though older chicks are fed increasingly on seeds.

Goldfinches are agile and lightweight, able to cling to a wobbling plant stem while attacking the seedhead with their bill – they will perch on larger seedheads and hold them steady with their feet as they peck out the seeds. They are very sociable when foraging, at all times of year, though flocks become particularly large after the breeding season – it is quite common for bird feeders to be completely taken over by Goldfinches for long spells. They may also forage alongside other finches, such as Lesser Redpolls, Chaffinches and Siskins; in the wider countryside they regularly move around in flocks more than 100 strong and frequently associate with Linnets.

Pairs form within flocks in late winter, and they engage in courtship displays with much posturing to show off the contrasting plumage colour patches on the face and in the wings. However, Goldfinches are not strongly territorial and several pairs will often nest close together in a loose colony.

The female builds the nest alone, weaving a compact, deep cup-shaped structure near the tip of a tree branch or in a bush. The outer structure is made of lichen and moss, and lined with soft thistledown and similar materials; spider silk is used to bind it in place. She lays a clutch of four to six pale, finely speckled eggs, and incubates them for about 12 days, while the male brings her food, delivering it directly into her mouth through regurgitation. The chicks are fed in a similar way, by both parents (but primarily the male at first, as the female stays with the brood to warm and protect them while they are still very small and naked). The young fledge at about 15–17 days old and continue to receive care from their father for another week or so, while the female begins to lay a second clutch. Most pairs have two broods in a year, and occasionally three.

Goldfinches in the UK are not great wanderers, but ringing recoveries show there is some regular spring/autumn movement of birds between the UK and the Low Countries, western France, south through Spain and into north-west Africa. Of these birds, the longest recorded movement was made by a bird that travelled 1,939km from Wiltshire to Morocco. However, another bird travelled even further, and in the 'wrong' direction, flying 2,070km south-east to Malta.

The oldest known UK Goldfinch was sexed as a male and caught as a first-year in 2006 in Suffolk. It was caught again at the same site 10 years and two days later. The European record is 14 years and one month, clocked up by a bird in the Czech Republic.

IN THE GARDEN

For some years, nyjer seed has been marketed as the 'Goldfinch magnet'. The seeds are so tiny that they need to be offered in a special feeder (they will simply fall straight out of conventional feeders, through the mesh or ports). Rich and oily, these seeds are highly attractive to Goldfinches, which are slim-billed and so prefer small seeds (and are expert at extracting them from the small oval slots in the nyjer feeders). However, Goldfinches are also very fond of sunflower hearts and black sunflower seeds, and some people find that their Goldfinches spurn nyjer seed completely if these are on offer. Like other seed-eaters, they are thirsty birds, so ensure the bird bath or other water source is kept topped up. You can also offer natural food for Goldfinches by having a wild patch in your garden where plants like Creeping Thistles *Cirsium arvense* and Wild Teasels can grow and seed.

It is fairly rare for Goldfinches to nest in gardens, especially as they like to breed in loose colonies and need a good-sized area of suitable habitat. However, they may do so if you have a large garden with some trees.

Nyjer seeds are rich in oil and very appealing to Goldfinches, as are sunflower seeds.

MYSTERIOUS MULES

There is a long tradition of keeping certain British songbirds as pets, and the Goldfinch is probably the most popular species, thanks to its colours and pleasant song. Caged native birds must wear a closed leg-ring to prove they are captive-bred (these rings can be placed only on small nestlings). There are, unfortunately, still cases every so often of wild British birds being illegally trapped for the caged bird trade.

Some birdkeepers produce hybrids between different species. Hybrids between native British finches and domestic canaries are known as 'mules' (after the horse x donkey hybrid). Escapee Goldfinch mules and other hybrids such as Goldfinch x Greenfinch turn up with some frequency in gardens and cause many a head-scratching moment for the people who spot them, as they show some aspects of the distinctive Goldfinch plumage pattern but are clearly not the same as a 'real' Goldfinch. If a peculiar-looking but rather Goldfinch-like bird wearing a leg-ring turns up in your garden, it is probably a mule or a hybrid that escaped from a cage or aviary.

Bullfinch
Pyrrhula pyrrhula

16cm
21g
AMBER

This handsome, large finch is a rather shy species. Although it is softly spoken and introverted in character, the male is one of the most colourful and striking of all garden birds.

Bullfinches are stunning when seen clearly, but it's more usual to glimpse just the white rump disappearing into a hedgerow.

INTRODUCTION

The Bullfinch is stocky with a short, very stout bill. It has a black cap, chin, wings and tail, with a neat, square white rump patch and a broad but somewhat faint pale wing-bar. Males have bright rose-pink cheeks and undersides, and dove-grey backs, while in females the underside is a more subtle grey-pink and the back is just a shade greyer, but showing little contrast with the underside. The legs and feet are dark pinky brown. Juveniles are like females but lack the black head markings, so look very plain-faced, with prominent dark eyes. In flight, the white rump patch is very striking.

The call is a soft, rather mournful-sounding short whistle – discreet and subtle, but still usually quite noticeable once you have learned its sound. The male's song is a few such whistles given together, sometimes with some squeaking or wheezing notes, but it is so simple and quiet that it is not even readily recognisable as birdsong.

DISTRIBUTION, POPULATION AND HABITAT

Bullfinches are found throughout most of the British Isles, though become very patchy in the upland parts of northern Scotland (especially in the breeding season) – they are also missing from most offshore islands, especially in the north, and from very open areas, such as around the Wash in East Anglia. The species' range extends eastwards across most of Europe and in a broad band through northern and central Asia to the Far East, with the most northern birds migrating south in winter but the majority being sedentary. The subspecies we have in the British Isles is *P. p. pileata*, but in autumn and winter variable numbers of the northern European subspecies *P. p. pyrrhula* arrive, particularly on northern and eastern coasts. Most winters only a handful are recorded, but occasionally there are mass arrivals or 'irruptions' of this subspecies. These events are linked to a poor crop of Rowan berries in their 'home' countries.

There are about 190,000 pairs of Bullfinches in the UK. The population was formerly considerably higher but suffered a crash around the mid-1970s, probably driven by changes in agricultural practices and in woodland management. The decline, which was most severe in England, slowed from the mid-1980s and numbers stabilised in the mid-1990s – they have fluctuated but generally increased somewhat since then. Overall, there was a 37 per cent decline between 1967 and 2015 but a 21 per cent increase between 2005 and 2015.

The beady black eye of the young Bullfinch is noticeable in its otherwise unmarked head. Its wing pattern is like the adult's.

This finch is most common around woodland edges, large natural hedgerows, copses on mixed farmland and similar habitats with a good variety of native plant types. It is most likely to turn up in rural gardens with plenty of shrubs and at least a few trees.

THE SOUND OF SILENCE

Many birdwatchers would have a hard time describing the song of the Bullfinch, as it is so indistinct and unimpressive. Early Victorian cage bird fanciers found the bird rather a disappointment, as it lacked a beautiful voice to go with its stunning appearance (and was also a little fragile and difficult to keep).

One of the reasons why Bullfinch males put so little effort into song may be that they are exceptionally monogamous. Pairs stick together through the winter, and neither sex invests much time in seeking sneaky matings with the neighbours, as most other songbirds do. The lack of sexual competitiveness is evident in Bullfinch physiology, too: the male's testes make up a mere 0.29 per cent of his total body mass (by contrast, those of the polygamous and extremely frisky Dunnock make up 3.4 per cent), and he also produces sperm with an unusual shape, less well adapted to fast swimming than those of other songbirds. All of these traits indicate that males are not strongly driven to compete against one another for female attention. As we know, songbird males do battle first and foremost with their voices, but the male Bullfinch's way of life means he has not had the need to hone his song into an impressive weapon.

However, the Victorian birdkeepers did discover that they could teach their pet Bullfinches to accurately imitate a simple whistled melody, or even two or three different tunes, if they started the lessons very early with a hand-reared male. Such trained birds were highly prized and changed hands for large sums of money.

TRUMPETING GIANTS FROM THE NORTH

The Bullfinch subspecies *P. p. pyrrhula* occurs widely in Europe and across northern Asia. Those breeding in the far north are migratory, heading south in winter, and sometimes they head more westwards than they might have intended and reach the British Isles. There is quite a marked difference between this form and our own *P. p. pileata* and in a 'good' year for *P. p. pyrrhula* they could turn up in gardens. If you notice a strikingly big, distinctly pale Bullfinch in autumn or winter, listen for its calls. The northern form has a distinctive call, often likened to the toot of a toy trumpet and quite distinct from the soft, sad whistle of *P. p. pileata*.

BEHAVIOUR

The Bullfinch is mainly vegetarian and has a particular appetite for unopened fruit tree flower buds, a habit that makes it very unpopular with anyone running commercial orchards as it can do significant damage. It takes other flower and leaf buds, too – the importance of buds in the diet all year round means that it needs a good range of different plant types to provide food through all the seasons. There is some evidence that individuals have their own particular tastes and preferences.

The bird also feeds on berries, such as those of Rowan and Blackberry, and the seeds of various trees such as elms, and herbaceous plants including Meadowsweet *Filipendula ulmaria* and Stinging Nettles. The bill is stout enough to crack quite hard seeds and crush fruit to a pulp, but its shortness makes it unsuited to dealing with plants whose seeds are buried deep in a spiky seedhead. In the breeding season, the diet is supplemented with small insects.

Bullfinches are usually seen in pairs, the male and female staying close together as they make their way along a line of trees, feeding as they go. Young unpaired birds will gather in larger parties in autumn and early winter, and these groups may be joined by bonded pairs as well. Bullfinches will assemble at spots where there is plenty of food, and will feed alongside other bird species at feeding stations, but they rarely actively join mixed feeding flocks.

Small soft fruits appeal to Bullfinches in autumn and winter – plant a range of native fruiting shrubs to attract them.

Because pairs of Bullfinches stay with one another and on their territory all year round, courtship behaviour is rather perfunctory. Both sexes may perform a simple dance involving rocking and bowing postures, prior to mating. Young birds find their mates within autumn and winter flocks, and separate out as pairs before the new year.

The nest, built high up within a large, dense shrub, is a cup of woven small twigs and grasses with some moss, and lined with small soft roots. In it the female lays a clutch of four or five eggs, and incubates them for about 15 days. The chicks fledge at about 16 days old. The pair will usually produce a second brood, and occasionally a third. Once the chicks are independent of their parents, a couple of weeks after fledging, they may join other families of juveniles and roam in foraging parties through early autumn and into winter.

Adult Bullfinches are very sedentary. Young birds may disperse some distance in their first autumn and winter, but long-distance movements are unusual, and there have been very few recoveries of British-ringed Bullfinches overseas (or vice versa). One adult ringed in Scotland in winter 1995 was found dead in Sweden nearly three years later, having covered a distance of 1,508km – this was quite likely a Swedish-born bird of the migratory northern subspecies. A few individuals have moved more than 200km within the UK, the furthest travelling 517km from Norfolk to east Scotland.

The oldest known British-ringed Bullfinch was ringed as an adult in autumn 1965 and found dead in early winter 1975 – an interval of nine years, two months and nine days. One Bullfinch in Germany was at least 12 years and seven months old, and there is also a record from Sweden of one reaching at least 12 years and six months of age.

IN THE GARDEN

The kind of garden most likely to attract Bullfinches will be rural, with plenty of trees (especially Apple *Malus domestica*, Pear *Pyrus communis*, cherries and other fruit trees) and shrubs, and close to mixed woodland with lush, well-vegetated edges. Offer mixed birdseed or sunflower seeds on a bird table or in hanging plastic feeders with perches and feeding ports (the birds are not particularly agile and prefer this type of feeder to a perchless mesh feeder) and you are likely to see at least a pair of Bullfinches. Although they are usually quite shy and timid, they are unhurried when feeding if they don't know they're being watched, and you should have good views. They may opt to breed in your garden if you have some large, dense shrubs offering secure nesting sites.

NIP IT IN THE BUD

It is hard for us to imagine, but the beautiful and timid Bullfinch has, historically, been considered a serious pest because of the damage it can do to the flower buds of fruit trees. Although the bird's precipitous decline has been fully appreciated and the species has full legal protection, fruit-growers may apply for, and be granted, a licence to kill Bullfinches if the depredations of their local birds are harming their livelihood and non-lethal preventative measures have proven to be unsuccessful. During the winter of 1996 to 1997, a general licence to kill Bullfinches was issued to commercial fruit-growers in Kent meaning that they could do so without making a formal application. However, studies have shown the problem is better managed by removing dense cover from the edges of orchards – Bullfinches are always more comfortable when there is a large thorny bush nearby into which they can dive should danger threaten.

If Bullfinches are damaging your fruit trees, you can try to discourage them by tying plastic carrier bags in the trees for the few weeks that there are unopened flower buds – the sound and movement the bags make as the wind blows them about should be enough to keep the finches away. You can also offer your local finches plenty of seed to distract them from other food sources.

Siskin
Spinus spinus

12cm
15g
GREEN

This delightful little finch is a relative newcomer to the garden birdwatching scene. Its recent population increase and the expansion of its breeding range have, without doubt, been partly driven by the species learning to use garden bird feeders, a habit that began only towards the end of the 20th century.

INTRODUCTION

Siskins are about the same size as Blue Tits and have a similar compact build and lively, agile character. They have long wings and quite deeply forked tail-tips. The male is brightly coloured (though there is considerable variation in colour intensity), with a yellow face and breast, fading to white on the belly and with some bold blackish streaks on the flanks. He has a leaf-green back, black crown and bib, and black-and-yellow patterns on the wings and tail. Females are drabber yellow-green with brownish streaking over the whole body plumage, this becoming thick and bold on the rear flanks. The wings are patterned like the male's, but less brightly coloured. Juveniles resemble duller and browner females. The greyish bill is relatively long and thin, and the legs are a dark pinkish colour.

The Siskin's call is a rather wheezy high note; flocks going overhead draw attention with their frequent calls. Similar notes are included in the male's song, which also has high-pitched trills and twitters.

Siskins are most likely to nest in areas of pine woodland but become much more widespread in winter.

DISTRIBUTION, POPULATION AND HABITAT

Siskins breed throughout Scotland, including on most islands, and across most of Wales and Ireland. In England, they breed mainly in the north, south-west and along the south coast, and also in the Thetford Forest area of East Anglia. In winter, they can be found almost anywhere in the British Isles.

COUSINS ABROAD

The Siskin does not normally occur in North America, although there have been occasional records from the last century. However, there is evidence that it (or at least its fairly recent ancestors) did manage to reach North America and go on to become established there. The founder populations would have come either from western Europe, crossing the Atlantic, or far eastern Asia via Alaska.

DNA evidence indicates that 'our' Siskin has existed in its present form for about 5 million years, while its American relatives diverged from it only some 200,000 years ago. One possible explanation for this is that Siskins from Eurasia reached North America some 2 million years ago (during their periodic 'irruptions') and became established there, spreading across the continent and south to Central America and the Caribbean. Subsequent ice ages would then have broken up the populations in North America into three groups, which over the millennia adapted more closely to their environments. In doing so, they became distinct forms, different to each other and also different to their 'parent' species. They are, today, classed as three distinct species: the Pine Siskin *S. pinus* of North America, the Black-capped Siskin *S. atriceps* of Guatemala, and the Antillean Siskin *S. dominicensis*, found on Hispaniola in the Caribbean.

They also breed across Europe and north-west Asia, moving to southern Europe, the Middle East and North Africa in winter in numbers that vary considerably from year to year – sometimes there are very large-scale 'irruptions' southwards and westwards. There is a separate breeding population in north-east Asia that winters in eastern China and Japan.

The Siskin is considered to be monotypic – it is not divided into any subspecies, as it shows no significant differences across its populations – which is unusual for such a widespread bird.

About 410,000 pairs of Siskins breed in the UK, with more arriving in winter. The bulk of the breeding population is in Scotland but numbers are increasing elsewhere, and the breeding population has sometimes spiked quite dramatically in years following a large influx of Siskins the previous winter. The UK population as a whole rose by 61 per cent between 1967 and 2015, with the strongest increase occurring since 2005 (a rise of 89 per cent between 2005 and 2015).

Siskins in the UK show a preference for breeding in coniferous forest, and thrive in the native Caledonian pine forests of the Scottish Highlands, but they can also do well in commercial spruce plantations. In addition, they may occur in mixed and deciduous woodland. In winter, roaming flocks often work their way along riversides and through wet lowland woodland, searching for Alder trees to feed on the cones (often in the company of redpolls). They are also frequent visitors to gardens through winter, even small urban ones.

Lightweight and acrobatic, Siskins often cling sideways or dangle upside down when feeding from Alder cones.

BEHAVIOUR

Siskins are seed-eaters through the autumn and winter, and in addition to attacking Alder cones they also enjoy the seeds of spruce, pine, larch and birch trees. They will also take the seeds of thistles, knapweeds and related herbaceous plants. In spring and summer, this diet is supplemented with some insect protein, and the young chicks are mainly fed on small insects, including beetles and caterpillars.

Siskins rarely feed on the ground. However, tired newly arrived migrants may do so. They are sociable in winter and flock readily with redpolls (Lesser and other types); they may also join groups of Goldfinches and, more rarely, other finches. Although they are one of the smaller species to visit feeding stations, they are feisty and often manage to hold their own against the likes of Greenfinches and Great Tits.

Siskins begin to pair up in late winter within their flocks, and if they have wandered away from breeding areas they return to them in spring together. Males

SUPER-SIZE ME

When Siskins began to visit gardens in the UK in large numbers in the 1980s, it was clear that the big draw for them was the red mesh bags of peanuts many people hung out for the birds at the time. These bags attracted various species of tits, which were able to cling to the mesh and pick out fragments of nuts, but Siskins are just as agile as tits and were soon taking advantage of the bounty.

It is sometimes theorised that these peanut bags attracted the attention of Siskins because they look rather like super-sized versions of the Alder cones that form such a key part of their natural diet in winter. Alder cones are reddish and hang downwards – the seeds within have to be winkled out from between the scales, much like a bit of peanut through plastic mesh. If you wander down an Alder-lined river in winter, you stand a good chance of finding a Siskin flock acrobatically tackling the cones, dangling upside down with ease as they work.

Today, red mesh peanut bags are not widely available and no food should be placed out for birds in soft plastic net bags anyway, as there is a serious risk they may catch their toes or tongues in the mesh. Happily, Siskins quickly learned to use other kinds of feeders.

compete for female attention, and females prefer the more highly coloured males with bolder and brighter wing patterns; however, they will always favour a male that they know from their own flock over a 'new' male, regardless of his colour intensity.

On returning to the breeding grounds, the male proclaims his territory with song and with a circling flight at treetop level; he also engages in courtship feeding, regurgitating seed when his partner begs for it with fledgling-like wing-fluttering. As with other birds that practise courtship feeding, this behaviour means the female gets extra food rations, which help her body prepare for egg-laying and strengthens the pair-bond. She builds the nest – a beautifully woven deep, compact cup – near the end of a small branch high in a conifer tree, using grasses, tiny twigs and some moss for the outer shell, and soft roots, plant down and other fluffy material as a lining. The clutch usually comprises four or five lightly mottled, pale bluish eggs.

The male brings the female food as she incubates the eggs, over the 12–13 days it takes for the chicks to hatch. At first the male brings all the food to the nest, but as the chicks grow older both parents leave them alone and go out foraging. The chicks fledge at about 14 days and continue to beg for food from their father for a couple more weeks, while the female is busy incubating her second brood.

The BTO's map of ringing recoveries for Siskins that moved between the UK and overseas shows that these little birds can wander considerable distances. Many have travelled here from (or go to) the Low Countries, Germany, Sweden, Denmark and Norway, but there is also considerable interchange between the UK and France, Spain, Portugal and northern Italy, and scattered records from further south and east.

Of several birds that moved more than 2,000km, the greatest traveller was an adult male ringed on his breeding grounds in Argyll and Bute that had moved 2,676km to Malta by late autumn in the same year. A close second was a Scottish-bred youngster that travelled 2,657km to Morocco. Movements of more than 800km within the UK are not unusual.

The UK longevity record is held by a male, ringed as an adult in the Netherlands in February 1988, which was recorded by a ringer in Surrey 12 years, one month and 22 days later. A ringed bird in Russia was recaptured 13 years and six months later.

IN THE GARDEN

Siskins will come to hanging feeders that offer sunflower hearts, peanuts and mixed birdseed, and will also take some suet-based foods. They often arrive in gardens in late winter and early spring, the time when natural foods are at their scarcest and the return migration to breeding areas is underway.

If you live in an area with breeding Siskins, they are likely to come to your garden feeders all year round. And if you have mature conifers in the garden, they may nest – if so, you're likely to spot the juveniles working out how to use the feeders when they fledge in summertime.

The yellow wing-bar revealed when a Siskin flies could lead to momentary confusion with a Goldfinch, but the two are otherwise quite different.

UNUSUAL SOCIALITY

The Austrian zoologist Konrad Lorenz (1903–89) was a great advocate for the Siskin as a pet bird, as he explained in his 1949 book *King Solomon's Ring*. The Siskin, he says, is 'of all the small birds I know, the only one which, even when captured in maturity, not only becomes tame, but also really affectionate'. He goes on to argue that the 'companionable tameness' of the Siskin, although it takes time to build, is more rewarding than the food-driven approachability or 'cupboard love'

demonstrated by, for example, the Robin.

Taking a wild Siskin as a pet today is illegal in Britain as well as ill-advised, but some people find their garden Siskins show signs of this behaviour, becoming quite unworried by the approach of the gardener and hanging around nearby while feeders are refilled. The species' strong sociality with its own kind and with other small bird species could explain its openness to build friendly bonds with human beings too.

Greenfinch
Chloris chloris

This sturdy, handsome finch has been a stalwart of UK gardens ever since people first began to put out seed and peanuts, and is a conspicuous and argumentative presence at the bird table. However, it has suffered a serious decline, particularly in gardens but also in the wider countryside, since the early 21st century. Its conservation status is likely to be changed to Amber in the near future if things don't improve for it soon.

INTRODUCTION

This finch is about the same size as a House Sparrow. It looks rather top-heavy, with a big, flat-topped head and stout bill, and rather featureless plumage. The male is a darkish, olive-tinted green, though he can look very yellow in certain lights – the underside is a little paler. There is a dark patch in front of the eye, giving a rather stern expression. The bill is pale yellowish pink and the legs a rather drab pink. The female is a paler, browner yellowish green with a more greyish bill, and she lacks a distinct dark patch in front of the eye, so her eyes are more prominent and her expression more 'gentle'. Both sexes have a yellow flash along the wing edge, and yellow edges to the tail. Juveniles are like females but drabber, and their plumage is rather faintly but extensively marked with darker streaks. In flight, the yellow wing and tail markings can be prominent, as is the notched tip to the tail.

The male's song is varied but its individual elements are quite simple. Commonly heard phrases include a monotone high twitter, and a long, nasal, downslurred *chweeeer*. The calls are similar to these elements of the song.

The green appearance is not produced by green pigmentation but a combination of blacks and yellows, plus the interplay of light.

HIDDEN DANGER

The catastrophic decline in our Greenfinch population has been caused, in large part, by the spread of a deadly and infectious disease – trichomonosis. This disease, nicknamed 'trich' (and also known as 'canker' in doves and pigeons), is caused by a protozoan (single-celled) organism, and affects the digestive tract – birds suffering from the condition are unable to swallow food properly.

A bird suffering from trich will often sit at a bird feeder for long spells, trying to feed but regurgitating what it eats – infecting the food as it does so. You may notice dried food stuck to its bill, and wet feathers on the face. The bird will be lethargic and may well not fly away even if you approach closely. Its eyes will be partly closed and its feathers puffed up – ironically, though birds with trich can look very fat because of their fluffed-up plumage, they are actually dying of starvation.

Trichomonosis is spread via contaminated food and water, and unfortunately bird-feeding stations create ideal conditions for it to be passed on. Good hygiene can help reduce the spread of other diseases – the RSPB's advice is as follows.

- Use feeders with drainage holes to prevent moisture building up.
- Use more than one feeding site to reduce the number of birds in one place.
- Rotate feeders around several locations to 'rest' each spot, in order to prevent build-up of infection on the ground underneath.
- Clean and disinfect feeders and water baths regularly,

rinsing thoroughly and allowing to air-dry completely – this itself will kill some diseases.
- Clean your feeders with a brush and bucket dedicated to this purpose and keep them outside.
- Sweep up droppings and spilt or old food, and dispose of them carefully in an outside bin.
- Change the water in baths frequently – ideally daily.
- Wash your hands carefully afterwards.

Should you notice any birds at the feeders that show signs of trich, the RSPB recommends that you stop feeding immediately and remove all feeding stations and water baths for thorough cleaning, only resuming feeding after a minimum of three weeks or when there are no diseased birds showing signs of infection. This helps to disperse the feeding birds and reduce the contact between sick and healthy individuals, thus slowing down the outbreak. The higher the concentration of birds at a feeding station, the greater the chance of another bird picking up an infected food particle and exposing itself to the infection.

DISTRIBUTION, POPULATION AND HABITAT

This finch is very widespread in the British Isles, present on most islands as well as everywhere on the mainland except the most open and mountainous upland parts of Scotland, Wales and Ireland. The subspecies *C. c. harrisoni* is present in the British Isles and nowhere else, while the migratory northern European *C. c. chloris* occurs in northern Scotland.

The Greenfinch's distribution beyond Britain encompasses most of Europe and extends into North Africa and western Asia, reaching the western Himalayas. The most northerly populations, in Scandinavia and north-west Russia, are migratory, and their winter range reaches the extreme north-east of Africa. The species has also been introduced to New Zealand.

This species' population has fluctuated considerably, reaching a high point in the early 2000s. There were an estimated 1.7 million pairs of Greenfinches in the UK in 2009, but there has been a considerable decline since 2005 (a 59 per cent fall across the UK was documented between 2005 and 2015). Numbers now are at their lowest ebb since national surveying began in the late 1960s.

Greenfinches are woodland birds, occurring in deciduous, mixed and coniferous woodlands, as well as more open habitats with some trees, and on the edges of conifer plantations. They will visit gardens of all sizes, even in city centres.

BEHAVIOUR

These finches are seed-eaters and can crack quite large and hard seeds with their heavy bills, supported by robust bones and jaw musculature. They also eat some berries, buds, shoots and invertebrates, some leaf matter and, sometimes, plant bulbs.

Greenfinches are often seen in flocks outside the breeding season and may join groups of sparrows, buntings and other finches when on the search for food. They will feed on the ground as well as in bushes, but they are not very agile and rarely forage among thin twigs in the treetops.

The cheerful song of male Greenfinches and their curiously bat-like circling display flight are evident in early spring, sometimes even as early as January, often around tall conifers as these are favoured sites for nest-building. The displaying bird glides on spread wings, fanning the tail to show off its yellow sides. Pair-bonding behaviour also includes courtship feeding, whereby the female begs like a fledgling and the male regurgitates food into her bill. Neither of the sexes is highly territorial and up to six pairs may nest close together in a loose colony.

The female selects a suitable spot – often in a high branch fork in an ornamental conifer – for the nest. She builds a largish, untidy bundle of small twigs, moss and grasses, with a neatly woven cup in its centre, lined with feathers, fur and similar soft materials. She lays four or five eggs, rarely six or seven. The eggs are, typically for finches, very pale with dark speckles that tend to concentrate at the broad end.

The female incubates alone for 14–15 days, and stays with the chicks while they are tiny, with the male bringing food. Later, both parents forage for the chicks, delivering food (mainly seed but some small insects too) by regurgitation. The chicks fledge at about 15 days old and the female begins a second brood while the male continues to feed the fledglings for another week or two until they

At feeding stations, Greenfinches are aggressive towards one another as well as to other birds, despite being quite gregarious.

COLOUR CURIOSITY

The Greenfinch's colours are made of two types of pigment – melanin, which provides black and dark brown tones, and carotenoids, from which the yellow tones are derived. The male's apparent green colour is produced by the combination of yellow and black, rather than a green pigment.

Greenfinches are quite popular pet birds, and breeders have developed a number of unusual colour variants. These are the result of genetic mutation affecting how pigment is deposited in the feathers, and the same mutations can occur spontaneously in wild birds as well.

Albinism, the lack of melanin pigment, usually results in an animal with white fur or feathers and pink eyes, but it does not affect carotenoid pigments. Therefore, an albino Greenfinch is not white but pale yellow, and retains very intense yellow coloration in its wing and tail markings. The result is a very striking-looking bird, and the same goes for mutations that dilute melanin pigment. These turn blacks to browns or creamy tones, but in Greenfinches the yellow markings are unaffected and look very bright against the rest of the plumage. You are most likely to observe unusually pigmented birds in late summer, among the year's crop of new fledglings. Sadly, natural selection works against them and they are less likely than most to survive very long – if a Sparrowhawk attacks a feeding flock of finches and one of the group stands out from the rest, it is likely to be targeted.

are competently feeding themselves. Some pairs may have a third brood – this is more likely among populations nesting in or near gardens where food is available all year round, as they begin breeding earlier.

Ringing recoveries of Greenfinches show that there is some movement of birds between Britain and mainland Europe, and also Scandinavia. The highest numbers concern birds moving between Norway and Britain – these are of the migratory subspecies *C. c. chloris*. There are also several records of birds moving between Britain and Denmark, though, curiously, not Sweden. These journeys are often in excess of 500km. However, the longest-travelled bird was born in Britain (Staffordshire) and moved south, being trapped in its first winter in Spain, 1,167km away.

Two British-ringed Greenfinches have lived to nearly 13 years old, while a bird in the Czech Republic was re-trapped 13 years and seven months after it was ringed.

IN THE GARDEN

Greenfinches are avid peanut-eaters, and will also take sunflower seeds (whole and hearts) and mixed birdseed, as well as suet-based foods. They consume a lot of water and will visit bird baths regularly – it's particularly important to keep water sources clean and regularly changed when you have visiting Greenfinches, to help prevent the spread of trichomonosis (see box, page 69).

These birds are rather aggressive at the feeders and may push out smaller birds; they may also visit in small flocks. Place extra feeders in other parts of the garden if you notice this problem, to give other birds the opportunity to feed undisturbed.

If you have tall ornamental conifers in your garden, you have a good chance of attracting Greenfinches to nest. Put out bundles of small, soft feathers or short pet hair to provide them with nest-lining material, and look out for fledglings visiting your seed feeders from early summer.

Lesser Redpoll
Acanthis cabaret

12cm
11g
RED

This charming little finch is a regular winter visitor to some gardens but its movements tend to be rather erratic and unpredictable. As a breeding species, it has declined significantly in recent decades, and over most of the UK you are rather unlikely to see it during the breeding season.

INTRODUCTION

The Lesser Redpoll has light brown plumage, paler on the underside, marked with dark streaks that are very prominent on the whitish flanks. It has long wings and a prominently notched tail. It is similar to the Siskin in general appearance but has no green or yellow tones. Instead, there is a red forehead patch, and a variable pinky-red flush on the breast (strong in adult males, absent in most females and in juveniles). There is a black patch between the eye and the bill, and a small black bib. The wings have two pale bars.

The call is a fast, high-pitched but rather dry-toned twittering; flocks are highly vocal, especially in flight. The male's song is a more lengthy and varied version of this.

DISTRIBUTION, POPULATION AND HABITAT

Lesser Redpolls breed quite widely in Scotland, Wales and Ireland, and also in northern England and parts of the south-west. They are resident over much of that range, but in the far north of Scotland they are summer visitors only, while they are winter visitors only over most of England. There is an introduced population in New Zealand.

The breeding population in the UK is about 220,000 pairs. It suffered a steep population fall in the 1980s and 1990s, particularly in England (falling by 85 per cent in England between 1967 and 2015). Numbers have risen modestly across the UK as a whole more recently – there was a 27 per cent climb between 1995 and 2015.

Male Lesser Redpolls show much variation in the pinkness of their breast but the crown-patch is almost invariably bright red.

SPLITTERS?

Classifying the world's various different types of redpolls has proved quite a headache for ornithologists. Redpolls can be found across northern Euruope and Asia and North America, with those breeding further north tending to be bigger and paler (from greyish to nearly white), and those further south smaller, with darker and warmer brown tones. This tendency is known as 'clinal variation', and is something we see in many kinds of widespread animals – the biggest and palest Peregrine Falcons *Falco peregrinus*, for example, occur in the Arctic, while those of tropical regions are much smaller and very richly coloured.

The difficulty comes in deciding whether all the variation represents different subspecies or different species, and with redpolls the jury is still out, with some taxonomists recognising five different species, some three, and some two or even one. Although there are distinct forms, there are also intergrades, and because redpolls are often quite migratory, different populations regularly come into contact. Some authorities classify the Lesser Redpoll, which occurs mainly in Europe, as a distinct species, while for others it is just a variation of the Common Redpoll A. *flammea*, which occurs across Eurasia and North America. Even DNA studies can't give us a definitive answer – they can show the extent of genetic divergence, but it is up to us to decide how much divergence warrants describing different populations as different species.

Lesser Redpolls breed in woodlands, particularly mixed birch and pine. Their decline in the last century is probably linked to changes in commercial woodland composition and management – birch was often used as a screening plant for pine plantations, and birch seed is a key part of their diet in winter.

BEHAVIOUR

The birds feed on seed in winter, especially that of birch and Alder. You may also see them taking grass seeds and those of herbaceous plants, particularly ragworts and related species. In the warmer months, they take some insects.

These birds are highly gregarious and forage in flocks that can be very large. They are often seen in company with Siskins, and feed with great agility on seeds hanging from twigs in the high treetops.

The Lesser Redpoll nests in small, loose colonies, with pairs tending to form while the birds are still within their winter flocks. The nest is a typical finch construction of fine twigs and grasses with some moss and a nest-cup lined with soft materials. The female builds it alone in a branch fork of a bush or tree, and incubates the clutch of four or five eggs for 12 days. The chicks are fed by both parents and fledge at a couple of weeks old. Pairs usually rear two broods, or sometimes three.

Young Lesser Redpolls ringed in Scotland regularly turn up in southern England in winter, and there is also some exchange between mainland Europe and Scandinavia. Several ringed birds have travelled more than 1,000km, from Sweden to the UK or vice versa.

The oldest British-ringed Lesser Redpoll was recorded at the same ringing site where it was originally ringed six years, 10 months and 11 days previously. The potential lifespan of redpolls is considerably longer than this, as demonstrated by recoveries of a 12-year-old Common Redpoll from Denmark.

IN THE GARDEN

Hanging a large tubular feeder filled with sunflower hearts often provides a good chance of attracting Lesser Redpolls – if you are lucky enough to draw in a flock, you might notice a Common Redpoll (larger and greyer than the Lessers) among them. A wild patch with some tall weedy plants left to go to seed is a natural food source that will appeal to them. If you live in a good area for the species and have some bushes and trees, a pair or two may nest in your garden.

Leaving dead flower-heads standing through autumn and winter provides food for seed-eaters like Lesser Redpolls.

Brambling
Fringilla montifringilla

14cm
24g
GREEN

This handsome, boldly patterned bird is closely related to the Chaffinch, replacing it in more northerly parts of Europe and Asia. It is a fairly common winter visitor to Britain, with most of those wintering here coming from Scandinavia. It often turns up in gardens with flocks of Chaffinches.

INTRODUCTION

The Bramblings we see in Britain are mostly in fresh autumn/winter plumage, which is less colourful than breeding plumage. The colour scheme combines grey, brown and black tones on the upperparts with an orange throat, breast-sides and wing markings. The flanks and belly are white with some black spotting close to the tail's underside, and the rump is also white. Males have scattered black plumage on the head, while the females are grey-headed. By spring many males show an almost completely black head. The call is a somewhat Greenfinch-like *dzeee* note with a nasal, jeering tone.

DISTRIBUTION, POPULATION AND HABITAT

Bramblings do not normally breed in the British Isles but can be found almost anywhere in the winter months. They are most frequent in northern and eastern areas. Numbers visiting the UK each year vary dramatically from year to year, from as few as 45,000 to as many as 1.8 million. If you keep an eye on bird reports from north-east coastal areas, such as the bird observatories on Fair Isle and at Filey and Flamborough in Yorkshire, Holme in Norfolk and Landguard in Suffolk, you will get an idea of how many Bramblings are arriving on our coasts as autumn progresses. (See Further reading, page 220, for more information on these locations.)

As spring approaches, the heads and backs of male Bramblings lose their scaly appearance and become progressively blacker.

The Brambling is monotypic (not divided into subspecies). Its breeding range is very extensive, encompassing northern Europe from Scandinavia northwards, and across the whole of northern Asia

VANISHINGLY RARE

The Brambling is one of several UK bird species that are quite familiar as non-breeding visitors, but do also have a tiny British breeding population. Others include our 'winter thrushes'– the Redwing and Fieldfare. All three have bred, most often in northern Scotland, but in tiny numbers. Details of very rare breeding species are collated by the Rare Breeding Birds Panel, which publishes its reports online (see page 220). From 2000 to 2014, only two confirmed breeding records of Brambling were documented, both in the Scottish Highlands.

to almost the far east of Russia. It breeds in pine and birch forest up to the tree-line, and is extremely common in parts of its range – the European population alone is estimated at between 30 million and 48 million individuals, although it is declining. All populations are migratory, moving south as far as northern India for the winter. Bramblings are also regularly recorded in Alaska.

BEHAVIOUR

Bramblings feed on seeds in winter, as well as some berries. The numbers moving from Scandinavia to the UK in winter depends on food availability – a poor beechmast crop, in particular, will bring them here in good numbers. They are gregarious (vast feeding flocks holding as many as 2 million are regularly noted in eastern Europe) and will forage alongside Chaffinches. Check Chaffinch flocks in winter – any Bramblings will particularly stand out when the flock is in flight and the Bramblings' white rumps show. In the breeding season, the species relies heavily on caterpillars of certain Arctic moth species.

Seen front-on, the white underside is striking and readily distinguishes female Bramblings from female Chaffinches.

Bramblings do not habitually breed in the UK. If you see any in the UK later than May, notify your county bird recorder, particularly if there are signs of breeding behaviour (for example, males singing or females carrying nesting material). Their breeding biology is similar to that of the Chaffinch, with one or two broods of five to seven young produced each year.

Bramblings are winter visitors to Britain. The main arrival period is October and November, and they linger into April before returning to their northern breeding grounds.

One adult male Brambling, caught and ringed in winter in Norfolk in 1967, was found 3,327km away in Russia three years later. There are several recoveries of birds that covered more than 3,218km, but the general picture is that most of our wintering Bramblings come here from Norway. Some of those that reach the UK in autumn may keep travelling and spend winter even further south in mainland Europe – one bird ringed in October 1975 in Cork was recovered in February 1976 in Spain, 939km away from where it was originally ringed. However, the tendency of Bramblings to make irruptive movements in response to food shortages means they will not necessarily spend successive winters in the same areas.

The oldest UK-ringed Brambling was a female ringed as a first-winter in March 1975 and recovered eight years, seven months and 16 days later in Italy. A Swedish-ringed bird lived for at least 14 years and nine months.

IN THE GARDEN

Bramblings are most likely to visit your garden if you live in Scotland and north-east England but in good years they can turn up anywhere. They often tag along with Chaffinch flocks and are more likely to feed on the ground than on bird tables or feeders. Any kind of seed mix could attract them, and cold weather may drive them from woodlands into gardens where there is a ready food supply.

Sparrows and buntings

Like finches, sparrows and buntings are seed-eaters with sturdy, cone-shaped bills that are perfect for the job. Most are less colourful than finches and some are classic 'little brown jobs', but they are sociable, lively and very interesting to watch. Sparrows belong to the family Passeridae, while buntings are in the family Emberizidae.

House Sparrow
Passer domesticus

14cm
34g
RED

This cheerful, sociable little bird is one of our most familiar species and has a definite propensity to associate closely with humans. Although it is still the most frequently observed garden bird species in the UK, its numbers have crashed catastrophically through the late 20th and early 21st centuries, and the reasons behind this decline are still not clear. Given the species' preference for breeding and foraging around buildings, there is much garden-owners can do to help support their local House Sparrow population.

INTRODUCTION

The male (left) and female House Sparrow are noticeably different in appearance, the female being an archetypal 'little brown job'.

The House Sparrow is a small but sturdily built bird, with a stout bill. The upperside plumage is brown with darker streaks on the back, while the underside is plain light grey-brown. The male has a grey forehead extending to the centre of the crown. The top of the head is otherwise dark brown, as is the nape. There is black surrounding the eye and extending onto the chin and upper breast as a bib; he also has a white wing-bar. The markings become bolder and the bib larger through the breeding season as the pale feather fringes of fresh autumn plumage gradually wear away; his bill also changes from yellowish in winter to blackish in spring and summer. The female is plainer, her head marked subtly in grey-brown with a pale eyebrow but no black markings, and she has no white wing-bar; her upperside is a paler, greyer colour than the male's. Juveniles are like females but show prominent yellow flanges around the mouth-edges; juvenile males often have a hint of a bib and more contrasting plumage than do young females.

House Sparrows with colour abnormalities occur rather frequently. The most common aberration is leucism, whereby some or all of the feathers are pure white. Others include dilutions of one or both melanin pigment types, resulting in birds with a pale, 'washed-out' or ghostly appearance, and melanism, where there is excessive melanin pigment, producing a darker-than-usual plumage, often with enlarged and exaggerated black markings. House Sparrow fledglings with a kind of developmental pigment loss, caused by a poor diet during the nestling stage, are also quite common – they show white 'zones' in the centres of the long flight and tail feathers, with normal pigmentation at the feather ends. Such birds will usually grow normally pigmented feathers if they survive their first year (unlike body plumage, which is replaced in the post-juvenile moult soon after fledging, the flight and tail feathers are not moulted until the bird is nearly a year old).

The species' calls are various pleasant, conversational chirps, chirrups, croons and chatters. The male gives a repeated, well-spaced, loud single *chirp* to serve as territorial song.

DISTRIBUTION, POPULATION AND HABITAT

House Sparrows occur throughout the British Isles, with the exception of the open uplands of north Scotland; they are present on nearly all offshore islands. However, they are no longer as ubiquitous as they once were; for example, they are now rather scarce in central London and are entirely absent from several central London parks. Given that they were commoner than any other small bird by far in the city centre through most of the 20th century, the change has been dramatic and shocking. The subspecies present in Britain is *P. d. domesticus*, and this form ranges across northern Europe and northern Asia; another 10 or so other subspecies exist.

Worldwide, the natural range of the House Sparrow extends throughout Europe and across northern, central and much of southern Asia, and also North Africa. In addition, there are large introduced populations over most of North America, central and southern South America, southern and south-eastern Africa, eastern Australia and New Zealand, and on some smaller islands, including Hawaii. Most of these introduced populations are considered invasive, and in some areas they may

Even in the urban jungle, House Sparrows manage to find enough suitable materials to build sizeable nests.

ENGLISH SPARROWS

In the USA, the House Sparrow is widely known as the 'English sparrow' and is generally viewed with some contempt. The species was introduced intentionally and repeatedly by settlers from Europe, who reasoned that House Sparrows back home were probably important pest-controllers in the urban environment. The species' willingness to live closely alongside people meant it colonised the nation's towns and cities rapidly and very successfully, and today it is very common.

In some quarters in the USA, the House Sparrow is blamed for declines in native cavity-nesting bird species, such as Eastern Bluebirds *Sialia sialis*, Purple Martins *Progne subis* and Tree Swallows *Tachycineta bicolor*. Native birds have robust legal protection in the USA, but House Sparrows do not, and it is quite legal to destroy them, their nests and their eggs. Many conservation groups encourage gardeners to do just this if House Sparrows take up residence in a nest box. However, there is no clear evidence that House Sparrows are directly responsible for the decline of any native species in North America, and indeed there have been recent declines in some introduced House Sparrow populations as well as in native populations.

The House Sparrow clean-up crew is often on hand at places where humans dine al fresco.

threaten native bird species, for example by outcompeting them for nest sites.

In the UK, we have about 5.3 million pairs of House Sparrows. But although the species is still very abundant, it has suffered a decline of about 60 per cent since the mid-1970s. The overall decline has slowed through the 21st century but continues in England, while in Scotland, Wales and Northern Ireland there has been an increase in population since 1995. The general degradation of urban habitats as places for wildlife is a likely driver of the decline. Gardens are increasingly concreted over and the remaining plants treated heavily with pesticides. This means there are fewer places for invertebrates to live and therefore less food for baby sparrows. Lack of nest sites is another factor, particularly as this species does best when it can breed in colonies.

House Sparrows occur mainly in urban environments, and also around farms, barns and other rural buildings; historically, they were common and often problematic around grain stores on farms. They frequently nest in cavities within buildings, and also like to build their nests within dense climbing plants like Ivy on walls.

BEHAVIOUR

The House Sparrow's diet is very varied – it is adapted to eat seeds of all kinds (and is one of the few small birds that will eat grains like wheat) but it also takes other vegetable matter and insects, which are vital food for nestling House Sparrows. It will glean foliage for caterpillars, and hawks flying ants with reasonable skill. It also eats all kinds of discarded food around human habitations. It gathers at places where other animals are fed, including zoos, and town parks with collections of ornamental wildfowl.

The House Sparrow lives and forages socially, and feeding flocks can be huge. It will also associate with other seed-eating birds, including finches and buntings. Curious and intelligent, it is quick to spot and exploit new feeding opportunities. In many cities, if you eat a sandwich on a park bench, you'll soon be joined by several House Sparrows ready to mop up the crumbs, darting nimbly between the feet of the Feral Pigeons. In many urban areas, the local House Sparrows become very tame and will flock to a human hand if seed or other food is on offer.

INFANTICIDE

It is well known in nature for males of certain species to practise infanticide. The classic example is when a new male Lion *Panthera leo* takes over a pride and kills off all the young cubs, then impregnates the lionesses himself. House Sparrow males will move in on nests where the incumbent male has died and kill the chicks, then mate with the widowed female and have a brood of young with her. More unusually, female House Sparrows also practise infanticide, though under different circumstances. Bigamous male House Sparrows are attempting to provision two nests at once, thus doubling their reproductive output, but for the two females involved the male's input is halved, so it is in their interests to put a stop to this by destroying the rival female's brood. Most often, the male's primary mate will kill the chicks of the secondary female, so the male can invest all his energy into his one remaining brood.

In spring, male House Sparrows 'sing' by chirping repeatedly close to an active or potential nest site. Males with the largest bibs and blackest bills have higher blood testosterone levels and tend to be dominant socially, as well as more attractive to females. Successful pairings can persist over two or more years. However, bigamy is quite frequent in this species, the 'best' males often pairing with another female in addition to their main partner. The nest is an untidy mass of grasses and other dry material, lined with feathers, built in a cavity or within dense vegetation. The female typically lays four to five eggs, which hatch after 14 days of incubation, and then both parents tend the young for 16 days in the nest. After fledging, the chicks are fed by their father primarily, as the female will be incubating the second of her two to three broods.

House Sparrows are very sedentary. Of more than 40,000 UK ringing recoveries, only half a dozen have involved birds moving out of the country or arriving from abroad. The longest journey recorded took place within the UK: a young female that travelled 657km from Oxford to north-east Scotland. The longest journey overseas was a bird ringed in Dungeness, Kent, which travelled 445km to France. The oldest House Sparrow documented in Britain was ringed at Pontypool in Wales, and re-found there 12 years and 12 days later. A bird ringed and re-found in Denmark lived for at least 19 years and nine months – this individual is one of the oldest small songbirds ever documented.

IN THE GARDEN

House Sparrows will take almost anything you might think to put out on a bird table or in feeders, including all kinds of seed, peanuts, suet foods and kitchen scraps. They will forage on the ground as well. Offer water for drinking and bathing. They also enjoy dust-bathing – try offering an area of dry loose soil, large enough for several birds to bathe together and contained by a circle of stones.

A hole-fronted nest box with an entrance hole of at least 32mm will attract House Sparrows. Try placing several quite close together, on walls with some sort of sheltering cover from climbing plants. The 'sparrow terrace' nest boxes that are widely available offer three nesting spaces in a single large box, and you may have success with one of these if you have a good population of House Sparrows, though the birds tend to prefer not being quite so close to their neighbours. If you already have House Sparrows nesting on or in your house, try to avoid changing the spot where they nest if at all possible, but if you need to remove the Ivy or plug the space into the loft, do so outside the breeding season and put up some nest boxes nearby. Maintain a diverse wildlife-friendly garden if you have nesting House Sparrows, as nestlings need soft-bodied invertebrates, such as small caterpillars and aphids.

Because it evolved in the arid environment of the Middle East, the House Sparrow is as happy to bathe in dust as in water.

Tree Sparrow
Passer montanus

14cm
24g

RED

This bird, in many ways the 'country cousin' of the House Sparrow, has undergone an even more serious decline through the last few decades. As with the House Sparrow, its fortunes can be much improved through the efforts of gardeners in the areas where it still occurs. Conservation actions on farmland and nature reserves are paying off for this species, and its numbers are slowly beginning to recover, though they still remain well below historical levels.

INTRODUCTION

The Tree Sparrow is easily distinguished from its close relative as long as you can get a clear view of its head pattern.

The Tree Sparrow is the same size in bill-to-tail length as the House Sparrow but weighs considerably less, and its slighter build is apparent when you see the two species together. It is more brown and white and cleanly, contrastingly marked than the House Sparrow, lacking the latter's grey tones. It resembles the male House Sparrow in pattern but the crown is entirely chestnut brown, the black bib is rather small, and the whitish cheek is marked with a large black spot. The upperside is warm bright brown with dark streaks and a whitish wing-bar, while the underside is off-white. Males and females

SAVING SPARROWS

The 1970s and 1980s saw some dramatic changes affecting the UK's open landscape, as farms implemented new ways to boost productivity. These included removing hedgerows and planting to the fence-line to create larger fields, more efficient harvesting methods, and the increased use of highly effective selective herbicides. All of these changes seriously harmed arable farmland as a wildlife habitat, and farmland birds began to decline dramatically as they struggled to find food. In addition, the wide-scale renovation of old farm buildings and removal of old trees on farmland deprived cavity-nesting birds of nest sites.

The Tree Sparrow was affected particularly severely, and rapidly went from a common bird to a rarity in many areas. However, when it comes to conservation management, it is in some ways one of the easier species to help. The RSPB runs working farms on several sites, and has had success with bolstering Tree Sparrow populations.

It offers the following advice to farmers:
- Use low-input crop management, field margins or wetland features to create insect-rich habitats.
- Use over-wintered stubble or wild birdseed mixtures to provide seed food throughout the winter.
- Ensure nest-holes are available in trees and farm buildings, or use nest boxes.

Like House Sparrows, Tree Sparrows are usually colonial, and the more pairs you can encourage to nest in a particular area, the easier it is to attract more, so lots of nest boxes placed quite close together is the way to go. You can see successful Tree Sparrow 'villages' at RSPB reserves such as Old Moor and Bempton Cliffs in Yorkshire.

look alike, and juveniles are similar too, though their colours are more muted and they show a yellow gape flange.

The species' various calls are very like those of House Sparrows, perhaps a little higher pitched but not particularly easily distinguished.

DISTRIBUTION, POPULATION AND HABITAT

Tree Sparrows are still quite widespread in the British Isles, but their range has contracted considerably and they are now scarce in southern and north-central England; they are also rare in western and central Wales, much of Scotland (except the east coast) and central parts of Ireland. They are absent from most islands and island groups. The subspecies in the British Isles is *P. m. montanus*, the same form found across the whole of Europe and through northern Asia.

The Tree Sparrow's world range is very extensive, encompassing almost the whole of Eurasia except the far north and south, reaching Japan. It also has a toehold in North Africa. It has been introduced to Australia and South East Asia; there is also a small introduced population in Iowa, USA.

There are about 200,000 pairs of Tree Sparrows in the UK. Its decline has been perhaps more extreme than any other species – a fall of 96 per cent in England between 1967 and 2015. The population crash began in the late 1970s. Since the mid-1990s numbers have stabilised and begun to increase – surveys recorded a rise of 119 per cent across the UK between 2005 and 2015 (but it must be remembered that this is from a very depleted population, reduced to just 4 per cent of its pre-1990s numbers, and the species is still at a very low ebb relative to its position in the 1970s).

In the UK, Tree Sparrows are most common in lowland farmland, particularly in areas where more traditional farming methods are practised, and where there are set-aside fields that encourage insects in summer and provide weed seeds in winter. They can also thrive in lush, well-vegetated wetland areas, provided there are suitable nest sites around. They are regular garden visitors in rural areas close to suitable wild habitat. Elsewhere in their range they are common urban birds, taking the place of the House Sparrow as the ubiquitous 'city sparrow' in some areas.

THE GREAT SPARROW CAMPAIGN, CHINA

In 1958, only a few decades before UK conservationists were desperately trying to save the Tree Sparrow from eradication, a diametrically opposed plan was initiated in China. The government at the time had declared that Tree Sparrows, along with rats, flies and mosquitoes, were the most serious and injurious of animal pests, and should be entirely eliminated in China. The sparrows were targeted because they ate rice and grain.

Citizens could claim rewards for handing in dead sparrows, and used all manner of methods to kill them – including forcing them to stay in flight by scaring them with loud noises, until they literally dropped exhausted from the skies. Their efforts drastically reduced China's Tree Sparrow population, and very soon the consequences of this became apparent. Rice yields, predicted to increase, instead fell because there were no longer any sparrows to eat the various insects that attacked the rice crop, and locust numbers in particular were rising fast. The leaders ordered an end to the campaign against the sparrows in 1960 but it was too late to prevent the Great Chinese Famine of 1959–61, which killed between 20 million and 45 million people.

大家都来打麻雀

BEHAVIOUR

Tree Sparrows are seed-eaters in the colder months but take an increasingly high proportion of invertebrates through spring and summer, and they feed their young chicks almost exclusively on small, soft-bodied insects. They will feed on various types of seed, including cereal grain, but prefer smaller seeds on the whole. They fare best when they can access a good supply of weedy herbaceous plants through autumn and winter, or are given supplementary food in the form of birdseed mixes.

Like House Sparrows, Tree Sparrows are gregarious and forage in flocks outside the breeding season. Often, the flocks include some House Sparrows, and other seed-eaters will also flock with them, including the likes of Greenfinches and Reed Buntings.

Pair formation can occur within winter flocks or later into spring. Males set themselves up at a suitable nest site and 'sing' from close to its entrance with repeated chirps, to warn off other males from that site and to attract a female if they are not yet paired up. Nest sites are cavities in dead trees or in buildings, and increasingly in the UK the birds use purpose-built nest boxes. These may be fixed to walls or trees, but in open areas it's possible simply to mount the boxes on the tops of poles driven into the ground. Tree Sparrows may also nest within the dense twiggy depths of a bush or shrub but do so more rarely than House Sparrows.

The female does most of the nest-building, using grasses and twigs to build the untidy outer part of the nest, and feathers and fur to line the cup in which she will lay her eggs. Despite the male's close attendance at the nest through the egg-laying period, extra-pair matings happen regularly and 9 per cent of chicks are fathered by a different male to the one paired with their mother. A typical clutch is of five to six eggs, pale greyish in colour with copious spots. Both sexes incubate the eggs, taking turns while the off-duty parent stays nearby. The chicks hatch after 12 or 13 days, and are fed by both parents until they fledge at 15–18 days old. Then the male cares for them until they are feeding independently, a week or so later, while the female lays another clutch of eggs. She will produce up to three broods through spring and summer. For birds nesting in colonies, breeding success is higher with first broods than subsequent ones, while solitary pairs seem to do better with their later broods.

Tree Sparrows in Britain are highly sedentary. The same goes for their populations further east – only those breeding in the most northerly parts of Siberia show a marked tendency to migrate. There have been a few recoveries of birds moving between the UK and mainland Europe but most involve movements of no more than 200km – the longest journey involved a bird ringed in Belgium and found in Nottingham, having travelled 541km over the four years that elapsed in between. Within the UK, one bird moved 478km from Yorkshire to north-east Scotland.

The UK longevity record was set in 1996 by a bird that lived 10 years, 10 months and 20 days after being ringed as a chick – it was recovered just 3km away from where it had hatched, which is pretty typical of this unadventurous species. The European longevity record is 13 years and one month, but there is no reason not to suppose that this species has the potential to live into its 20s, like the House Sparrow.

IN THE GARDEN

If you live close to farmland you may be lucky enough to have Tree Sparrows visiting the garden. They behave much like House Sparrows, frequenting hanging feeders, bird tables and ground feeders alike, and taking peanuts and all kinds of birdseed. They may be dominated by their heftier cousins at the feeders, so make sure you have two or more feeding areas to give them space.

Nest boxes for Tree Sparrows should have a 28mm entrance hole, and it's best to place at least a couple fairly close together.

Tree Sparrows are just as gregarious as House Sparrows, particularly in winter, when they form large foraging flocks.

CROSS PURPOSES

Being closely related, with similar habits and often living in close proximity, House and Tree Sparrows will sometimes pair up together rather than with their own kind, and produce hybrid chicks. Such hybrids show traits of both parents, but it is unclear whether or not they are themselves fertile to any extent. Hybridisation in songbirds is generally quite rare, but there are many documented cases of House x Tree Sparrow hybridisation. And, in southern Europe, House Sparrows have hybridised so readily with Spanish Sparrows *P. hispaniolensis* that a stable 'hybrid swarm' exists in Italy – the 'Italian Sparrow' was originally thought to be a distinct species, but studies of its DNA indicate it arose through hybridisation. Italian Sparrows now prefer to mate with other Italian Sparrows over either of their 'parent' species.

Yellowhammer
Emberiza citrinella

16cm
31g
RED

Probably the best-known member of the bunting family in Britain, this beautiful bird is associated with farmland and other open habitats but is a regular visitor to more rural gardens, especially in winter. It, like many other farmland birds, has declined seriously in Britain since the 1970s, hence its Red list status.

INTRODUCTION

This bird is a little larger than a House Sparrow and looks sleeker and more elegant, with a rather long tail. The adult male Yellowhammer is unmistakable, with his bright butter-yellow face and breast standing out against the streaky brown body plumage. Males usually have dark lines on the crown, through the eye and outlining the cheek, while the underside fades to whitish with dark streaks on the flanks. Females have streaky brown plumage on the head and breast, and just a faint tint of yellow; juveniles are similar but show little or no yellow. In flight, both sexes show a bright chestnut rump and white outer-tail feathers. The bill is light greyish, and the legs dull pink.

The call is a rather dry single *dzee* note. The male's song is an emphatic, fast, dry and rattling chatter, slightly descending the scale and ending with a long, drawn-out single *dzeeeee* note – it is sometimes transcribed as 'a-little-bit-of-bread-and-no-cheeeeeese'.

DISTRIBUTION, POPULATION AND HABITAT

The head colour of male Yellowhammers can be quite subdued, especially in 'fresh' plumage after the annual moult in late summer.

The Yellowhammer is a widespread resident bird in rural parts of the British Isles, though it becomes rather scarce away from the coast in Scotland, northern England, Wales and Ireland. Two subspecies occur in the British Isles: *E. c. caliginosa* over Ireland and western and northern Britain, and the western European *E. c. citrinella* in southern England. The species is found widely across central and northern Europe and well into Asia, with the most northerly populations being partial migrants.

About 700,000 pairs breed in the UK – this follows a UK-wide decline of 56 per cent between 1967 and 2015. The decline was most severe between 1980 and 1995, but numbers continue to fall over most of the UK, with a decrease of 26 per cent in England between 1995 and 2015, and of 57 per cent in Wales over the same period. In Scotland over the same period, however, the population increased by 37 per cent. The decline is most likely driven by changes in farmland management – the loss of hedgerows and weedy field margins, and the increased use of pesticides, has resulted in reduced food and nest sites.

These buntings are most common in farmland, both mixed and arable, where fields are relatively small with weedy margins and set-aside fields, and have dense mature hedgerows for nesting. They also occur on heathland, scrubby meadows, and in some larger open parks with scrubland – golf courses can also offer good habitat for them.

BEHAVIOUR

Yellowhammers feed on plant matter, especially small seeds from weedy plants, and on insects and other invertebrates, with animal food being particularly important during the breeding season. They flock with other small seed-eating birds such as sparrows and finches in the winter months.

Male Yellowhammers hold territory and sing from early spring. The female builds the nest on or near the ground within tussocky grass at the base of a hedgerow or bush, and in it lays a clutch of usually three or four eggs. These are pale with irregular, dark, 'scribbled' markings. She incubates for 14–15 days, and the chicks fledge at about 15 days old. Yellowhammers produce two or three broods of chicks.

This species is sedentary. Very few ringing recoveries have involved overseas movement, and movements within the UK rarely exceed 100km, though there is one record of a Norway-ringed bird travelling 1,005km to reach Kent, in 1986. The oldest UK bird was a female ringed as a first-winter and found again 11 years, nine months and 28 days later, while a ringed German bird lived to at least 13 years.

IN THE GARDEN

Rural gardens close to farmland may well attract Yellowhammers in winter, especially if mixed seed is on offer. They are more likely to be seen feeding on spilled seed below bird feeders; the inconspicuous females may be overlooked in a flock of House Sparrows. A somewhat wild garden may attract them at other times of year, perhaps even to nest.

Some male Yellowhammers have extremely vivid head coloration, rivalling any other British birds for beauty.

BONUS BUNTING

If you live in the countryside in south Devon or Cornwall, there is a chance you could encounter another colourful bunting in your garden. The Cirl Bunting *E. cirlus* is a close relative of the Yellowhammer and, like it, suffered a population crash and range contraction in the late 20th century. It now occurs only in Devon and Cornwall, following a highly successful RSPB and Nature England-led reintroduction project, but it is increasing and spreading, and may in due course return to other parts of southern England. Male Cirl Buntings have bold black-and-green face and breast markings, while females are very like female Yellowhammers. The best way to tell them apart is to look at the colour of the rump when they take flight – bright rufous chestnut in Yellowhammers, but more olive brown in Cirl Buntings.

Reed Bunting
Emberiza schoeniclus

16cm
21g
AMBER

This elegant little bird is closely associated with marshes and other wetlands during spring and summer. However, it is a regular visitor to gardens in winter, and even ventures into towns well away from its breeding habitat.

INTRODUCTION

The Reed Bunting is a slim, fairly long-tailed bird, with beautiful though subtle body plumage patterned in shades of brown, cream and grey. The back and wings are brown with darker and paler streaks, the underside is whitish with some dark flank streaks and the outer-tail feathers are white. Males in breeding plumage have a jet-black head, throat and upper breast, with a white collar around the back of the neck and a small white 'moustache', while females have a brown head with quite prominent pale 'eyebrows'. In autumn and winter, males' heads are not solid black but mottled with brown, as the pale fringes of their freshly grown feathers are yet to wear away. Juveniles have female-like plumage.

The calls are simple dry chirping or buzzing notes. The male's song (unlikely to be heard in gardens) is a simple short phrase of a few slow notes followed by a brief rattle.

DISTRIBUTION, POPULATION AND HABITAT

This species is a widespread resident that may be seen throughout the British Isles, except in the northern Scottish Highlands and other open upland areas in Wales, northern and south-west England and Ireland. The subspecies *E. s. schoeniclus* is present in the British Isles, and its distribution continues to encompass most of Europe. The species' range continues across most of northern and central Asia – most northern European and Asian populations are migratory and move to southern Europe, North Africa and southern Asia for winter.

There are about 250,000 pairs breeding in the UK. The population fell rather sharply in the 1980s but has since shown a gradual (though fluctuating) upward trend; as a result, in 2009 the species was moved from the Red category of conservation concern to Amber. It breeds mainly in wetland areas, including fresh and saltwater marshland, boggy heathland, reed beds, riversides and around large natural and artificial lakes, and also increasingly on farmland. In winter, many individuals that breed in wetlands will move to farmland, scrub and gardens, where food is easier to find.

The Reed Bunting's typical breeding habitat is marshy, reedy wetland, where the male's monotonous song is a characteristic springtime sound.

SURVEYING THE SCENE

Most of the UK's available bird population trend data are derived from two BTO surveys in particular – the Common Birds Census (CBC) and Breeding Birds Survey (BBS). The CBS ran from 1962 to 2000, while the BBS is ongoing, having been launched in 1994. Both surveys rely on volunteers who conduct regular bird counts in their local area, during a walk along a set route through a pre-assigned 1 × 1km square.

Population data for the Reed Bunting has been drawn from other surveys as well: the Waterways Bird Survey and Waterways Breeding Bird Survey (WBS and WBBS), and the Constant Effort Sites monitoring (CES). The former involves mapping birds seen along stretches of river and stream, while the latter comprises data provided by bird ringers on the birds they catch at sites they visit regularly.

All of these data sources for Reed Bunting indicate the same general trend – of decline in the late 20th century followed by a period of some fluctuation but with an overall increase.

BEHAVIOUR

Like many small seed-eaters, the Reed Bunting switches to a more insectivorous diet in the breeding season. It feeds its young on various wetland insects such as damselflies and mayflies, but in winter it feeds mainly on seeds, including reed seeds as well as those of herbaceous plants like ragworts and thistles. It often forages alone but in winter will join flocks of finches, sparrows and other buntings.

Male Reed Buntings proclaim their territory from an elevated perch, sitting still for long periods as they deliver their monotonous but far-carrying song. The female builds the nest in thick vegetation, including in reed beds and also in fields of tall crops such as oilseed rape. She lays four or five eggs, which take 13 days of incubation to hatch. The chicks, which are fed almost entirely on invertebrates of various kinds, fledge after another 13 days. There is a very high rate of extra-pair copulation in this species – DNA testing has shown that more than 50 per cent of chicks are not fathered by the male that rears them.

Reed Buntings are quite prone to wandering, and those in northern Europe are habitually migratory. The ringing recoveries data show that many birds move between the UK and north-west Europe, as far as Scandinavia; there is also some movement between the UK and south-west Europe. The longest distance travelled by a ringed Reed Bunting was 1,919km and involved a Finnish-bred juvenile that moved to Somerset in its first winter.

In summer, with a nest full of growing chicks to feed, Reed Buntings become opportunistic hunters, even tackling dragonflies.

The oldest British-ringed bird was ringed as a first-winter in 1968 and re-trapped just 3km away, nine years, 11 months and 18 days later. A Swiss-ringed Reed Bunting was caught by another ringer 12 years and three months later.

IN THE GARDEN

The most likely time to see a Reed Bunting in the garden is during cold winter weather, and the most likely garden to attract the species is rural, close to farmland and already drawing in flocks of other seed-eaters such as sparrows. Reed Buntings will take seed of all kinds, and will feed on the ground, on bird tables or on hanging feeders.

The chances of this species breeding in your garden are slim but it could happen if you have a very large garden with some standing water that has well-vegetated edges. Note that both sexes are more boldly marked in summer than winter; some summer females are nearly as black-headed as males.

Thrushes

All but one of Britain's thrushes are habitual garden visitors that particularly appreciate a worm-rich lawn and an abundance of berry-bearing shrubs. They are large for songbirds, and most have particularly beautiful songs. They don't usually use bird feeders but appreciate cut-up apples and other fruit, and are expert controllers of slugs, snails and other garden pests.

Blackbird
Turdus merula

24cm
100g
GREEN

This is our most common and familiar species of thrush, and can be found in gardens of all sizes up and down the British Isles. It is easy to encourage Blackbirds to feed and breed in your garden, and you will find them to be useful controllers of pests like slugs. This species is a characterful and lively bird that is always interesting to watch, and the male's lovely song is a true natural masterpiece.

INTRODUCTION

The Blackbird is a medium-sized thrush, a little larger than a Song Thrush but smaller than a Mistle Thrush. It has graceful proportions, with a long tail that it characteristically holds raised a little higher than the wings and lifts up dramatically after landing from a flight. The male is unmistakable, with uniform coal-black plumage that has a soft sheen but lacks any colourful iridescent gloss or pale markings. He has a bright yellow bill and eye-ring (sometimes tending towards orange or even reddish), and dark pinkish legs. The female is dark brown, a shade paler on her belly and with faint darker spotting. Female plumage is variable – some have quite light-coloured underparts with prominent spotting. Her bill and eye-ring are dark greyish. Juveniles are like females but are brighter rufous brown with slightly paler dappling on the upperside; juvenile males have black flight and tail feathers.

Calls include soft clucking sounds and a more ringing *chink* note, given repeatedly and rapidly when the bird is alarmed or mobbing a predator. Blackbirds have a habit of alarm-calling at length close to dusk, even in the absence of any apparent threat. There is also a higher and thinner single-note

This is the only British garden thrush in which the sexes look different. The female's cryptic plumage helps camouflage her when she incubates her eggs.

A patch of turned-over soil is a happy hunting ground for a Blackbird, with earthworms a favourite prey.

alarm call, given when the bird is in potential danger itself and is hiding – for example, when a Sparrowhawk is around. The male's song is fluting, rather slow-paced and low-pitched in the main, but with some higher and faster trills, and very melodic, with each phrase clearly different from the last. It can be heard at most times of the year, and is often the first birdsong to be heard at daybreak.

DISTRIBUTION, POPULATION AND HABITAT

This bird is found throughout the British Isles except on the highest and barest mountains of north Scotland. Subspecies *T. m. merula* is found in the British Isles and through Europe except the south-east. The species also occurs in North Africa and into western and central Asia, with the most north-easterly populations migrating south for the winter, towards south-central Asia.

There are about 5.1 million pairs of Blackbirds in the UK – it is one of our most common wild bird species. In addition, variable numbers of migrants from mainland Europe visit us in the winter months. Numbers declined here between the 1970s and mid-1990s but have since increased again, though have not yet returned to their pre-1970 level – overall, there was a decline of 16 per cent between 1967 and 2015, but a rise of 13 per cent between 1995 and 2015.

Blackbirds are naturally woodland-dwellers, preferring woods with a good shrub layer and plenty of leaf litter; they also forage at woodland edges, and in scrubland and other more open habitats. They do very well in gardens of all sizes and are also common in parks, on playing fields and in other urban green spaces.

BEHAVIOUR

This bird has a diverse diet, which includes many kinds of insects and other invertebrates, especially earthworms, but also berries and other fruits, and some seeds. It will occasionally catch small vertebrates such as immature lizards and newts, and some individuals become skilled at taking tadpoles from the margins of garden ponds. Windfall apples and other orchard fruits are important in the winter diet, and Blackbirds will explore soil turned over by farm machinery or a garden spade to find soil-dwelling invertebrates.

You may notice Blackbirds poised on the garden lawn with their heads tilted; they can hear the movements of earthworms just underground. They are not especially agile but can quickly strip a bush of berries as they clamber and hop from branch to branch. When foraging on the ground, they move with a rapid series of bounding hops rather than by walking.

These are not sociable birds, by and large, and indeed both sexes are fiercely territorial at most times, but in cold winter weather they may suspend hostilities to maximise feeding time, so you could see half a dozen during such periods. They may also temporarily join flocks of the more social migratory thrushes (Redwings and Fieldfares).

Often the male will take care of the first brood of fledglings while the female starts to incubate a new clutch.

Blackbirds form enduring pair-bonds, though 'divorce' is more likely if they have a failed breeding season. The male sings almost all year round to defend his territory, but when courting a mate he also performs displays on the ground, running to and fro and giving a strained version of his usual song, with the bill open to show off its bright colour.

The female builds the nest on her own, usually within a deep, thick bush but sometimes in a small cavity or on the ledge of a building. Large, open-fronted nest boxes designed especially for Blackbirds are available from suppliers of garden bird products. The female uses various materials to construct the nest, including twigs, strong grasses, leaves and moss, and uses mud to hold the structure together. The eggs, which are deep blue-green with darker speckles, are laid on consecutive days, and the 13-day incubation – which is undertaken by the female alone – begins when the last or second-to-last egg is laid. Clutches of up to seven eggs have been recorded, but three or four are most typical.

The parents feed their young on soft-bodied invertebrates. The chicks grow rapidly and fledge at about 15 days old, though many nests are destroyed by predators such as corvids before the young reach fledging age. The chicks are flightless and small when they fledge and scatter to suitable hiding places in the undergrowth while the parents continue to feed them – within another couple of weeks, the youngsters have reached adult proportions and are feeding themselves. They moult into adult-like

EARTHBOUND

Blackbird chicks, and those of other thrush species, leave the nest when still rather small and somewhat helpless, with short flight and tail feathers. They cannot fly, and rely instead on keeping hidden – they can hop along at high speed as well, which would be enough to protect them from some opportunistic ground-dwelling predators but, sadly, not the domestic cat.

The value of fledging early is that the brood can disperse and hide on their own, making them individually less vulnerable than when they are all packed inside the nest together. But gardens don't tend to offer the extensive ground cover of woodland, and it is easy work for a cat to find and kill a whole brood of Blackbird chicks over one afternoon. Keeping cats in from dawn to dusk can dramatically reduce the number of birds they kill, but if you have fledgling Blackbirds bouncing haplessly and flightlessly around your garden, keeping the cat indoors for a few days could save all their lives. It will also save you from endless noisy alarm-calling from the parent Blackbirds whenever they catch sight of your cat.

CONTINENTAL BLACKBIRDS?

Some of the male Blackbirds we see in our gardens in autumn and winter don't have the bright yellow eye-ring and bill that we expect. Instead, the bill is blackish and the eye-ring is also dark, making it inconspicuous. These birds are males in their first winter – the bright colour of their bare parts will develop over the weeks ahead.

However, there's a persistent myth that all dark-billed male Blackbirds are of Continental origin: migrants from Scandinavia or elsewhere in northern mainland Europe, which are overwintering here. It's possible, indeed probable, that some of them are. However, all Blackbirds in north-west Europe are of the same subspecies (so there's very little variation between them), and (more importantly) all young male Blackbirds are dark-billed, whether home-grown or

visiting from abroad. A more reliable way to tell them apart could be behavioural – on mainland Europe, Blackbirds are not ubiquitous garden birds and so they may be flighty, shy and less easily approached.

plumage a few weeks later. Blackbirds normally produce two or three broods, but may have up to five on occasion – they will begin nesting very early in the year if conditions are mild enough and may be on their first clutch of eggs as early as March.

We don't think of Blackbirds as migratory birds, but ringing recoveries show that there is considerable movement of birds between Scandinavia and the UK. More than a thousand Blackbirds ringed in the UK have been recovered in Norway, and nearly a thousand in Sweden, with numbers making the reverse journey also high. There is also movement between the UK and mainland Europe.

The longest journey recorded by a Blackbird ringed in the UK was 2,005km, made by a first-winter female bird ringed in 1980 and recovered in Albania in 1984. Another young female ringed on Fair Isle travelled about as far as she could have done without leaving the UK, turning up in southern Dorset a few months later.

The oldest British-ringed Blackbird lived to be at least 14 years, nine months and 15 days old, but there are a few records of birds aged over 20 from Europe, including a bird ringed in Germany and caught 21 years and 10 months later by another ringer. The BTO notes a bird ringed in Sweden in 1959 whose ring was recovered in Norfolk 56 years and six months later – but there was no trace of the bird's body and rings are quite durable, so the individual in question could have died decades before (and almost certainly did).

IN THE GARDEN

In all likelihood, you already have at least a pair of Blackbirds visiting your garden. To encourage the species, put out food like dried fruit, raw pastry (see Introduction, page 13) and quartered soft apples – but most garden Blackbirds will find ample natural food. Encourage invertebrates by having a diverse garden with wild areas and shelter like stone or log piles, and areas where leaf litter and bits of fallen wood can decay. If you have fruit trees or berry-bearing shrubs, so much the better.

Blackbirds like to nest in dense and thorny bushes, and they often choose gardens. If you suspect you have a nesting pair, leave well alone and resist any temptation to check the nest's progress – however careful you are, predators could follow your scent trail and avian predators like Magpies are always on the alert for interesting human activity that could lead them to a meal. Offering live mealworms, though, will probably be appreciated.

Song Thrush
Turdus philomelos

23cm	
83g	RED

A much-loved garden bird, the Song Thrush is popular thanks to its charming appearance, exuberant song, and ability to rid the herbaceous border of snails and slugs. Its fortunes in the UK have taken a steep downturn over the last few decades but its population is now showing signs of recovery – partly because gardeners have become more aware of the harm that garden pesticides can do to this species and others.

INTRODUCTION

The Song Thrush is smaller and more compact than the Blackbird, and significantly smaller than the Mistle Thrush, with a shorter tail. The upperside is warm mid-brown, with yellowish feather tips on the greater coverts forming a narrow wing-bar. The underside is whitish with a light brown wash on the breast-sides and flanks. It is marked with small, neat blackish spots that become more elongated and teardrop-shaped on the flanks, often forming lines rather than looking haphazard. They fade away on the lower belly centre, leaving this area clean white. The stoutish bill is brownish yellow, and the feet and legs pink. In flight, the bird shows orange-brown 'armpits'. Juveniles have creamy spotting on the upperside.

The song is rich, loud, emphatic and fluty, and consists of short phrases, each repeated sometimes several times. It has a high, thin flight call and a softly clucking alarm call, which can become more rattling when the bird is very agitated.

This most welcome garden bird has sadly been declining for several decades, but gardeners can do much to improve its fortunes.

SONG OR MISTLE?

Seen side by side, our two common thrush species don't present much of an identification challenge, as the Mistle Thrush is much larger than the Song Thrush; they are also easy to tell apart by song. But one thrush on its own, keeping quiet, can be much more tricky. Here are the key features to check, in order of usefulness.

Wing feathers The larger wing feathers have pronounced pale borders in the Mistle Thrush, giving a stripy look. The wing feathers are uniform brown in the Song Thrush except for the very narrow yellowish wing-bar.

Spots on the lower flanks and belly These are round, blobby and scattered rather evenly across the whole underside in the Mistle Thrush, but are teardrop-shaped, form lines and fade away on the belly centre in the Song Thrush.

Body proportions The Mistle Thrush looks pot-bellied, small-headed and long-tailed, while the Song Thrush looks shorter tailed and has a compact body.

Plumage tone The Mistle Thrush's upperside plumage is a paler, cooler sandy-grey shade of brown, while the Song Thrush's is a darker, warmer brown.

Underwing and tail In flight, the Mistle Thrush shows white underwings and tail corners, while the Song Thrush shows orange-tinted underwings and a uniform brown tail.

Song Thrush

Mistle Thrush

DISTRIBUTION, POPULATION AND HABITAT

The Song Thrush is found throughout the British Isles, though it is absent from open mountainous parts of the Scottish Highlands and also the far north of Shetland. In the far north-west of Scotland, including the Hebrides, and in western Ireland, the subspecies *T. p. hebridiensis* occurs. Elsewhere in Britain, we have the subspecies *T. p. clarkei*, which is also found over mainland western Europe.

Further east, Song Thrushes of the migratory subspecies *T. p. philomelos* and, further east still, *T. p. nataliae* occur widely across northern, north-eastern and central Europe, and across northern and central Asia. They migrate south to the Middle East, southern Europe and North Africa. The species has also been introduced to Australia and also to New Zealand, where it is now extremely common.

There are in the region of 1.2 million pairs of Song Thrushes breeding in the UK. Numbers fell by 50 per cent between 1967 and 2015, but the most significant phase of the decline occurred between 1970 and the mid-1990s. The population then rose by 13 per cent between 1990 and 2015. The Song Thrush has shown a particularly strong recovery in Northern Ireland. Its decline is probably mainly due to changes in farming practices, but increased use of slug pellets in gardens has also caused losses.

This thrush naturally occurs in woodlands and woodland edges, and in more open, scrubby habitats as well. It can be found in urban areas wherever there is some green space – it frequently forages on lawns, sports fields and other areas of mown grass, and is quite common in town parks as well as in gardens.

BEHAVIOUR

Like other thrushes, Song Thrushes have a varied diet that tends to be mostly of animal origin between mid-spring and late summer, with more vegetable matter taken in autumn and winter. They are expert hunters and finders of invertebrates of all kinds, especially earthworms, slugs and snails, but also woodlice, spiders, centipedes and other insects. Come autumn, they feed heavily on berries and larger fruits such as apples, and will visit orchards to feed on windfall fruit.

Song Thrushes usually forage alone, though they may be seen with flocks of other thrushes when they gather to strip a berry bush or to feed on fallen apples. You might notice them on the ground, hopping rapidly before pausing to listen, head tilted, for invertebrates moving in the grass or just underground.

Male Song Thrushes can be heard singing from mid- or late winter. They often begin their song well before first light and sing beyond dusk. Unpaired males sing more during daylight hours, to attract a mate. Once paired up, they sing before their mate has woken for the day – the song's purpose is to inform other local Song Thrushes (particularly rival males) that the territory is occupied.

Berries of plants like Rowan are vital food for Song Thrushes and many other birds in the cold winter months.

The female builds the nest on her own, choosing a well-hidden spot low in a dense bush or even on the ground. The outer structure is a neat cup-shaped mass of twigs, grasses, leaves and moss, held together with plenty of mud, and with a smooth mud lining to the inner cup. It takes her up to three weeks to complete the nest, during which the male helps supplement her diet through courtship feeding.

SMASHING SNAILS

If you notice a stone on the ground in your garden that's surrounded by shards of broken snail shell, you have found a 'thrush's anvil'. The Song Thrush is the only British bird (and one of only a handful of bird species worldwide) that habitually breaks open snails by bashing them against a rock – it does this by gripping the snail by the lip of its shell and using a vigorous, rapid head-flick to whack the shell against the rock.

Experiments with hand-reared Song Thrushes suggest that the tendency to lift and flick objects is instinctive rather than learned by example. Young Blackbirds show similar behaviours but differ from Song Thrushes in lacking persistence, so do not get to the point where they know that if the object is a

snail and if it's flicked against a rock, the shell will break. The Song Thrush chicks can take a couple of weeks to make this connection and learn to perform the skill well, but they keep at it until they do.

POISON PILLS

It goes without saying that a wildlife garden should be kept as free of chemical pesticides as possible. However, slugs are particularly pernicious garden pests and it's not surprising so many gardeners turn to slug pellets to combat these nocturnal vegetable-munchers. The toxins in slug pellets, though, will also kill animals that eat the poisoned slugs and snails. This affects many species, particularly Song Thrushes and also Hedgehogs *Erinaceus europaeus* – two of the most beloved and beleaguered of our wild garden visitors.

You'll help protect these animals if you make the commitment never to use slug pellets. Other control methods might be a bit more labour intensive, but on the plus side, a healthy population of mollusc-eaters will help you out.

The female lays three or four dark-spotted blue eggs, and starts to incubate after the last egg is laid, ensuring the brood hatch at more or less the same time, 14–15 days later. She remains with the chicks most of the time and through the night for as long as they need to be kept warm, but within a week they are large and their feathers have developed enough to maintain a safe temperature without her help. Both parents fetch food (invertebrate prey of all kinds) for the young. The chicks fledge at about 14–15 days old, or perhaps a day or so sooner by 'exploding' from the nest as a defensive mechanism if disturbed – this habit is another good reason to avoid going anywhere near an active nest.

Once fledged, the young hide separately and are fed individually. They are small, with tufts of down on their heads and short wing and tail feathers, but the remaining feather growth is rapid, and within a few days they are able to fly and begin to feed themselves. The parents produce another brood or two through summer, often reusing the same nest.

There have been many recoveries of British-ringed Song Thrushes in mainland Europe, primarily along the western coasts of France and Spain, and further north through the Low Countries and western and southern Scandinavia. There have also been a few recoveries from North Africa, Italy, and east through the Baltic states and into Russia. The longest journey was made by a first-winter bird ringed on North Ronaldsay in the Orkneys in autumn 1987 and recovered in Morocco in January 1991 – a distance of 3,522km. This individual was almost certainly not born in Britain, though, but would have been mid-migration from somewhere further east when it called in at North Ronaldsay. The same goes for most other well-travelled Song Thrushes ringed in the UK and recovered abroad (or vice versa).

Most British-born Song Thrushes, by contrast, do not wander far from the place they were hatched. The oldest Song Thrush ringed in Britain is a case in point – it was ringed as a two-year-old in summer 2001, and re-trapped at the same ringing site almost exactly 11 years later. A Danish bird lived longer, reaching at least 17 years and six months.

IN THE GARDEN

Song Thrushes are most likely to visit your garden if you have some areas of lawn and bare soil for them to search for worms, and a good variety of native berry-bearing shrubs and insect-attracting herbaceous plants. Woodpiles, compost heaps and drystone walls are also happy hunting grounds, and if you have an Apple tree, fallen fruit may attract them. If you don't, just put out some halved soft apples. Other food that will attract them are mealworms (dried or live), dried fruit and suet-based foods.

Any dense prickly or bushy shrubs in the garden could provide nest sites for Song Thrushes. If you suspect they are nesting, give the area a wide berth so as not to draw the attention of nest predators such as Magpies and Jays. As with other thrushes, the chicks fledge before they can fly, so it's very important to keep cats indoors if you notice baby thrushes around, as they are very easy prey for even the slowest cat.

Mistle Thrush
Turdus viscivorus

27cm
130g
RED

This is the biggest of our thrush species, and is a rather imposing and aggressive bird, as well as a very handsome one. It is not as common a garden bird as the Song Thrush and Blackbird, but it is quite likely to turn up if you have an expansive lawn, some tall trees, or both. It has shown a steady decline in numbers since the mid-1970s, and was moved from the Amber to the Red list of species of conservation concern in the UK in 2016.

INTRODUCTION

This thrush is a markedly bigger, paler and more boldly spotted species than the Song Thrush (see page 97 for guidance on thrush identification). Compared with smaller species, it looks fat and big-bodied with a relatively small head and a long tail. It moves with fast, bounding hops and has an undulating flight. The upperside is a light greyish-sandy shade of brown, with conspicuous whitish edges to the larger wing feathers, giving the wings a defined stripy pattern. The upperside tail corners are white, and it shows strikingly white 'armpits' in flight. The underside is marked with bold blackish spots, which are smaller and arrow-shaped on the breast-sides but become rounder and blobbier on the lower flanks and belly. Juveniles are like adults but have pale spotting on the upperside, which is particularly noticeable on the head. Mistle Thrushes are sometimes confused with Fieldfares but are much plainer in colour, and have a more 'open' facial expression, lacking the black-and-whitish facial markings of the Fieldfare.

The Mistle Thrush's very powerful song has the same fluty timbre to the Blackbird's, but shows less variety and virtuosity, the phrases varying rather little and with few pace changes or high silvery notes.

A front-on view reveals dense, 'blobby' blackish spots spread across the whole belly, characteristic of the Mistle Thrush.

STORMCOCK AND MISSEL-THRUSH

The old nickname 'stormcock' for the Mistle Thrush is one of the most evocative traditional names for a garden bird, and reflects the male's tendency to continue singing even in the wildest weather. Other names referencing its rather harsh voice include 'shrite' and 'screech'.

Older books spell the English name 'missel' rather than 'mistle', but both versions have the same root – the plant Mistletoe *Viscum album*, once called 'misseltoe'. The bird's scientific species name, *viscivorus*, also means 'mistletoe-eater'. The Mistle Thrush greatly enjoys the white berries of this parasitic plant, which grows in spherical bundles on high tree branches. When it attempts to excrete the mistle seed, though, it has some difficulty because of the seeds' very sticky coating. The bird is often forced to wipe its backside on a tree branch. The stuck-on seed can then germinate and grow – and in this way the mistletoe plant spreads from tree to tree. In an ironic twist, mistletoe seeds are a traditional component of bird-lime, a sticky substance spread on branches to catch birds when they land, and this link between the plant and the Mistle Thrush inspired the Latin proverb *Turdus malum sibi ipse cacat* ('The thrush himself excretes his own trouble').

It usually sings from a high vantage point and is noted for continuing to sing in weather bad enough to force most other birds to quieten down and take shelter. Its alarm call is a loud, hard, clacking chatter, like a football rattle.

DISTRIBUTION, POPULATION AND HABITAT

The Mistle Thrush is a widespread resident species in the British Isles, absent only from the high open uplands of northern Scotland. It does not breed on most northern Scottish islands (though it regularly visits them in winter). The subspecies in Britain is *T. v. viscivorus*, which occurs throughout western Europe and east across much of northern and central Asia. In the far east of Asia it is replaced by *T. v. bonapartei*, while the localised *T. v. deichleri* occurs in north-west Africa and on both Corsica and Sardinia. In north and central Asia and Scandinavia, it is a summer visitor only, migrating south to spend the winter in North Africa, south-east Europe, and parts of the Middle East and south-western Asia.

There are about 170,000 pairs of Mistle Thrushes breeding in the UK. The population declined by 55 per cent between 1967 and 2015, and by 24 per cent between 2005 and 2015; there was a particularly steep fall between 2005 and 2010. Very recently, there has been a small upturn (a 3 per cent rise between 2010 and 2015) but it is too early to assess whether the general downward trend has been halted. The decline has been most significant in England, and the species is doing rather better in Scotland, with a 28 per cent rise between 1995 and 2015. The intensification of farming practices is the likely cause; loss of hedgerows and reduced biodiversity on arable farmland in general will have had a negative affect on the species.

Mistle Thrushes nest in tall trees but prefer to forage in more open settings, such as scrubland, forest edges, farmland with hedgerows and copses, and open grassland. They are common in parkland, including town parks with playing fields and some mature trees, and also in larger gardens. Wandering flocks visit moorland and heathland.

BEHAVIOUR

Mistle Thrushes take a wide variety of animal and plant food. Like other thrushes they are expert earthworm-catchers and also take plenty of slugs and snails. Other invertebrates are taken opportunistically, and the birds will also catch and kill small vertebrates such as tadpoles and other amphibians, juvenile slow-worms and even, on occasion, the chicks of other small birds.

Fruits are widely taken in autumn and winter. Soft windfall apples, pears and other fruit are particularly popular, as are the berries of Mistletoe, Holly, Rowan and Ivy. The Mistle Thrush is an important seed-disperser for many berry-bearing trees and shrubs. As winter progresses and berries become scarcer, it will visit ploughed fields in search of worms and other soil invertebrates.

The male Mistle Thrush sings almost year round, with song becoming more frequent from late winter. Song is used to attract a mate and to proclaim territory, which can be very large – up to 17 hectares, with the area around the nest site defended with particular vigour. Pairs that bred successfully in one year will often re-form the following season, and established pairs in particular can begin nesting very early, sometimes even in February.

The female builds the nest on her own, choosing a secure spot in a branch fork or where a branch joins the tree trunk. Often the nest is quite high, sometimes up to 20m and very rarely lower than 2m. It is a large cup-shaped structure of twigs, grasses, leaves and moss with a coating of mud inside, lined with feathers and other soft materials.

The female lays four eggs on average – these are a blue-green shade with some dark spots. She incubates alone for 15–16 days, during which time the male stands guard near the nest and may bring her food at times. Fledging occurs when the young are between 14 and 17 days old, and the male then feeds them for a further 15–20 days while the female lays and incubates her second clutch. There is occasionally a third brood. After the breeding season, young Mistle Thrushes often disperse in small flocks and may be encountered in more open, treeless countryside as well as in typical breeding habitat.

Mistle Thrushes are generally rather sedentary, though recoveries of a few birds ringed as nestlings in Scotland show that they are capable of quite lengthy dispersal. One Highlands-born bird reached the Isle of Man, 449km away, while another travelled 352km to Lancashire. Of foreign-ringed birds recovered in Britain, the rather sparse data include one extreme outlier – a chick hatched in Estonia that was found three years later in Essex, 1,737km away. There are a few records of UK-ringed birds reaching France and Belgium, and one Dutch-ringed chick was found the winter after its birth in the UK, in Kent.

TOP OF THE TREE

In autumn and winter, Mistle Thrushes can be quite gregarious, benefitting from having many pairs of eyes searching for food. They will also join up with wandering flocks of other thrush species, such as Redwings and Fieldfares. However, they have another feeding tactic that is much more antisocial. Sometimes, a single Mistle Thrush will monopolise a particular berry-bearing tree, such as a Holly, or any tree with plenty of Mistletoe clusters. The bird defends this tree from all comers and attempts to monopolise the fruit for as long as it can. This works well if there are not too many other thrushes around, as the Mistle Thrush 'outranks' all other species through its size and aggression. However, it may be forced to abandon its tree if a large flock of Fieldfares turns up, as it would have to expend more energy trying to drive them all away than it could replace by feeding.

GUARDIAN ANGELS

Mistle Thrush nests are targeted quite frequently by Magpies, Carrion Crows, Jays and squirrels, due to their relatively exposed positions. The thrushes, though, are far from helpless and both sexes will furiously attack any intruders, diving at them repeatedly while giving their ear-splitting football-rattle alarm call. It is quite common for Chaffinches to nest close to Mistle Thrushes, exploiting the latter's vigorous nest defence to keep danger away. In turn, the Chaffinches provide an early-warning system for the thrushes, as they are highly alert to any approaching threat.

The oldest British-ringed Mistle Thrush was at least 11 years, four months and nine days old, having been ringed as an adult in May 1971 and found dead in October 1982 just 6km away. The species has the potential to live much longer, though, as evidenced by a Swiss-ringed bird that was found dead at the age of at least 21 years and three months old.

IN THE GARDEN

Mistle Thrushes are not particularly regular garden visitors in many areas, and are most likely to visit larger, rural gardens and those close to parkland where they are nesting. They use tall trees both for nesting and for vantage points to sing from, so look out for them in nearby treetops. They may be attracted by halved apples or other soft fruits, and by both dried and live mealworms.

A large earthworm-rich lawn with some bare earth in the borders will appeal to them, as will berry-bearing shrubs and trees. They are only likely to nest in your garden if you have tall trees. Nesting thrushes of all kinds require some mud to cement and line their nests, so if it is a very dry spring you may want to keep a patch of earth wet so that mud is easily available to them.

An outer covering of moss helps hide this nest against the broad branch on which it is built.

Redwing
Turdus iliacus

21cm
63g
RED

As the days grow shorter and the nights colder, Redwings begin to stream into the British Isles. They make landfall on the east coast and spread across the country, descending in marauding swarms on berry-laden hedgerows. They are timid unless hunger and cold get the better of them, when you can get closer views and fully appreciate their beauty and character.

INTRODUCTION

The Redwing is a shade smaller than the Song Thrush, with a more compact, short-tailed shape – almost recalling a Starling in silhouette. Its upperside plumage is darkish brown, and the underside is pale with spots that coalesce into bold streaks along its breast-sides and flanks. It has rich rusty-red underwings (obvious in flight) and flank sides. The facial pattern is distinctive, with a dark eye-stripe and a broad creamy supercilium (eyebrow), which extends down to form a pale surround to the dark-streaked cheek. Its bill is yellowish with a black tip, and the legs are a dull pink.

The flight call is a short, thin, high but oddly grating *seee*, often heard at night in autumn as migrating flocks pass overhead. In spring, you may hear it singing; it produces a short, somewhat monotonous phrase that combines fluting warbles and rapid chattering.

DISTRIBUTION, POPULATION AND HABITAT

The Redwing is an extremely rare and declining breeding bird in Britain – this accounts for its Red list status. Almost all breeding records come from the Scottish Highlands, and there has been a steady decline in numbers since the 1980s (when a peak of 121 pairs was recorded in 1984). Since 1990, only a dozen or two pairs are recorded in most years. These birds are of the subspecies *T. i. iliacus*, which also breeds across Scandinavia and extensively through north-eastern Europe and northern Asia, across into eastern Siberia. They are migratory, wintering across much of Europe and into North Africa and parts of south-west Asia.

The face pattern of the Redwing, with its bold pale 'eyebrow', is unlike that of any of our other thrushes.

ICELANDIC REDWINGS

The Icelandic subspecies of Redwing, *T. i. coburni,* also breeds on the Faroe Islands and marginally on Greenland. It has a much more restricted distribution than the mainland Eurasian *T. i. iliacus,* and a much smaller population. However, Icelandic birds also winter in Britain, particularly in the north-west and Ireland. With care you can tell the two forms apart. The Icelandic birds are a little larger than the mainland birds, and have darker plumage, with a blackish-brown upperside and a dusky look to the heavily marked underside.

As a winter visitor, the Redwing is very numerous, with some 8.6 million birds arriving each year, mostly from Scandinavia and further east. We also receive birds from Iceland, which are of a different subspecies – *T. i. coburni.*

Redwings nest in pine and birch forest and forest edges. In winter, they wander the countryside and could turn up anywhere where there are berry bushes, lawns and ploughed fields – they are frequent visitors to gardens and urban parks, as well as rural hedgerows and scrubland.

BEHAVIOUR

When they are in the British Isles, Redwings are most often seen feeding on berries and other fruits, such as windfall apples. Later in the winter, when many bushes have been stripped, you are likely to see them foraging on pastures and other grassy places, looking for worms and other invertebrates.

Redwings are highly social, forming flocks both large and small. The flocks may include other thrush species, such as Fieldfares, and Redwings will also join flocks of Waxwings.

It is not unusual to hear male Redwings singing in spring. The few pairs that nest in Scotland are rarely seen, as their breeding habitat is usually rather remote.

The female builds the nest, low down in a bush or on the ground among dense vegetation. She lays four or five eggs and incubates them alone for 11–15 days. Both parents then rear the young, which fledge at about 14 days old.

Ringing recoveries show the long migrations undertaken by this thrush, and reveal that many birds that reach the British Isles come here from Scandinavia, while many more that visit our shores at the start of winter go on to move further south, reaching France, Spain and other Mediterranean countries, including several travelling well east of Britain. There are also a number of ringing recoveries involving birds moving between the British Isles and Iceland.

The longest migrations recorded involved birds ringed in Britain in early winter that were recovered in Asia later that same winter – one bird travelling 4,365km to Iran, and another covering 4,282km to Azerbaijan. The oldest British-ringed Redwing was an adult ringed in Northumberland, which was shot in Portugal 11 years, 10 months and seven days later. A Finnish bird was recovered 17 years and four months after it was originally ringed.

IN THE GARDEN

As they wander long distances around the countryside, Redwings will visit any gardens they encounter where food is to be found. If you have Holly or Ivy, Rowan trees, cotoneaster, pyracantha or other berry-bearing shrubs and trees, flocks may visit and stay until they have eaten all the berries. Encourage them to linger by putting out halved soft apples, dried fruit and similar foods.

Fieldfare
Turdus pilaris

26cm
100g
RED

This is our most colourful thrush and sometimes turns up in very large numbers in autumn, often alongside its fellow winter thrush, the Redwing. Fieldfares are bright, bold and bossy, with a distinctive call that draws attention as they fly swiftly overhead in streaming flocks, or descend mob-handed to strip shrubs and trees of their berries.

INTRODUCTION

The Fieldfare is nearly as large as the Mistle Thrush, and its proportions are like those of the Blackbird, with a rather long tail and deep chest. The head and rump are blue-grey, the wings and tail black, and the back a rich mahogany brown. Its underside is white with a variable orange flush to the upper chest, and is marked with black spots on the breast, which turn into dense chevrons on the flanks. The centre of the belly is bright white, as are the undersides of its wings. A black patch in front of the eye gives a frowning expression. The bill is yellowish with a black tip, and the legs are dark. Juveniles are drabber but have moulted to adult-like first-winter plumage by the time they reach us in autumn.

The call is distinctive – a slightly fruity, peevish double-cluck or chuckle. Flocks on the wing call often, and their voices can be picked up from some distance.

DISTRIBUTION, POPULATION AND HABITAT

Some Fieldfares are brighter than others, but the chevron-shaped dark markings on the flanks are always distinctive.

This thrush visits Britain in winter from its breeding grounds in Scandinavia. On average, close to 700,000 Fieldfares come to our shores, but numbers vary greatly from year to year – the highest numbers are in eastern England and Scotland. There are occasional breeding records as well, mostly from Scotland. The last documented instance of UK breeding at the time of writing was in 2012, when two pairs bred in Northumberland. However, these flamboyant thrushes become very shy and

inconspicuous when breeding, so it's possible that it occurs more frequently. The Fieldfare's rarity as a breeding bird is why the species is on the Red list of species of conservation concern in the UK.

The world range extends from Europe through northern Asia, reaching north-eastern China, with a total breeding population that may exceed 50 million individuals. Most migrate but those in central and eastern Europe are resident.

The preferred habitat at all times of year is a mixture of trees and open country. In the British Isles, Fieldfares are most often seen in farmland with ploughed fields and berry-laden hedgerows; they also regularly visit orchards and gardens.

BEHAVIOUR

Like other thrushes, Fieldfares are omnivores. In Britain, they are most often seen eating fruit (especially berries, but also often windfall apples and pears) or foraging for worms and other invertebrates in short-turfed or ploughed fields. They will forage in company with other thrushes (especially Redwings) and berry-eaters, including Waxwings.

As with the Mistle Thrush, sometimes a lone Fieldfare will take up territory in a garden and defend a berry-bearing tree from other birds, to monopolise the resource for itself.

Where possible, Fieldfares nest close to other pairs and cooperate to defend the nest area from predators. The female builds a cup-shaped nest, often in plain view in a tree fork but sometimes nearer the ground, and lays five or six eggs. The chicks hatch after about 14 days' incubation by the female, and both parents feed the young in the nest for 14 more days, then another week or two after fledging. There are one or two broods, depending on latitude.

Many Fieldfares ringed in Britain in winter have subsequently been re-found in Norway, Sweden and Finland, and vice versa. Many autumn-ringed birds have been re-found in France, northern Italy, Spain and Portugal; a few more go east to reach Greece and the Balkans, such as one ringed in Yorkshire in February 1996, which then turned up in Turkey, 2,859km away, in November of the same year. There have been several recoveries in Britain of Russian ringed Fieldfares, which travelled distances exceeding 2,000km.

The oldest Fieldfare ringed in Britain lived for 14 years and eight months. A Finnish bird beat this record, having reached 18 years and one month.

IN THE GARDEN

You could attract Fieldfares with some halved soft apples, particularly in the coldest weather. Bushes such as pyracantha or cotoneaster will also appeal to them. They are very active and often aggressive towards smaller birds, so if you do have a flock visiting, you can help keep the peace by distributing food over a wide area.

Fruits are vital winter food for Fieldfares, especially when snow cover makes it hard to find worms and other soil invertebrates.

DIRTY PROTEST

The Fieldfare's method of nest defence is inelegant but highly effective. When a predator such as a corvid comes along, all of the pairs in the area leave their nests and dive-bomb the intruder, sometimes even striking it, but invariably spattering it liberally with faeces. This unpleasant bombardment is often more than enough to encourage the predator to change its plans, though is less effective against a mammalian attacker.

Small insect-eaters

In this section, I cover a mixed bag of unrelated songbirds that are mainly insectivorous and regularly visit gardens. It includes some of our best-known and most beloved species – Robin, Wren and Starling. All of these birds particularly thrive in gardens where native plants grow and areas are left untidy – the more natural the garden, the more insects there are for them to eat.

Robin
Erithacus rubecula

14cm
18g

GREEN

This little bird is one of our most familiar garden visitors, and is much loved for its apparently friendly disposition as well as its beautiful song. Most gardens in the British Isles have their 'own' Robin, and keen gardeners in particular will know just how easily a Robin can become confident enough to approach a human closely when there might be a free meal in the offing. The darker side of Robins is also well known – their fierce territoriality leads to many a dramatic confrontation along the fence-lines and sometimes even a fight to the death.

The large eyes and long legs reveal the Robin's expertise at finding and chasing insect prey on the ground.

INTRODUCTION
The Robin is about the size of a House Sparrow but weighs much less. The plumage is warm brown on the upperside, whitish on the belly, and with the red breast that extends up to cover the forehead, cheeks and around the eye. There is often a bluish border between the red of the throat and the brown of the neck-sides. Robins have proportionately very large, dark brown eyes, dark bills, and pinkish or dark pink legs.

RED FLAG

Robins aggressively posture and display at other Robins that approach or enter their territory, and the red breast-patch is a powerful trigger and a symbol of strength in these ritualised showdowns. When confronting another, a Robin sings vigorously, adopts an elevated position relative to its enemy and assumes a head-up posture to show off the red breast to its best advantage. If this fails to work, though, physical attacks begin. Studies with stuffed models show that Robins are not bothered by a model with its breast-patch obscured, but will violently attack a model that just consists of a clump of breast feathers. Up to 10 per cent of Robin deaths are attributable to territorial fighting.

Juvenile Robins' lack of red breast coloration, therefore, not only helps them evade predators through camouflage but also keeps them safe from assault by other Robins, including their own parents.

Juvenile Robins lack their parents' trademark red breast, though are often easy to recognise anyway by their leggy, upright, droop-winged stance and big eyes. Their plumage is uniform brown with extensive golden scalloping on the face and breast, and golden feather centres on the back, giving a streaky appearance. The first traces of a red breast appear a few weeks after fledging.

The most often-heard call from a Robin is the *tick* call, which becomes more frequent and insistent when given in alarm or aggression. The song, which may be performed by both sexes, is a sweet, wistful warbling, with some fast twittered phrases. It is probably the most familiar British birdsong, as it can be heard at any time of year.

DISTRIBUTION, POPULATION AND HABITAT

Robins live throughout the British Isles, including nearly all islands, though they become less common in open, cold places and mountainous regions. We have an estimated 6.7 million pairs in the UK. In winter, some of our breeding Robins depart, but we also have arrivals from further north and east. The subspecies that breeds here is *E. r. melophilus*, which is also present over most of western Europe.

The Robin's global range is mainly confined to Europe and covers nearly the whole continent. It also just reaches North Africa and the Middle East (mainly in winter), and into western Russia. Its world population is somewhere between 130 million and 201 million individuals. The various subspecies across its range include two distinctive forms found in the Canary Islands – *E. r. marionae* on Gran Canaria and *E. r. superbus* on Tenerife. These Robins are very striking, with bright white bellies and eye-rings, and together may form a distinct species.

Pigment abnormalities seen in Robins include a lack of reddish phaeomelanin pigment. The result is a 'Robin whitebreast'.

FOLLOWING THE HERD

The tendency of Robins to follow gardeners closely conveys much of their charm. The classic perch for a Christmas card Robin is not a branch but a spade handle, from which it eagerly watches its human companion at work with the trowel. As the earth is turned, the Robin descends to the ground to snap up an uncovered worm or centipede.

This behaviour long predates gardens and gardening. In their natural woodland habitat, Robins follow a different big mammal around – the Wild Boar *Sus scrofa*. As the rooting pigs ruck up the ground with their hooves and snouts, they expose soil invertebrates in just the same way. To a Robin, a gardener is just a foraging pig – on two legs.

Robins will happily use nest boxes with open fronts, as well as all manner of less conventional nest sites.

The natural habitat of the Robin is woodland and woodland edges, and other habitats with trees and bushes and a good understorey in which to forage. In the British Isles it is very much a garden bird, but is much shyer and less frequent in gardens further south and east.

BEHAVIOUR

The Robin is a predator, primarily, hunting all kinds of invertebrates, from earthworms to flies, beetles and spiders. It will also feed on berries and other fruits, will take some seeds, and eats most of the various foods we put out on our bird tables and in feeders.

The Robin's large eyes are well adapted to spot movement, even in low light – Robins can start foraging in the morning before most other birds, and carry on until later in the evening. They often wait on a low perch, dropping to the ground when they see prey. They will also search within foliage, will investigate disturbed soil, and can catch flies on the wing. In urban areas you may see them picking squashed insects from tarmac or even car grilles.

Robins are not particularly avid eaters of berries, lacking the agility and power of larger birds to wrestle the fruit free while dangling from a branch, but in cold weather in particular they will turn to this food source.

Unlike most of our birds, Robins are territorial all year round, and territory-holding birds (of both sexes) will sing through autumn and winter to discourage rivals. The male's song becomes more avid as spring approaches, while the female's lessens and then ceases once she has found a mate. Often a male and female will meet in winter and form a pair-bond, and then associate relatively little with one another but peacefully share the territory until early spring when nesting activity begins. However, a substantial proportion of British-breeding female Robins migrate south in winter, and will then seek a 'free' male on their return in spring.

This species is notorious for nesting in peculiar situations. Although it will build its cup-shaped nest in a bush or tree fork, it prefers some surrounding shelter and often picks a hollow on the ground or a crevice in a stone wall. In gardens, Robins will use nest boxes, and will also enter outbuildings and nest in abandoned flower pots or coat pockets. There is even a record of one female coming into a bedroom through an open window and beginning to build her nest in the folds of an unmade bed.

The female builds the nest and incubates with little or no assistance from her mate, but he will help her keep her energy levels up through courtship feeding. It is common to see a pair foraging quite near one another, and whenever the male captures a sizeable prey item, his mate will begin to beg like a fledgling and he will feed her.

The female lays a clutch of four or five eggs that are pinkish white with brown mottling (the expression 'robin's-egg blue' describes the eggs of the unrelated American Robin *Turdus migratorius*). Incubation lasts 15 days, and the chicks fledge at about 14 days old. Given a sufficiently early start to the breeding season, Robins can produce three broods a year.

Though we may be right to suppose that 'our' garden Robin is *in situ* all year, for its whole life, many of our breeding Robins – females especially – do migrate, mainly to southern France, Spain and North Africa. Robins from Scandinavia migrate to Britain, sometimes in large numbers. In western Europe the species' movements are variable, driven by weather as well as availability of territories, but Robins breeding in northern and eastern Europe are always migratory.

There have been several UK records of Robins covering more than 2,000km on migratory journeys. The furthest distance travelled by a ringed bird was 2,460km, by a young bird ringed in Russia and recovered in Kent; a Scottish-born bird nearly equalled it with a 2,388km migration to Morocco.

The oldest Robin ringed in Britain was not a traveller – it was found dead in winter at the same site in Lancashire where it had been ringed as a juvenile eight years and four months previously. This record is completely eclipsed by a bird in the Czech Republic, which reached at least 19 years and four months old.

IN THE GARDEN

The Robin is one of those species that may well live and nest in gardens whose owners do nothing in particular to encourage birdlife. Although they will come to bird tables and feeders, and will use nest boxes, the needs of these birds are often completely met by the facilities available in an average garden – a bush or shrub to nest in, and some turf and bare soil in which to find prey.

To enhance your garden's Robin-appeal, make sure to include a wide variety of insect-harbouring corners – log piles, drystone walls and open compost heaps are all good. Turning over the soil in winter will make life easier for them, especially if there has been snow cover. Robins are most likely to use open-fronted nest boxes, placed within sheltering vegetation (within Ivy on a wall is good). When they come to the bird table, they will take suet-based bird foods and some smaller seeds, but to convince them to hang around, offer their favourite – mealworms. Dried mealworms are acceptable but fresh are particularly enjoyed – you can buy them alive and wriggling (or see the Introduction, page 13, for instructions on how to establish your own mealworm colony).

A BIRD ON THE HAND

Robins quickly become quite fearless in the garden, especially if thrown the occasional unearthed worm, and most can be persuaded to feed from your hand if you wish. Once 'your' Robin seems confident in your company and you can tell it is watching you, try encouraging it nearer by placing food items closer to you. The next stage is to offer food on an outstretched hand, resting on the ground or close to the fence where the bird perches. This means the Robin can hop up and take the food from your hand without having to step onto your fingers. Once it is accustomed to this, you can start encouraging it to fly to your hand.

Dunnock
Prunella modularis

14cm
21g

AMBER

This shy little bird is the only native British representative of the accentor family, a group of birds mainly found in central and eastern Asia. However, it is often confused with the sparrows (and is even sometimes known as 'hedge sparrow'). Dunnocks are common residents in many gardens throughout the British Isles, and their rather quiet and unobtrusive manner belies a private life full of intrigue and subterfuge.

INTRODUCTION

The Dunnock has brown body plumage, which is a shade paler on the underside. The back has strong blackish streaking, and there is fainter darkish streaking on the flanks as well, sometimes spreading up to the breast-sides. The upper breast and head are blue-grey with brown streaking on the crown and cheeks; this is quite variable, with some individuals looking almost entirely grey-headed and others much browner – the most extreme grey-headed birds are often male and the streakier brown ones female, but there is much overlap. The slim bill is black, the eyes are dark red and the legs are pink.

Juvenile Dunnocks are like adults but lack blue-grey entirely and have a more marbled and spotty yellowish look. They can be confused with juvenile Robins, but their general shape and manner reveal their identity – in particular, they have rather small eyes whereas Robins look very wide-eyed.

The song of the Dunnock is an enthusiastic and pleasant-toned but somewhat unexciting shortish twittering warble, lasting about three seconds and given in repeated phrases. Singing birds often deliver their tune from a high, exposed perch, which can lead to identification confusion, as it is so different to the bird's usual furtive skulking at ground level. Its calls include a shrill *tseep* note.

The juvenile Dunnock is more streaky and speckled than an adult, and its eyes are dark brown rather than reddish.

DISTRIBUTION, POPULATION AND HABITAT

Dunnocks occur throughout the British Isles, including on most islands, though are rare or absent in the bleakest upland areas. About 2.3 million pairs breed in the UK. There are two British subspecies: *P. m. occidentalis* (found in Britain except the Hebrides, and also in western France), and *P. m. hebridium* (found on the Hebrides and throughout Ireland). Another six or so subspecies occur in other parts of its range.

The species has an extensive European range, and also reaches north-western Russia and south as far as North Africa; it occurs patchily through South East Asia as far as Iran. It has also been introduced to New Zealand, where it is very common and widespread – this population is probably of *P. m. occidentalis*. The total population in Europe is thought to be in the region of 25.4 million to 45.5 million individuals.

In the UK, Dunnock numbers began to fall substantially after the mid-1970s. The crash was steepest between 1975 and 1985, after which it slowed down and numbers stabilised. There has been a modest increase since the end of the 20th century but numbers still remain much depleted – between 1967 and 2008, the overall decline was 34 per cent, with a 5 per cent rise between 1983 and 2008. The recent increase has been strongest in Scotland and Northern Ireland. The cause of its decline is not known but is probably related to changes in woodland management, and increased numbers of deer preventing woodland regeneration and understorey development.

This is a bird of woodland, scrub, heath, moor, marsh and any other habitat with a good level of low-growing vegetation. As a timid and mostly ground-feeding bird, it takes well to more natural gardens with some bushes and other hiding places.

BEHAVIOUR

Insects and other small arthropods make up the bulk of the Dunnock's diet. They locate their prey on the ground and may also forage within bush foliage. In the colder months they take some small seeds and berries – these can make up well over 50 per cent of the total diet in mid-winter.

Dunnocks forage mainly on the ground, moving slowly and investigating around and under leaf litter and rocks. They may also pick prey from shrub stems and leaves. They are usually seen feeding alone.

Dunnocks begin to sing in earnest in late winter and to seek out mates. Because they are sedentary, they may pair with the same partner year after year, but things are rarely this simple.

Dunnocks are most often seen hopping rather furtively on the ground, searching for insects and other invertebrates.

INTERLOPER

The chances of ever seeing a Cuckoo *Cuculus canorus* in your garden are not high, but are much improved if you have nesting Dunnocks. There are three main host species for Cuckoos in the British Isles – the Meadow Pipit, the Reed Warbler *Acrocephalus scirpaceus* and the Dunnock. Female Cuckoos specialise in just one host species, so a female Cuckoo that is a Dunnock-specialist will need to seek out as many Dunnock nests in her local area as she can during the month or two that she'll be able to lay eggs (she may lay 20 or more in a season). Once the Cuckoo's egg is in place, the Dunnocks' own offspring (whether hatched or not) are doomed, as the nestling Cuckoo's first act is to hoist any other chicks and eggs out onto the ground below.

Cuckoos that lay their eggs in Meadow Pipit or Reed Warbler nests produce eggs that look very like the host's, and studies show that most host species will eject alien eggs that are not good mimics of their own. However, a Cuckoo egg in a Dunnock's nest is obvious at once – it is speckled brown, while the host's own eggs are clear blue. Why Dunnocks don't seem able to spot the Cuckoo egg alongside their own is unknown.

The display behaviour of the Dunnock is elaborate and sometimes frenetic, with wing-flicking a key feature.

The sex life of the Dunnock is famously convoluted, and led to the coining of a new term – polygynandry. This word combines polygyny (one male pairing with two or more females) and polyandry (one female pairing with two or more males), and describes a system in which up to six Dunnocks can form 'pair-bonds' with one another. Dunnocks may form monogamous, polygynous, polyandrous or polygynadrous arrangements, depending on population density and the balance of the sexes, and behaviour of the same individuals shifts from year to year according to these factors. Where food is abundant and females can make do with smaller territories, polygyny is more frequent.

The most common arrangement, though, is polyandry, with one female pairing up with two males, one of which is dominant to the other. This alpha male therefore has more mating opportunities than does the beta male. In more complex arrangements, a male Dunnock could be alpha to one

BUM-BITING

Males attempt to ensure paternity of the eggs their mate or mates lay by pecking at the female's cloaca before mating – this may encourage her to eject any sperm from a recent previous mating. There is little else he can do, though, besides trying to prevent any other males from getting close to the female. Once there are chicks to feed, males have no way to tell whether they are caring for their own offspring or not, and they feed all the chicks in the nest the same amount, alongside any other males also helping at the nest. However, the total amount of effort any male puts into provisioning the nest is dictated by how many matings he had with the female whose nest it is.

In terms of reproductive success, the sexes' interests are not aligned. For a female Dunnock, polyandry is the 'best' system, as she has two males to help her rear her young, so their survival chances are improved. For a male, polygyny is better as he has a chance of having two (or more) broods of chicks that are definitely his own.

OTHER ACCENTORS

The family Prunellidae is small, holding just 13 species, all in the genus *Prunella*. Most of these birds occur thousands of kilometres east of Britain. However, two of the Dunnock's cousins have reached our shores, albeit as extremely rare vagrants.

The Alpine Accentor *P. collaris* is like a large and colourful Dunnock, with tints of rust red on its belly and a speckled black-and-white throat. It is a montane species, occurring in the Alps and Pyrenees as well as further east. Like the Dunnock, it is polygynandrous, and is noted for being one of very few species in which the female attracts males through song.

The Siberian Accentor *P. montanella* looks like a very yellowish Dunnock except for its head, which bears a black crown and eye-mask. It breeds across northern Russia, in sparse birch and coniferous woodland near the tree-line, but moves south and west in winter. In October and

November 2016, extreme weather conditions drove large numbers of Siberian Accentors much further south and west than usual – the first ever individual recorded in the UK was found in Shetland in early October, but before the year was out another 13 had been discovered. Many of them lingered for weeks on end, and brought much joy to British birdwatchers.

female partner and beta to another. Dominance conflicts between males are characterised by energetic wing-flicking displays, but physical fighting is rare.

The female builds the nest alone and incubates her clutch of four or five eggs without help from any partner. The nest is a tidy cup-shaped affair made of twigs and lined with softer material, often close to ground level within a dense bush or shrub. The chicks hatch after 14 days of incubation and fledge another 14 days or so later. There may be three broods in a season but two is more usual.

In Britain, Dunnocks are very sedentary birds. Further east in Europe they are partial or full migrants, and there are several records of birds from Scandinavia reaching Britain and vice versa; there is also some exchange between Britain and the Low Countries. Long-distance movement is rare. The longest documented journey concerns a bird ringed on Fair Isle, Scotland, and re-trapped in southern France, 1,810km away (but given that Dunnocks do not breed on Fair Isle, this bird's true journey was at least a little longer).

The longest-lived Dunnock in Britain reached more than 11 years and three months (it was ringed as an adult, so its true age is not known). The European record-holder, though, a bird from Denmark, is notable for being the only wild small songbird in Europe known to have lived into its 20s – this Dunnock lived 20 years and 10 months after being ringed.

IN THE GARDEN

Dunnocks are likely to visit any garden that has some bushes, some sheltered turf or some dark corners full of leaf litter. They are unobtrusive, easily confused with sparrows if you don't look too closely, and tend not to visit bird tables or bird feeders very often. However, their interesting social behaviour rewards the time it takes to look out for them.

To attract Dunnocks, keep a reasonably untidy and wildlife-friendly garden, with plenty of dark nooks and crannies where invertebrates can shelter, and have a few prickly bushes in which the birds can nest. As insectivores, they particularly appreciate suet-based foods that contain insects, and both dried and live mealworms.

Wren
Troglodytes troglodytes

`10cm`
`10g`
GREEN

Small but mighty, the Wren is a characterful and feisty songbird that makes an appearance in most gardens, despite rarely being interested in anything on offer at the bird table. The wren family is large and native to the Americas, where today there are nearly 90 other species of true wrens. The ancestors of 'our' wren are thought to have crossed to Eurasia from north-western North America when the two land masses were connected at the Bering Strait, some 2 million years ago. *Troglodytes troglodytes* remains the only true wren to occur anywhere in the world outside of the Americas.

INTRODUCTION

The Wren is very small and warm rufous brown, a little paler and duller on the underside than the upperside. The body plumage is marked extensively – including the flight and tail feathers and most of the underside – with fine darker barring. It has a broad pale supercilium separating the dusky, streaked crown and cheek, and the throat is pale. Its tail is markedly short and square, and often held cocked right up over the bird's back. It has dark eyes, a rather long, slim bill with a very slight downcurve, and pinkish legs and feet – for its size, the feet and claws are large. Its wings are very short and very rounded, which is striking when the bird is seen in flight.

Juvenile Wrens recently out of the nest are like adults but a little darker and more rufous, with a less prominent supercilium, and narrow yellow fleshy mouth-edges.

The various vocalisations include a hard *tack-tack* alarm call, which may be given as a rapid machine-gun chatter, or *churr* when the bird is very agitated. This same chatter forms part of the song, which is a long phrase consisting of fast trills at various pitches, delivered with surprising power and force. If you spot the songster you may notice it vigorously shivering its wings and tail in an apparent ecstasy of emotion.

When very excited and hormonally energised, a male Wren opens and shivers his wings as he sings.

AMERICAN WRENS

Until the early 2000s, 'our' wren was considered to be the same species as the Winter Wren *T. hiemalis* and the Pacific Wren *T. pacifica*, which occur extensively in eastern and western North America, respectively. There are another nine or so wrens in the genus *Troglodytes*, and another 18 genera in the wren family Troglodytidae. While most wrens are rather like ours, in being small and a rather nondescript brown, a few are boldly marked, such as the red, white and black Bay Wren *Cantorchilus nigricapillus* or the white-spotted Canyon Wren *Catherpes mexicanus*. Several others are noted for their lovely voices, including the aptly named Musician Wren *Cyphorhinus arada*, two species of nightingale-wrens, and the Flutist Wren *Microcerculus ustulatus*.

DISTRIBUTION, POPULATION AND HABITAT

The Wren is Britain's most abundant breeding bird – a fact that surprises many, as it is not necessarily very obvious, except when delivering its deafening song. It can be found throughout the British Isles except the most unvegetated and cold upland areas, and is present on many island groups. The total UK population is in the region of 17 million individuals. Its population is prone to short-term fluctuations – numbers can crash in severe winter weather – but the general trend since 1970 has been a steady increase.

There are about 29 recognised subspecies across the Wren's extensive world range, which encompasses nearly all of Europe, parts of North Africa and the Middle East, and stretches across south-central Asia as far as eastern China, Japan and the Kamchatka Peninsula in far eastern Russia. In all, its population is thought to be somewhere between 10 million and 500 million individuals. The subspecies found over most of the British Isles is *T. t. indigenus*; it is not present in mainland Europe, and some of the Scottish island populations have been separated as distinct subspecies.

Wrens are very adaptable and occur in all kinds of habitats, dry or marshy, upland or lowland, provided there is a reasonable amount of ground vegetation. They are most frequent in woodland and scrubby habitats with leaf litter and fallen wood to forage among, and they are regular visitors to most kinds of gardens.

BEHAVIOUR

These little birds feed almost entirely on arthropods, particularly those that live on the ground or in and around crevices in wood. The species preys heavily on spiders and beetles, and in winter will also take some seeds, but it rarely visits bird tables and feeders. Its reliance on invertebrates for food and its very small body size render it more vulnerable than most small birds to the effects of bad weather, especially prolonged freezing temperatures and snow cover.

Wrens are experts at hunting down insects and their larvae from cracks and hollows in decaying wood.

The Wren's foraging style involves careful but fast exploration of promising spots such as tree stumps, piles of rocks and within leaf litter, where it searches for crannies in which spiders and other invertebrates may hide – it can recall a mouse as it moves discreetly and often rapidly over the woodland floor. Less often, it picks prey from tree and shrub foliage or bare soil, but is rarely seen searching turf. Its large feet and strong claws make it a competent scrambler but it is not especially agile.

This little bird is aggressively territorial all year round, with both males and females defending a 'patch' of their own. Male Wrens sing all year round but especially energetically from late winter to attract neighbouring females. About 50 per cent of male Wrens are monogamous, but polygyny is

ISLAND WRENS

The most famous Wren subspecies is the St Kilda Wren *T. t. hirtensis*. The little group of uninhabited islands that form St Kilda are the most remote of the British Isles, lying about 66km west of Benbecula in the Outer Hebrides. A couple of hundred Wrens live on the islands – they are distinctly bigger and darker than any other Wrens, and make a living in the islands' sparse shrubs and around the old drystone walls.

The Wrens found in Shetland, on Fair Isle and in the Outer Hebrides are also often regarded as distinct subspecies – they are *T. t. zetlandicus*, *T. t. fridariensis* and *T. t. hebridiensis*, respectively.

common in this species, with one male pairing with two, three or even occasionally four females. The male builds the outer structure of the nest, which is a ball of moss, grasses and leaves, in a bush, or stuffed into a tree hole, a space between tree roots, a crack in a wall or another crevice of some kind. Males build several such nests in their territory ('cock nests'), and the female or females then selects one from these, adding a soft lining to it.

The female lays a clutch of five or six brown-speckled white eggs and incubates them without her mate's help. They hatch after 17 days, and then both parents feed the young in the nest until they fledge at about 16 days old. They receive a few more days' care before they start to become independent. Most females produce two broods in a season, but within polygynous trios (or quartets or quintets) the females tend to start egg-laying at different times. This makes life a little easier for the male, as he is not required to feed two or three nests of well-grown chicks at the same time.

Wrens are not strong flyers and are generally very sedentary. There are a few records of long-distance movements, though, mostly concerning birds hatched on mainland Europe. Most notably, a young bird ringed in Russia in September 1996 was found dead in West Sussex in March 1997, having travelled 1,528km. One bird ringed as a chick in Germany travelled 1,282km in five months to reach Cornwall in November that year. Another ringed Wren covered more than 1,000km during its life in the opposite direction; ringed as a first-year in Kent in October 1988, it was re-caught in April 1989 in Sweden, 1,174km away.

Ringing recoveries suggest the Wren is naturally a short-lived species, with the record-holder caught at the same site (Bardsey Island, Wales) almost every year in the late 1990s and early 2000s. The last record of this bird was October 2004 – seven years, three months and six days after it was ringed as a juvenile in 1997. No ringed European Wren has beaten this record to date, though several other British-ringed Wrens have lived into their sixth year.

IN THE GARDEN

Although the Wren is a very abundant bird, it is often overlooked in the garden because of its skulking habits. However, the male's loud song, mainly heard in spring but also at other times, does grab attention, especially as singing Wrens often choose quite elevated and conspicuous perches. Otherwise, look out for them foraging among deadwood, rocks and the undergrowth. Leave plenty of cluttered wild areas to appeal to Wrens – deadwood is particularly good for them as it harbours a multitude of small creepy-crawlies.

Wrens are not easy to attract to the bird table but may be tempted by suet pellets or mini-mealworms. They will, however, use nest boxes both for roosting and nesting. For nesting, they are most likely to use open-fronted boxes, but for roosting any type will do. They will also use the wicker basket 'roosting pouches' that are sometimes sold in garden centres, both as roosting spots and as nests.

Wrens thrive in damp habitats and often hunt along the edges of puddles, streams and ponds.

BOXED IN

Keeping warm overnight makes the difference between life and death for tiny birds with a fast-running metabolism. In sub-zero weather, finding a sheltered place is not necessarily enough and Wrens overcome their natural territorial disposition to bed down together, sharing crannies and crevices to pool their body heat. This is a good reason to leave bird nest boxes out through the winter – they may attract gatherings of roosting Wrens and save the little birds' lives on the coldest nights. The groups can be very large – one observer counted 60 Wrens entering the same nest box at dusk on a freezing night. However, it is more usual for the roosting group to number up to 10 birds.

Roosting sites are traditional, used year after year by the local Wrens, which may travel a kilometre or two to reach them. Because Wrens hold territory all year round, the roost will be within one bird's own territory, and this individual summons others to the roost through loud song – it benefits from its bedmates' warmth after all, even though such closeness is in other ways against its very nature. Perhaps for this reason, it 'polices' which others are allowed to use the roost – some will not be permitted inside. Which particular birds are chosen, and why, is not yet clear. Perhaps those that are excluded are the territory-holder's most significant rivals – but more research is needed.

Goldcrest
Regulus regulus

9cm
6g

GREEN

If you have conifers in your garden, you have a good chance of seeing a Goldcrest now and then, as this tiny bird is a specialist at winkling prey items out from between pine needles. It is utterly charming to watch as it flits, bounds and hovers among the trees, and is often almost fearless, its attention entirely focused on its ceaseless search for food.

INTRODUCTION

This is Britain's smallest bird, and has a compact, almost neckless body shape, though the wings and tail are proportionately longish. It is drab olive or leafy green in general colour, paler on the underside. The wings are darker and marked with two whitish bars. The crown of its head bears a narrow yellow stripe, bordered by black – displaying males flare out their crown-stripe to reveal orange feathers at its centre. The face is otherwise plain apart from a short dark, downturned line from the mouth-edges – this, along with the large dark eye, give the face a somewhat woebegone expression. Juveniles are like adults but lack the black-and-yellow crown marking. The bill is black, shortish and fine, and the legs pinkish with rather yellow feet.

Goldcrests call frequently as they feed, uttering a single thin note. The song is a similarly high-pitched, slightly grating short twitter. Older people cannot always hear its calls because of the high pitch.

With its little gold 'crown' and rather woebegone expression, the Goldcrest's charm far outweighs its physical size.

DISTRIBUTION, POPULATION AND HABITAT

Goldcrests occur throughout the British Isles, except the open high uplands in Scotland. They don't breed on all offshore islands but their migratory habits mean they can turn up nearly anywhere. The

GOLD AND FIRE

The Goldcrest's close relative the Firecrest *R. ignicapillus* may also visit gardens. It is a much rarer bird in general, but its movements are unpredictable and in some winters it is quite abundant, its numbers boosted by visitors from mainland Europe. To tell the two apart you need a good look at the head – the Firecrest has a conspicuously stripy face, formed by a white supercilium and black eye-stripe. It also has a more colourful look overall, thanks to a yellowy-bronze patch at its shoulder. The two species' common names are misleading, as the Firecrest's crest is not really any more fiery than the Goldcrest's – males of both species have some orange feathers in the crown-stripe.

UK breeding population is about 1.2 million individuals, and many more may visit in winter. Numbers fluctuate considerably and can take a severe hit after a run of harsh winters (as happened in the 1960s), but the general trend since 1970 is for stability.

The subspecies *R. r. regulus* occurs in Britain and over most of Europe into western Siberia. Most of the other 14 or so subspecies are endemic to particular island groups. The Goldcrest occurs over most of Europe and much of central Asia, as well as parts of south and South East Asia – it is also a winter visitor to northernmost Africa. The world population is estimated at between 98 million and 165 million individuals.

The preferred breeding habitat of Goldcrests in Britain is coniferous woodland, though one or a few isolated large conifers can often be enough. It is therefore frequent in parks and also larger gardens. In winter, it ranges more widely and may be found in any kind of woodland, as well as scrubland, hedgerows and marshes.

BEHAVIOUR

This species specialises in tiny soft-bodied prey such as aphids and small spiders that hide between pine needles, but can handle bigger items too, and is adept at flycatching. It climbs and dangles with great agility, often hovers to examine the tips of fine twigs, and will forage on the ground as well. It may drink sap from damaged tree bark and occasionally comes to bird tables to feed on suet. In winter, Goldcrests often forage in small flocks, sometimes with other species such as tits and Chiffchaffs.

The male's silvery song may be heard from early spring, after foraging flocks break up and territories are established. Both sexes build the delicate cup nest, which is usually woven into the tip of a conifer twig and bound in place with cobwebs. The female incubates her clutch of six to eight eggs for about 17 days before they hatch, and then both parents feed the chicks until they fledge at about 20 days old. During this time the male may also build a second nest, in which the female lays her second clutch of the season, incubating these while her mate is still caring for the first-brood fledglings.

Newly fledged Goldcrests stick close together and may be seen sitting in a tight row along a twig, waiting for their next food delivery.

Despite their size, Goldcrests regularly migrate long distances. There have been many recoveries in Britain of birds ringed in Scandinavia, and several from the Baltic countries and Russia. On autumn mornings following easterly gales, very large 'falls' can occur along the east coast of England and Scotland. One Goldcrest ringed in Slovakia travelled 1,764km to reach the Orkneys.

The longevity record for Goldcrests in Britain is five years and one month. A Danish bird reached five years and five months.

Lacking the adults' bold head markings, juvenile Goldcrests are rather featureless, though their pink bills are striking.

IN THE GARDEN

Goldcrests are most likely to visit gardens with tall conifers (and may well nest in them). They occasionally come to bird tables and feeders, especially suet cake in a hanging 'cage' feeder, which encourages their natural tendency to climb and hover.

Blackcap
Sylvia atricapilla

| 13cm |
| 21g |

GREEN

The story of the Blackcap as a British garden bird is rather surprising. This dapper warbler is a common summer visitor that migrates south to Iberia and North Africa for winter. Since the 1960s, though, increasing numbers have been observed here in winter, often in gardens. Ringing recoveries show that these are not our own breeding birds but are migrants themselves, coming here from eastern Europe.

INTRODUCTION

The Blackcap is a sleek, rather long-tailed warbler with ash-grey plumage that is paler on the underside. Males have a black cap, while the female's cap is warm brown. Juveniles resemble females. All birds have a slimmish dark bill and dark legs. Males could be confused with Marsh or Willow Tits but can be told apart, given a good look at their heads, by their grey rather than white cheeks, and the fact that their black cap is confined to the top of the head rather than extending down the back of the neck.

The rich, fluty song of the Blackcap is much celebrated, giving rise to the nickname 'mock nightingale'. It is similar to that of the Garden Warbler *S. borin,* but that species' song is less varied, more hurried and includes longer phrases. The alarm call is a hard, tuneless *tack*, like pebbles being knocked together.

DISTRIBUTION, POPULATION AND HABITAT

This is a softly coloured, rather plain-looking bird, especially in the case of the brown-capped females and juveniles.

Blackcaps breed over most of the British Isles, though they are scarcer in Scotland and in upland areas. There are about 1.2 million pairs in the UK in summer. In winter, at least 3,000 birds are present, most abundantly in southern England but increasingly further north too. As a breeding bird, the Blackcap has increased dramatically of late, with a rise of 288 per cent in the UK between 1967 and 2016.

The subspecies *A. a. atricapilla* breeds in Britain and most of Europe. Four more subspecies are found elsewhere in the species' range. Blackcaps breed across Europe, north-west Asia and North Africa. They winter in Iberia, northern and western Africa, and parts of eastern Africa south to Malawi.

The breeding habitat includes deciduous woodland, woodland edges, scrub and parkland, also larger rural gardens. In winter, though, Blackcaps visit even urban gardens, provided there is food.

BEHAVIOUR

Blackcaps are mainly insectivorous in the breeding season, feeding on all manner of insects and also other small invertebrates. Towards autumn, as they prepare to migrate, they consume large numbers of berries and other fruits.

The Blackcaps that visit us in winter will also feed on fruits, berries and some seeds, but they appear to be most reliant on foods offered at garden feeding stations, particularly suet-based foods.

Our summer-visiting Blackcaps start to return through late March. The males soon establish a territory and begin to sing, and by mid-April most have attracted a mate. The nest is well hidden, often low in a dense prickly shrub such as a Blackberry bush. In it the female lays four to six eggs, which she incubates alone for about 11 days. The chicks take another 12 or so days to grow to fledging age, under the care of both parents. In southern Britain, pairs often produce a second brood.

Blackcaps in Britain are all migratory. Summer breeding birds winter mainly in southern Spain, Portugal and north and north-west Africa, a distance often exceeding 3,000km. A few appear to head east instead to reach Italy, Greece and even the Middle East. Our wintering birds come to us from Germany, Poland and adjacent countries – few if any of the birds here in winter are breeders that stayed on. The longest journey recorded was a juvenile female that was ringed on Fair Isle in September 1999, and caught again in the Gambia in January 2000; she had flown 4,999km.

The British longevity record for the Blackcap is 10 years and eight months, set in 1988 by a bird found dead in Spain, which had been ringed in the UK as a first-year in 1977. In Europe, a Czech-ringed Blackcap was re-caught 13 years and 10 months later.

IN THE GARDEN

A visiting Blackcap in winter often monopolises the suet-cake feeder and fiercely chases away any other small birds that try to get close. You may have a male and a female Blackcap visiting together and tolerating one another, but the aggression they show to other birds is remarkable, especially considering how shy they can be when breeding. Berry-breeding shrubs and plenty of safe cover will also help make your garden appealing to wintering Blackcaps.

Blackcaps can be heard singing from mid-April and are among the sweetest-voiced of all Britain's wild birds.

EVOLUTION IN ACTION

The phenomenon of Britain's wintering Blackcaps has attracted much attention from ornithologists, sparked by the discovery (thanks to ringing recoveries) that they are not 'home-grown' but migrants from further east. This behaviour is a recent development – previously, eastern European Blackcaps migrated to Africa, just as ours do. Now, a small but growing part of the population heads west rather than south-west, and reaches Britain.

It is known that a single genetic mutation can change the way a migratory bird orientates itself. This usually means the bird ends up in an unsuitable place to overwinter (or is lost at sea). For the Blackcaps, though, the combination of Britain's relatively mild winter climate and the availability (in gardens) of plenty of high-energy food improves survival rates. Carriers of the new gene have thrived and bred successfully. Moreover, they are more likely to breed with one another than with the traditional south-west migrators, as they return to their breeding grounds earlier. This separation is driving the earliest stages of an evolutionary split in the Blackcap population, and differences in plumage colour and anatomy have already been noted between the two 'types'.

Starling
Sturnus vulgaris

22cm
78g
RED

A bird of forceful character and striking beauty, the Starling is not always as welcome in gardens as it should be, thanks to its appetite and tendency to travel in large, noisy gangs. Starlings are still common birds in the British Isles and are frequent garden visitors, but their numbers both here and in northern mainland Europe have crashed since the 1970s and are showing no sign of recovery.

INTRODUCTION

This is a robust bird with a proportionately short tail and an upright, strutting gait when moving on the ground. In flight, the wings show a distinctive pointed, triangular shape. The adult Starling in breeding plumage is plain black at first glance but any light striking the plumage reveals iridescent greens and violets. A closer view shows a sprinkling of whitish or creamy-brown spots on the flanks, belly and rump, becoming elongated streaks on the back and chevrons under the tail. The wing feathers are brown-edged. Females are more spotted than males. The legs and feet are pinkish, and the bill is yellow with a black tip – the bill base becomes blue in breeding-condition males, but is yellowish pink in females. The sheen of the Starling's plumage, its shape and its manner of moving make it readily distinct from the male Blackbird.

In their fresh winter plumage, Starlings are more heavily white-spotted, with extensive speckling over the head and neck. These spots are at the feather tips, so disappear gradually through wear. Juveniles are plain light brown when they fledge, with a whitish throat, a black bill, and a black patch in front of the eye. They soon start to develop adult-like white-spotted black feathers on their bellies and, gradually, over their entire body plumage, though their heads remain somewhat brownish well into winter and their bills blackish, making them distinguishable from full adults.

Male Starlings produce an extraordinarily varied, rambling song, which combines rattles, bubbling trills and thin metallic notes with mimicry of all manner of other sounds, natural and non-natural. The species also makes various grating and chinking calls.

Starlings will use soft leaves as nest-lining material, as well as animal hair, feathers and bits of grass.

TICKLED PINK

A second species of starling occurs in Britain – rather rarely, but it does turn up in gardens and towns more often than in other habitats, nearly always teaming up with a flock of 'our' Starlings. The Rose-coloured Starling or Rosy Starling *Pastor roseus* is found in Asia and is rather nomadic by nature. Several individuals reach our shores every year, most of them young birds that arrive in autumn.

It is much the same size and shape as the Starling but is unmistakable in its black-and-pink adult plumage, with its long, floppy crest and smallish pink-toned bill. In juvenile plumage, though, it is rather less impressive looking and very similar to a juvenile Starling. It is a few shades paler, with more contrast between its darker wings and light fawn-brown body plumage, and its smaller bill may be

noticeable. The biggest clue, though, is that the youngsters that reach us in autumn are still in full juvenile plumage, many weeks after our own Starlings are well on the way to their adult-like first-winter plumage.

DISTRIBUTION, POPULATION AND HABITAT

Starlings are found almost everywhere in the British Isles, though are scarcer in more open uplands and absent from mountainous regions. There were about 1.8 million breeding pairs in the UK in 2009 but this number has probably fallen over the last nine years, as the BTO's surveys suggest an ongoing decline. Between 1967 and 2016, the total decline in the UK was 51 per cent, and in England it was a shocking 89 per cent. The decline appears to be mainly down to a reduction in the number of young birds making it through their first winter, probably due to changes in farming practices reducing the amount of food available. Also, nest sites are becoming scarcer, as old buildings are repaired or demolished; competition for tree holes with the introduced and fast-spreading Ring-necked Parakeet may also be a factor in parts of England.

Starlings are fully protected in the UK, but over much of Europe, they have no protected status and are considered pests or are even shot for food, despite the fact that they are declining in almost every part of their natural range.

The subspecies of Starling found over most of the British Isles and most of Europe is *S. v. vulgaris*. However, Shetland and the Outer Hebrides have a different form, *S. v. zetlandicus*, distinguished from *S. v. vulgaris* by its less spotty plumage. There are another 11 or so subspecies across the Starling's world range, which encompasses virtually the whole of Europe and extends well into central and south-western Asia. The winter range reaches North Africa and the Middle East. Within its native range, the Starling's population is in the region of 105 million to 191 million individuals. There are also introduced populations of Starlings in North America, South Africa, south-eastern Australia, New Zealand, parts of South America and on some island groups.

Starlings are often associated with human habitation. They can be common in villages, towns and cities, and around farmland. However, they are also frequently encountered in the wider countryside, especially open lowland areas such as marshland. Reed beds can hold large winter roosts of Starlings.

BEHAVIOUR

Starlings are omnivores but obtain a significant part of their food from underground; they are avid eaters of leatherjackets (cranefly larvae) and earthworms. All other kinds of invertebrates are taken, along with the odd small vertebrate. In winter, vegetable matter such as berries, seeds and grains

BLAME THE BARD

The presence of Starlings in North America is down to an imaginative but unwise idea to establish every bird mentioned in the works of Shakespeare in the USA. This was the brainchild of the American Acclimatization Society, and in 1890 members of the group released Starlings in the New York area.

There are now Starlings throughout the USA as well as much of Canada and northern Mexico. There are 140 million of them (45 per cent of the total world population). They displace native cavity-nesting species such as bluebirds from their nest sites, they compete with native birds for food, and they can be very destructive to crops. Vast numbers are killed each year by state governments as well as individuals and private concerns, but the species is now far too widespread and established for any realistic attempt at eradication.

At dusk in winter, Starling flocks join up into large murmurations, which perform dramatic swirling sky-dances before going to roost. Each time one bird makes a small change in direction, the movement ripples through the whole flock so it moves as one, confusing any birds of prey nearby.

make up a larger proportion of the diet, and all year round Starlings will search pavements, roads and rubbish dumps for discarded food items. They may even raid other birds' nests on occasion.

The birds unearth soil invertebrates by pushing their bill into the earth and then opening it to make the hole larger – they use a similar technique to break into plastic rubbish bags. They are also skilled at catching flies and winged ants in mid-air, as well as chasing beetles and the like on the ground. They are fairly agile and able to climb and hang from mesh- and cage-type bird feeders. Highly social at all times, Starlings usually forage in flocks, which can be very large, and may forage alongside thrushes on the ground.

Towards the end of winter, adult male Starlings start to seek out and defend breeding territories, centred on a suitable nest site (in a cavity of some kind), in which they start to build a nest. Only a small area around the nest-hole is defended – about 50–100cm radius, so pairs may nest very close together. Both sexes try to return to the same nest site they used before, so the same pairs will often re-form.

Both parents incubate the four or five eggs for about two weeks, and both feed the chicks until they fledge at around three weeks old. Their father continues to feed them for a few days outside the nest while the female lays again (though not all pairs attempt a second brood); after this, the juveniles from all nearby nests flock together and forage as a group. They are very noisy when fresh from the nest, and can often be seen and heard chasing after the adults both in flight and on the ground, giving loud, grating calls as they beg for food.

Ringing recoveries show that there is a great deal of movement of Starlings between Britain and north-eastern Europe and north-western Russia. For example, there have been 434 recoveries in Norway of British-ringed Starlings, and 247 in the other direction. The figures from Sweden and Finland are similar. Exchange with countries further south is less frequent, but British-ringed Starlings have reached Spain, Italy, Greece, Turkey and even Azerbaijan – this last journey, at 3,934km, is the longest on record.

The longest-lived Starling in Britain was 20 years and eight months old. In Europe, a Danish bird lived to the age of 22 years and 11 months.

IN THE GARDEN

Starlings are common visitors to most gardens, especially those with a short-turf lawn, which they will ransack for leatherjackets. If you offer fat balls or other suet-based foods on a bird table or feeders you may attract numerous Starlings, especially in winter and right after the local pairs fledge their first brood of chicks.

Nest boxes for Starlings should be made in the conventional style, with a round entrance hole, and fixed to a tree trunk or wall out of direct sunlight. The box should be about 30 × 23 × 15cm with a hole of 45mm diameter.

Starlings compete for their tree-hole nests with various other species, such as Nuthatches and Ring-necked Parakeets.

BAD BREEDING BEHAVIOUR

If you find a solitary and intact blue egg on your lawn it was probably left there by a Starling. Those female Starlings that do not have a pair-bond with a territory-holding male, or that lose their mates or nests after mating, will try to pass on their genes anyway by laying an egg or two in another Starling's nest. The nest-owner does not seem to notice the alien egg. If they are caught in the act or can't find a nest in time, they will just lay wherever they can.

There is also evidence that female Starlings will attack other Starlings' nests and injure or even kill the chicks. This behaviour is probably sparked by a shortage of suitable nest sites, leading to deadly competition.

Pied Wagtail
Motacilla alba

18cm
21g
GREEN

The British Isles is home to three breeding species of wagtails; of these, the Pied Wagtail is the one most associated with towns and villages. However, it is still not a particularly common or frequent garden bird – you're more likely to spot it on the roof than down on the lawn or patio. It is a distinctive and attractive little bird, which is most likely to turn up in gardens in bad winter weather.

INTRODUCTION

The Pied Wagtail is a small but very long-tailed bird with smart black-and-white plumage. It has a fast-running gait and the habit of bobbing its long tail constantly when standing still. Adults have black upperparts and a white face and belly, with a broad black breast-patch. In breeding plumage, the throat is also black. The wing feathers have white edges, as does the tail. Males are, in general, more neatly marked than females, with more intense and extensive black plumage. Females often have white neck-sides and can look dark grey rather than black on the back. All birds have a strongly undulating flight pattern.

White Wagtails (the European subspecies *M. a. alba*) also occur in Britain. Telling White Wagtails from Pied is sometimes quite difficult, but White are always paler and have less extensive black markings. Juvenile Pied Wagtails are quite uniform dusky grey, with no black. They show white wing-bars and a pale yellowish face and chin.

The usual call is a bright, ringing, two-note *chissik*, often given in flight. The rather jumbled song incorporates this note as well as other hurried twittering notes.

DISTRIBUTION, POPULATION AND HABITAT

The Pied Wagtail breeds throughout Britain and Ireland, though it tends to retreat to the lowlands in winter. It is present on nearly all offshore islands, even some very small ones (for example, it is one of only three songbirds to nest on the sparsely vegetated and tiny Farne Islands off Northumberland). The breeding population in the UK is about 470,000 pairs, and the population trend is generally

This busy little bird draws attention with its confident fast walk and non-stop tail-bobbing.

stable, though like many small insectivores this species is affected by short-term fluctuations in response to weather conditions in winter.

The subspecies *M. a. yarrelli* occurs in the British Isles. Over Europe it is replaced by the White Wagtail, a regular migrant to Britain, and there are about seven other subspecies across the rest of its range. The species occurs over virtually the whole of Eurasia (wintering in southern Asia) and is also present in winter over much of the northern half of Africa (with a small breeding outpost in north-west Africa). Its world population is between 135 million and 221 million individuals.

Flat roofs and car parks offer good foraging grounds for Pied Wagtails, as do open areas of short turf such as sports fields, but they are also found around farmland, by upland streams and in wetland areas.

BEHAVIOUR

These birds eat insects, particularly flies that they catch in mid-air with agile, fluttering leaps. They also pursue prey on the ground and around water, and will pick up squashed insects from roads and on car grilles. They occasionally capture fish fry and will scavenge along strand-lines on beaches for invertebrates such as sandhoppers. They sometimes forage in loose groups.

Male Pied Wagtails sing to proclaim their territories from March or April, when they begin the nest-building process – this is completed by the female. The nest is built inside a crevice, often a hole in a riverbank or a wall, or a crevice in a rock face. There is also a marked tendency to nest in unsuitable places, such as in a space on a piece of farm machinery that is sometimes in use. The species will use open-fronted nest boxes. The clutch is usually of four to six eggs; they are whitish with dense brown speckling.

The female does most of the incubation, which takes about 13 days. The chicks fledge at two weeks old and their parents care for them for another week or so. Most pairs will go on to have a second brood.

Pied Wagtails are largely sedentary, but White Wagtails are migrants over much of their range and are regular passage migrants in Britain. Most ringing recoveries concern birds ringed in Britain that moved south to the western parts of France and Spain, with a few travelling to north-east Africa. Birds breeding in Iceland also regularly turn up in the British Isles.

The longest migratory journey of a British-ringed Pied or White Wagtail was a juvenile ringed on Fair Isle in August 1957, which was shot two months later and 4,776km away in Mauritania. There are also several records of birds moving more than 900km between Scotland and southern England.

The oldest ringed Pied Wagtail in Britain was at least 11 years and three months old, having been ringed as an adult in 1977 and found dead only 2km away in 1988. A ringer in the Czech Republic re-trapped the oldest known European bird 13 years and eight months after it was first ringed.

IN THE GARDEN

The usual bird-table fare is unlikely to attract Pied Wagtails, but they may be tempted by insect-filled suet cakes or pellets, especially in freezing weather. They may also forage on the lawn and around the edges of the garden pond. A standard-sized open-fronted nest box may encourage them to stay and breed.

Pied Wagtails form communal winter roosts, often in towns, which tend to be warmer than the surrounding countryside.

Crows

Despite their size and lack of musical talent, crows are technically classified as songbirds. Not always popular in the garden, they are nonetheless beautiful and entertaining visitors that will make short work of any garden scraps you care to throw out for them. Crows belong to the family Corvidae, and most British species visit gardens regularly.

Carrion and Hooded Crows
Corvus corone/C. cornix

46cm
510g
GREEN

The Carrion Crow is the familiar large all-black crow that you'll see over most of Britain. In north-west Scotland and Ireland, it is replaced by the Hooded Crow, which is grey and black but otherwise very similar. These two crows were until recently considered to be subspecies of the same species, and where their distributions overlap, they will interbreed quite freely. They are opportunists, and will visit gardens as well as all other kinds of habitats if there is food to be had.

INTRODUCTION

Where their ranges overlap, Carrion and Hooded Crows interbreed, and the hybrid young look like Hoodeds with extra black patches.

The Carrion Crow is a large, robust and gracefully proportioned crow with entirely black plumage, dark eyes, a black bill and blackish-grey legs. The head is rather flat-topped and the plumage sleek, with a subtle blue gloss. The bill is strong and sturdy with a slight downward curve along its top edge. In flight, the bird shows a square-ended tail and has a somewhat laboured, 'rowing' flight style.

The Hooded Crow or 'Hoodie' has the same shape and proportions as the Carrion Crow, and has a black tail, wings and bare parts, but its body plumage is mostly warm mid-grey, with just a black head and upper breast. Hybrids between Hooded and Carrion Crows have more black in their plumage than pure Hooded Crows. Juveniles of both species have the same plumage colours as the adults.

WHITE-WINGED

It is quite common to see Carrion Crows with extensive white in their wings and tail, revealed when they are in flight. The whiteness takes up the central parts of the long flight feathers, giving the appearance of broad white wing-bars and a white-centred tail. The feathers are the usual black at their bases and tips. The phenomenon is most common among crows living in towns and cities.

This is a kind of leucism (plumage depigmentation) but is developmental rather than genetic. If the chick in the nest is not well nourished, the deposition of melanin in its feathers can be affected, and this is most likely to occur in the biggest and longest feathers. The result is a strikingly black-and-white-patterned crow, which may lead you to suspect the bird to be part Magpie. However, these birds

are 100 per cent Carrion Crow, and provided they survive their first year and have a good diet, they will replace their depigmented juvenile flight feathers with normal solid black ones during their first full moult.

The typical call of both crows is a low, flat and dry cawing, but some individuals have higher-pitched voices. They are capable of mimicry.

DISTRIBUTION, POPULATION AND HABITAT

The Carrion Crow is present throughout most of Britain, including island groups as far north as central Scotland; it is absent from far north-western Scotland and the Hebrides. It is also found along the eastern coast of Ireland, and in winter will visit Shetland and Orkney. Its UK population is about 2 million, and has risen steadily for some decades (an 18 per cent increase UK-wide between 1995 and 2016). Its population in England increased by 138 per cent between 1967 and 2016.

Hooded Crows are found throughout Ireland, and in north-western and northern Scotland, including all island groups. In winter, Hooded Crows from mainland Europe visit north-eastern and eastern coasts in varying numbers, sometimes reaching East Anglia and even Kent. In the UK, there are about 260,000 pairs; the species showed a 31 per cent decline in Scotland between 1995 and 2016.

Carrion Crows of the subspecies *corone* are found in the British Isles and western Europe, from Spain and Portugal east as far as Austria. The Hooded Crow (of the subspecies *cornix*) replaces it in Scandinavia and eastern Europe, its range extending through north-western Russia and south (represented by three other subspecies) through southern Europe to parts of the Middle East. In central and eastern Asia, Carrion Crows of the subspecies *orientalis* take over, occurring right across Siberia to Sakhalin, Korea and Japan. The International Union for Conservation of Nature (IUCN) estimates the two species' combined world population to be in the region of 58.7 million to 110 million individuals.

Both crow species may be found in all kinds of habitats, though they are more common in open landscapes than in woodland. They will both visit beaches, marshland and urban environments, and are regular in gardens, especially larger ones with an expanse of short turf.

BEHAVIOUR

Both of these crows are omnivores, and are highly intelligent. They feed on all kinds of animal prey – although they are not specialists in the task, they will frequently catch and kill small mammals and

The Carrion Crow's nest is a sturdy structure, able to contain up to five wriggling, well-grown fledglings.

other vertebrates, and sometimes two or more will cooperate to kill larger prey. They also scavenge roadkill, scour the strand-line, raid birds' nests and fishmongers' stalls, and eat food waste from streets and rubbish dumps (and will rip up bin bags given the opportunity). They probe the ground to uproot worms and other soil invertebrates, and will eat fruit, seeds and other plant-derived food. They will also pick up shellfish and drop them from a height to break them.

Hooded and Carrion Crows may forage alone or in small parties (Hoodies are more likely to be social). A good food supply, such as a large mammal carcass, will attract plenty of them. They will try to steal kills from birds of prey, and will also aggressively chase and mob any raptors they encounter.

These crows are inclined to form long-lasting pair bonds and stay together on their territory through the year, although they will wander more widely and tolerate others of their species in winter. In some areas, they will nest in loose colonies, and sometimes chicks from the previous year will remain in their parents' territory and assist at the new nest. Pair-bonding behaviours include bowing displays and mutual preening.

ONE SPECIES OR TWO?

The IUCN is one of several bodies that consider the Carrion Crow and Hooded Crow to be forms of the same species. This is in part because the birds will interbreed and their hybrid offspring are fertile. However, studies have shown that in northern Italy, where the two forms come into contact, Hooded Crows still preferentially mate with other Hoodies, and the same goes for the Carrion Crows. There is also evidence that hybrid crows breed less successfully than 'pure' ones of either species, producing fewer eggs and having lower chick survival. The two forms also show slight but consistent differences in the habitats they prefer, with Hoodies better able to make use of poorer-quality, wilder and more rugged habitats.

This evidence has persuaded the British Ornithologists' Union to recommend that the two crows be considered separate species. And the differences in their habitat preferences may explain why, in Scotland, the Carrion Crow has been spreading its range and moving into traditional Hoodie areas, while Hoodies are becoming rarer – as more land is farmed, the landscape in western Scotland becomes more Carrion Crow-friendly.

CAUSE OF DEATH

Nearly all the ringing recoveries for crows of both species concern birds that were ringed in the nest and re-found after being either shot or trapped. This is in contrast to smaller passerines, which are most often caught and then re-caught by bird ringers using mist-nets. These nets are usually set low down across a gap between trees or clumps of shrubs, so open-country birds like crows rarely encounter them. Even if they do, they are likely to be either too clever to be caught or too powerful to stay caught.

However, the nature of crow ringing recoveries also reflects the fact that these birds are on the General Licence – they may be legally killed without first applying for a special licence, provided there are legitimate reasons for doing so, and that non-lethal control measures have failed. Gamekeepers kill thousands of Carrion and Hooded Crows every year, and conservation bodies also sometimes need to control their numbers to protect vulnerable breeding birds. The necessity and ethical justification for this is hotly debated, but both crow species are currently faring well despite the large numbers killed each year.

The pair works together to build the nest. This is a large, untidy structure of sticks, built high in a tall tree, on a crag or sometimes on a building, and occasionally on the ground. The outer structure is held together with some mud, and the nest cup is lined with fur, feathers, soft grasses and similar materials. The female lays three to five eggs and incubates them alone for about 19 days, while the male feeds her on the nest, particularly in the early part of the incubation period. She may leave for short spells to forage for herself as the hatching day approaches.

The female feeds the hatchlings by regurgitation, and after the first few days the male also directly feeds the young. The chicks take about a month to reach fledging age, and about the same again to reach independence – the parents only have time to produce one brood per year. The chicks are not normally ready to breed until two years old and so may spend their first year in the parents' territory.

Carrion Crows in Britain are very sedentary, with few movements of more than 100km ever observed, and no recoveries overseas. The same seems to be true of our home-grown Hooded Crows, but populations of this species in north-eastern Europe are somewhat migratory and a few have reached Britain, including two from Norway and two from Sweden, which travelled more than 1,000km. The longest journey was of 1,627km, a bird ringed as a chick in Sweden in 1919 and found in Suffolk two years later.

The oldest known British Hooded Crow was 10 years old, and the oldest Carrion Crow 17 years old. A Swiss Carrion Crow was observed alive 19 years and two months after it had been ringed, and the longevity records from other large corvids suggest that Hooded and Carrion Crows should both be capable of living into their 20s.

IN THE GARDEN

You are likely to see crows (Carrion, Hooded or both, depending where in the British Isles you live) flying over your garden, and if you have a good-sized lawn they will probably regularly descend to explore and probe the turf. Though they are clever and agile, they are simply too big to use most hanging bird feeders, but are likely to come to open bird tables and to food offered on the ground. Despite being quick to notice an opportunity, they are wary birds and may avoid roofed bird tables and any other feeding stations that require them to go into a space that feels too confined.

Crows will eat almost anything you care to put out, including conventional bird foods but also kitchen scraps of all kinds. If you feed your dog or cat outside, there's a good chance a crow will raid their bowl. If your garden has some very tall trees, you may also attract the birds to nest.

Rook
Corvus frugilegus

| 45cm |
| 430g |

GREEN

This is a large crow with a somewhat loose-plumaged, shaggy look. It is more of a countryside dweller than the Carrion Crow (with which it is often confused), but quite regularly turns up in larger, more rural gardens, especially those close to farmland. Like all crows, it is a clever and inventive bird and an entertaining garden visitor.

INTRODUCTION

The Rook is about the same size as the Carrion Crow, but is slimmer, with loose 'baggy trousers'. Its plumage is black with a blue-violet sheen. The bill is long, slim and whitish, with an area of pale bare skin around the base, including the chin and almost reaching the eye. Its crown is peaked and, in flight, its tail tip is slightly diamond-shaped. It is quite agile and flamboyant in flight.

Young Rooks have fully feathered faces and dark bills, so are much more like Carrion Crows. They are best identified by the different bill and tail-tip shape, and are usually seen with adult Rooks.

The call is a harsh, rather desolate cawing. Breeding colonies generate a great deal of noise.

DISTRIBUTION, POPULATION AND HABITAT

Rooks are found throughout lowland Britain and Ireland; they are absent from the high uplands of Wales and Scotland, and also from the inner London area and large city centres generally. The UK population is about 1.1 million breeding pairs. The population fell by 21 per cent between 1995 and 2016. This places the species close to the threshold for inclusion on the Amber list of species of conservation concern.

The species' distribution is extensive, including almost all of Europe (except northernmost Scandinavia) and continuing in a broad band through central Asia to the far east of Russia and

Rooks love company and it's unusual to see one on its own, but pairs are also closely bonded, staying together all year round.

PROBLEM SOLVER

Examples of corvid intelligence are frequent in the media. One such observation concerned Rooks at a motorway service station. These clever birds learned how to access the contents of partly full rubbish bins without having to jump inside. The birds would perch on the open top of the bin and grab the plastic bin liner in their bill, pulling up a fold of it. They would secure this fold and then another with a foot, and then gradually winch up the bottom of the bag until they could reach its contents.

Rooks also work together to solve problems. Respondents to the BTO's 2014 Garden Rook survey noted cooperative feeding, whereby one Rook moved a bird feeder within reach of another, or emptied a feeder onto the ground where other Rooks were waiting.

China and across to Japan. Just two subspecies are known – *C. f. frugilegus* in the west, and the migratory *C. f. pastinator* in the north and east of Asia. Rooks were introduced to New Zealand in the late 19th century. The world population is between 54 million and 95 million individuals.

In the British Isles, Rooks favour lowland farmland and pasture, with some woodland or copses for nesting. They are sometimes common around villages and small towns, but tend to avoid very built-up areas.

BEHAVIOUR

The Rook's species name, *frugilegus*, means 'fruit-gathering' and reflects the somewhat more vegetarian diet of this species compared with other crows, though it prefers grain to fruit. It also eats soil invertebrates, its relatively long, narrow bill being well adapted for probing and digging.

It is a part-time scavenger, of human food waste as well as natural carrion, and flocks often visit service stations, rubbish dumps and car parks in search of food. It will at times raid birds' nests and catch living prey, and will search the tideline for living invertebrates as well as carrion. Large flocks of Rooks forage in pastures or stubble fields, sometimes along with Jackdaws.

Rooks nest socially, in large, long-lasting colonies called rookeries. The clusters of large stick nests are easily spotted in late winter when the trees are still bare and the colony occupants very active. Rooks are monogamous and affirm their bonds with display flights and mutual preening at the start of the breeding season. A pair may renovate and reuse the previous year's nest, or construct a new one.

The female incubates her clutch of three or four eggs while the male feeds her. Incubation lasts about 16 days, and the chicks fledge at around 33 days old. They rely on their parents for some weeks afterwards, and adults and juveniles alike then join other local colonies to form very large foraging and roosting flocks.

British Rooks are mostly sedentary, but birds from overseas occasionally turn up here. The longest journey was made by a bird ringed as a chick in Finland, which travelled 1,759km in the same year to reach Suffolk. The oldest British (and European) Rook was 22 years and 11 months old.

IN THE GARDEN

Rooks are most likely to visit your garden if you have a good area of open lawn and live near farmland. They will eat household scraps as well as all kinds of bird food, but nesting is unlikely unless you have several very tall mature deciduous trees.

In spring and early summer you'll often see Rooks with a swelling under the bill. This is a full gular pouch, a pocket of loose skin in which the bird carries food, to be delivered to its chicks in the nest.

Jackdaw
Corvus monedula

34cm
220g
GREEN

This bird, the smallest of our black-plumaged crows, is a conspicuous and noisy inhabitant of towns and villages all through the British Isles, as well as in the wider countryside. It is one of the birds most likely to nest on (or more likely in) our homes and can be a frequent garden visitor; unlike larger crows, it can feed quite easily from hanging bird feeders. It is not closely related to the other crows in the genus *Corvus* and is sometimes classified in a new genus instead – *Coloeus*.

INTRODUCTION

A sturdy little crow, the Jackdaw is easily recognised by its white eyes and black 'mask' contrasting with the greyer neck.

Jackdaws are markedly smaller than Carrion Crows and Rooks, and have a compact shape with a proportionately small and chunky bill. The plumage is black but becoming grey on the neck and breast-sides. It is palest at the back of the head, where it contrasts with the sharply delineated black forecrown and front of the face. The legs and bill are blackish grey and the eyes white. Young Jackdaws are blacker than adults, and have light blue rather than white eyes.

In flight, the Jackdaw shows a round-ended tail. The head looks rather blunt because of the small bill. It could be confused at a glance with a dark Feral Pigeon but is a little larger and bigger-headed, with less pointed wings. Its flight manner is agile, light and graceful, with quicker wingbeats than a Carrion Crow.

Jackdaws are named for their calls, which include a crisp ringing *cheeack*, the usual contact note given between members of a pair and a flock, as well as a more typically crow-like cawing note, given in alarm. Youngsters begging for food have a shrill screech.

BEAST FROM THE EAST

Our Jackdaw has only one close relative – the Daurian or Eastern Jackdaw *C. dauuricus*, which is found in far eastern Asia. This bird is Jackdaw-like in size and shape but has different coloration – it rather resembles a Hooded Crow, with pale grey body plumage contrasting with a black face, breast, wings and tail. However, it is variable and in young birds the grey parts of its plumage are much darker, making it very Jackdaw-like indeed. Whatever its plumage is like, the Daurian Jackdaw can always be recognised by its dark (as opposed to pale or white) eyes.

The Daurian Jackdaw is a very rare visitor to Europe, and those that have occurred here have been found among flocks of normal Jackdaws. However, if you find a Jackdaw with unusual pale plumage, the chances are much more likely that it is a normal Jackdaw with leucism (unusually pale pigmentation) rather than a Daurian.

DISTRIBUTION, POPULATION AND HABITAT

Jackdaws are very widespread in the British Isles, being scarce or absent only in the bleaker uplands of northern and western Scotland. They are present on nearly all offshore islands too, though are scarce in the Outer Hebrides. The UK population is about 1.4 million pairs; these birds are of the subspecies *C. m. spermologus*, which is also present in western and southern Europe and, sparsely, in northern Africa. In the UK, Jackdaws have increased considerably over the last few decades, with a rise of 130 per cent between 1967 and 2016.

This species is resident throughout most of lowland Europe, though rare in Scandinavia. Its range extends eastwards as far as Mongolia, with the easternmost population being migratory – these birds are the subspecies *C. m. soemmerringii*. The subspecies *C. m. monedula* is found in most of Europe and western Russia, and *C. m. cirtensis* in Algeria. There is quite a lot of minor variation in appearance across the species' range and there may be a case for separating some other Jackdaw populations as separate subspecies – some authorities recognise as many as 11 more besides those already named. The world population is between 39 million and 85 million individuals.

Jackdaws are found in all sorts of habitats, including farmland, woodland edges, marshes and urban areas. As cavity-nesting birds, their presence is dictated by the presence of nest sites. They are notorious for nesting in chimneys, but are often very common in parks with large mature trees that have some holes suitable for nesting, and around sea cliffs and quarries that offer an abundance of crannies and sheltered ledges.

Jackdaws prefer to stay close to their partners, even in the air. It's often easy to pick out the pairs within a flying flock if you watch for a few moments.

BEHAVIOUR

Like other corvids, Jackdaws are omnivorous and opportunistic. They are most often seen feeding on the ground, on short grazed (or mown) turf, searching for beetles and other invertebrates, and sometimes probing the soil for worms. They will turn over animal droppings and catch flies that come to feed on cowpats. They scavenge at carcasses, take eggs and chicks from birds' nests and occasionally catch other small vertebrate prey, clean up human food waste, and also take some vegetable matter, including grains – they will eat grit to help process harder foods like these.

Jackdaws forage in groups and will also feed alongside other birds, including other corvids (especially Rooks), but also pigeons, Starlings, gulls and waders. Within a flock, there is a very definite and stable dominance hierarchy, and when a male pairs with a female she attains the same social rank as him – so females will select the highest-status mate they can. Social status is communicated through various displays; tilting up the head shows appeasement, while pointing the bill down shows aggression.

Where possible, Jackdaws prefer to nest communally, in loose aggregations. This is easier in some habitats than others – for example, it's generally easier to find nest sites on a rock face than in a woodland. Young Jackdaws seek out mates when they are in their second year, and if a pairing lasts for a few months then almost invariably it will persist until one of the pair dies, even if the birds fail to breed successfully for two or more years in a row. Genetic tests also show that matings outside the pair-bond are virtually non-existent.

The nest is built in a crevice, hole or other sheltered space. The Jackdaws may have to do battle with other hole-nesters, such as Tawny Owls, Kestrels and Stock Doves to secure a site. Once the nest is established, it may be used and augmented by the same Jackdaw pair year after year, becoming very large over time. The base is made of large twigs, which the birds drop into a crevice if it is too deep, to form a platform on which the nest proper is built. The nest cup is lined with grasses, feathers and animal hair – in spring, Jackdaws can often be seen perched on the backs of sheep or deer, pulling out wool or hairs to use as nesting material.

The clutch usually comprises four or five eggs. The female incubates them for 20 days or so, and both parents feed the youngsters for 32 days in the nest, then a few more weeks post-fledging. Only one brood is produced per year.

In Britain, Jackdaws are not very inclined to travel. Most will stay close to home but lack of nest-sites may force them to disperse. Movements of more than 200km are unusual; the longest journey within the British Isles of a British-ringed bird was 375km, made by a bird ringed as a first-winter in County Wexford, Ireland, which moved to Yorkshire.

GIFT-GIVING

Altruistic behaviour in animals is much studied, and its frequency disproves the theory that every living thing is out for itself. Jackdaws have very close social bonds, and their food-sharing behaviour is very egalitarian. A study on juvenile Jackdaws showed that the birds shared food with others regardless of sex and closeness of relationship. They were more likely to share their favourite types of food than less favoured items, and (most unusually) the initiative was taken by the giver, rather than by the receiver showing begging behaviour.

FIREPLACE FLEDGLINGS

Every year, many householders are startled by the sudden arrival of a baby bird in their (hopefully not currently in use) fireplace, after a nest built in the chimney has collapsed. Worse is when an adult or a young bird becomes trapped in the flue, and a complicated rescue is required. The species involved is almost invariably the Jackdaw, and anyone living in an area where Jackdaws breed should fit a mesh guard over the chimney top to prevent birds nesting and keep them safe from any harm. Instead, put up a large nest box (see below) high on a wall.

Jackdaws of more northerly and easterly populations in Europe are somewhat migratory. A few British-ringed birds have been recovered in Scandinavia, and because most of these were ringed as adults in winter and then re-found in the spring and summer months, they were almost certainly Scandinavian breeders overwintering in Britain. The longest journey of such a bird was an individual ringed in Norfolk in December 1966, which was found dead in May 1976 in Sweden, 1,023km away. A chick ringed in Sweden in 1939 travelled the other way, to turn up in Hertfordshire in late winter 1940, 1,055km away.

The oldest ringed British Jackdaw was – or possibly still is – more than 18 years old, having been ringed as an adult on its breeding territory in spring 1999 and then re-caught several times over the following years at the same ringing site, most recently in May 2017. A Danish-ringed Jackdaw has lived for at least 20 years and four months.

Roadkill is a great food source for Jackdaws and other corvids, and can also provide nesting material.

IN THE GARDEN

Jackdaws will visit any garden where food is on offer, particularly if there is an area of lawn where they can probe and search for invertebrates. They will take bird food and kitchen scraps, and are able to use hanging feeders provided the openings are large enough – cage-type feeders with fat balls will certainly attract them.

It is a good idea to keep Jackdaws from nesting in your chimney as this can cause problems for both you and them. They will readily use nest boxes – if you are building your own, make it about 45 × 20 × 20cm wide, and position it high up on a wall or a tree trunk out of direct sunlight. A box of this size could attract various other species besides Jackdaws, and the birds may also occupy boxes that you put out in the hope of attracting Tawny or Barn Owls, or Kestrels.

Magpie
Pica pica

45cm
220g

GREEN

This beautiful small crow is one of the most distinctive and instantly recognisable British birds, and would certainly be much admired and sought after by birdwatchers if it was a little more scarce. Magpies in the garden are a mixed blessing, as they can and do prey on baby birds and also take eggs. However, this is because they are opportunistic omnivores, and there is much you can do to protect garden-nesting birds from their attentions.

The showy, noisy and charismatic Magpie is one of Britain's most familiar and, in many ways, most spectacular birds.

INTRODUCTION

The Magpie is a smallish, short-winged crow with a long, graduated tail (the central feathers are the longest). It is black with large white shoulder panels and a white belly (but not undertail). The black areas of its plumage are a dense, slightly glossy black, but the wing and especially tail feathers show colourful iridescence – in strong light, the tail reflects a spectacular rainbow of colours, from green to violet. In flight, the bird reveals extensive white areas on the inner parts of the primary wing feathers. The eyes and bill are blackish and the legs are dark grey. Male Magpies are a little larger than females. Young Magpies look like adults but have paler, bluish eyes and less glossy plumage, and, for the first couple of weeks after they leave the nest, are shorter-tailed.

Magpies move on the ground with a strutting walk or sometimes a fast hop. In the air they look ungainly with their long tails and are not prone to the aerial agility of some other crows, such as Jackdaws. They have various squeaking and harsh chattering calls and are also capable of mimicry.

THE MEANING OF PIE

The original name for the Magpie was just 'pie', which derived from an old Indo-European word meaning 'pointed'. It probably referred to the bird's tail, but over the centuries has been assumed to mean 'black and white' instead, giving rise to the terms 'pied' and 'piebald' to mean anything patterned in black and white. Pied lives on with the black-and-white meaning in several English bird names, including the Pied Wagtail and Pied Flycatcher.

The addition of 'mag' to 'pie' apparently likens the bird's chatter to the voices of women talking, with 'Mag' being a shortened version of the name Margaret. Today, many birds and other living things with black-and-white coloration have the word 'magpie' in their names, including the magpie-robins, the Magpie Moth *Abraxas grossulariata* and the Magpie Inkcap *Coprinopsis picacea*, a strikingly patterned fungus.

DISTRIBUTION, POPULATION AND HABITAT

This species is very common and widespread in the British Isles, except for the north and central upland regions of Scotland. It is also missing from many Scottish islands. Its UK population increased strongly between 1970 and 1990, since when it has been generally stable at about 600,000 pairs (overall, it showed a 100 per cent increase between 1967 and 2016).

The Magpie ranges across Europe and much of Asia to the Far East, and is represented by six subspecies. The form present in Britain is *P. p. pica,* which is also present in most of Europe and into western Russia.

In Britain, Magpies are most common in mixed lowland habitats with some trees and some open ground. They are common on farmland with patchy woodland, and also in parks and gardens; they can be found in city centres provided there is some green space around. They prefer to nest in tall trees, and mainly forage in soft ground with short turf or other vegetation, but are intelligent and adaptable enough to survive in a wide range of other environments.

BEHAVIOUR

Like the other crows, Magpies are true omnivores, taking seeds, fruit, grain, insects and other invertebrates, carrion and food waste left by people, and sometimes killing and eating small vertebrates. A study on urban Magpies found that up to one-sixth of their diet was dog faeces, and other mammalian droppings are also fair game. Other particularly important foods are soil invertebrates such as leatherjackets (cranefly larvae). Magpies are intelligent and observant birds that are quick to exploit new feeding opportunities – they will raid dustbins and food left out for pets and livestock, and will prey on any other animal they can subdue. Excess food is often buried for later consumption.

A horse's back is a fine vantage point for a pair of Magpies, and offers plenty of hair for lining their nest.

Magpies access a lot of their food by digging, using the stout bill and also the feet. They also pick fruits, tear flesh (holding the food item steady between their feet as they work) and pick parasites from the backs of large grazing mammals, and are agile enough to use hanging bird feeders, as well as reach birds' nests in tree holes.

Younger unpaired Magpies remain in flocks through summer, but most will seek a partner either in their first or second spring, and pair-bonds persist year after year. Courtship involves short chases and posturing to show off the white shoulder markings and tail colours.

145

A TRICKSY GENUS

The genus *Pica* has, at the last count, seven members, and all seven are very similar in appearance. The most distinctive is the Yellow-billed Magpie *P. nuttalli*, a rare bird found only in California. While this bird has both a yellow bill and a yellow eye-mask, its shape and pattern are the same as that of our own (Eurasian) Magpie. The Maghreb Magpie *P. mauritanica* of North Africa has a striking patch of violet-blue bare skin around its eye, but it, too, is in other respects like our Magpie, and the remaining four species lack facial ornamentation and are almost identical to Eurasian Magpies.

It is only since 2018 that some of the *Pica* species have been recognised as separate to Eurasian Magpies, as a result of genetic study. Because the *Pica* magpies are not strongly flying birds and are reluctant to disperse to new territories, their ancestral populations have long been kept separate by barriers such as seas and mountain ranges that have formed over time, and some of these isolated forms have become sufficiently different from others to be classed as distinct species.

The nest is very large, and usually placed on a high, stable fork in a tall mature tree. The base is formed by sticks stuck in place with mud, with a lining of softer grasses and roots. On top of the main cup is a roof of thorny branches. The birds access the inside of this ball-shaped nest by squeezing through a single inconspicuous opening on the side of the roof.

The female lays a clutch of five or six brown-speckled blue eggs and incubates them for about 20 days. The chicks remain in the nest until they are anywhere between 25 and 31 days old, and rely on parental care for at least the same time span again. The family will stay together during this time, and it's common to see the young birds play-fighting on rooftops and flying together between trees, with much raucous calling.

In winter, Magpies associate in loose flocks and will often forage together. They behave cooperatively to access food and to drive away predators. Their social bonds can be very strong. Some observers have noted behaviour suggestive of grief within a flock when one of their number is killed.

This bird is not inclined to wander far from its place of birth. Of 1,684 birds ringed in the UK and then recovered, none has ever left the country and only 108 moved from the county in which they were originally ringed. The longest journey was made by a bird ringed in its first winter in Essex and found in Somerset eight years later, a distance of 204km away. A handful of others travelled more than 150km, but this is very much out of the ordinary.

The oldest known wild British Magpie was ringed as a chick in 1925 and shot at the same location 21 years, eight months and 23 days later. This bird is also the oldest known Magpie in Europe.

IN THE GARDEN

Any garden with an area of lawn will probably attract Magpies at least some of the time. A large garden with a sizeable lawn and some mature trees will probably have Magpies around all the time and they may well stay to breed. They are useful birds to have in the garden as they eat a lot of destructive invertebrates and clean up carrion. Any food scraps thrown out onto the lawn will also be eaten. To keep them away from feeders intended for smaller birds, use cage-type guards with a rigid wire frame around the feeder itself.

Dense, prickly shrubs offer nest sites for small birds that are well protected from opportunistic Magpies. Always leave nests well alone and avoid searching for them – Magpies notice unusual human behaviour and will investigate anything that they see has caught your attention.

BRIGHT AND BEAUTIFUL

The brain of a bird is different in several respects to that of a mammal, and we are only now beginning to learn how it works and its potential in different species. The region of the avian forebrain concerned with higher functions, such as abstract thought, is called the nidopallium. It is similar to the neostriatum in the mammal brain, but in mammals, the neostriatum is concerned with less advanced functions, such as learning to avoid harmful stimuli.

All members of the crow family are known to be intelligent, with the ability to carry out complex tasks such as making and using tools, counting and retaining detailed memories. The Magpie's nidopallium is comparable, by its size relative to the rest of the body, to the parts of the brain concerned with higher functions in the great apes, making it likely to be one of the most intelligent of all living animals.

The notion that Magpies like shiny objects and will steal them at all costs comes from Rossini's opera *La gazza ladra* (*The Thieving Magpie*), in which the titular bird steals a silver spoon, almost causing the execution of a wrongly accused

servant. This isn't backed up by any real-life observation, however, they are curious birds and will investigate all unfamiliar objects, shiny or otherwise.

Jay
Garrulus glandarius

34cm
170g
GREEN

This is our smallest crow species and the only one not decked out in monochrome tones – instead, it is strikingly colourful, although its shy and wary nature means that we don't get to appreciate its beauty as often as we might like. Jays are most often encountered in rural gardens with woodlands nearby, but they do also occur in towns and even cities.

INTRODUCTION

About the length of a Jackdaw but lighter in build, the Jay has a strong bill, a medium-length tail and fairly short wings. Its body colour is a soft orange-pink, suffused with grey on the back. The undertail, throat, crown and front of the face are white, and there are fine black streaks on the crown and a broad black stripe running from the bill base under the eye to the cheek. Its wings and tail are black – the wings also have a white patch at the base of the secondaries, and patches of black-barred, bright blue feathers at the wing-bend. In flight, it reveals a large white rump patch. The legs are dull pink, the bill dark greyish, and the eyes mid-brown or light blue. Young Jays are very like adults but a little drabber.

The Jay's outline in flight is distinctive, with a round-ended tail and very broad, round wings. Its direct, rather laboured-looking flight pattern is also quite distinctive.

The usual call of the Jay is a very harsh screech, often given in alarm when the bird has noticed danger. It has a repertoire of other calls, including skilled mimicry, with the mewing note of the

The delightful colours and patterns of the Jay provide camouflage and break up its outline in its woodland habitat.

Buzzard *Buteo buteo* one of its favourite sounds to repeat. The mimicry is so note-perfect that many experienced birdwatchers will not be able to distinguish the call from that of an actual Buzzard – though if it originates from within a tree rather than the open sky, that is a strong clue that the caller is a Jay.

DISTRIBUTION, POPULATION AND HABITAT

Jays are widespread in the British Isles. They are absent from parts of western Ireland and significant expanses of northern Scotland and upland northern England, and are also absent from most northern islands. The UK population is about 170,000 pairs. The species' numbers have been broadly stable over the four or so decades that bird population surveying has been widely practised in Britain. Over the short term, some moderate fluctuations have occurred, with a strong increase noted in the UK between 1998 and 2012, followed by a fall.

The world range encompasses virtually all of Europe, a broad swathe of central Asia across to Japan, and north-western Africa and the northern Middle East. Its world population is estimated to be somewhere between 30 million and 66 million individuals.

Jays are woodland birds by nature and are most often found in lowland deciduous oak woods with some mature trees. However, they can also do well in habitats with more scattered trees, including farmland with copses, parkland and larger gardens. Provided there are enough trees around they will occur in large towns and cities. In busy town parks where people come to feed wild birds, Jays can overcome their naturally wary nature and become quite tame, in some cases even coming to take food from people's hands.

BEHAVIOUR

Like its fellow corvids, the Jay is an omnivore and a great opportunist. Its diet contains a very high proportion of seeds and nuts in autumn and winter, and it also eats fruits and other plant matter. In addition, its diet includes all kinds of invertebrates, especially beetles and caterpillars, and a variety of vertebrate prey, including the eggs and chicks of other birds.

Jays find much of their food on the ground, but they also search within tree foliage and bark for invertebrates. They will scan roadsides for carrion and will also visit garden bird tables and hanging feeders. It is unusual for them to forage in groups or to associate with other bird species.

JAYS OF MANY COLOURS

According to the *Handbook of Birds of the World*, there are 27 subspecies of Jays around the world. Some other authorities consider that there are even more than this. In the British Isles we have two – *G. g. rufitergum* in Britain (and also north-west France), and *G. g. hibernicus* in Ireland.

Among the other Jay subspecies are some that are strikingly different in colour to our own Jays. The central Asian *G. g. brandtii* has a rich orange head and upper breast, while *G. g. cervicalis* of North Africa is rather grey with a striking white head. The south Asian *G. g. bispecularis* has dark eyes and lacks white markings, while *G. g. atricapillus* has a solid black hindcrown, contrasting with its white face. The Japanese *G. g. japonicus*

has the darkest face of all, with the pale eye appearing very prominent in its black surround.

NATURAL REFORESTING

The easiest time of year to see Jays is the autumn. Look out for them flying overhead in their distinctive straight-line, steady-flapping style. A closer look will probably reveal that they are carrying an acorn (or two) in their bills. Jays collect vast numbers of acorns in autumn, carrying several in their throat pouch as well as in their bill. Each individual can pick up as many as 5,000 acorns, all of which it will stash in hiding places (usually buried in the ground in natural hollows) to provide a store of food for the winter months, over an area of several square kilometres.

The Jay remembers where it stores its bounty and will retrieve as many as it needs. Into spring, it can locate a buried acorn by spotting the sprouting seedling (and will then eat both acorn and sprout). Inevitably, though, some buried acorns will never be dug up, and in this way new oak forests can be established. In years with a poor acorn crop, you may see Jays carrying sweet chestnuts or beechmast instead.

Jays are among those species that often engage in 'anting' behaviour – lying on or near the nests of wood ants and allowing the insects to climb on and through their plumage, and sometimes even placing them within their feathers. They are not consuming the ants but instead using them for feather maintenance. The ants spray formic acid, which discourages parasites.

This is a notoriously shy bird and is particularly difficult to observe when it is nesting. In spring you might see several together, and pairs form within these pre-breeding flocks. The pair-bond may last for repeated seasons, though you are more likely to see Jays by themselves at all times of year. In their social encounters, their display behaviour includes erecting the crown plumage into a comically tall crest.

The pair builds its nest high in a fairly large tree within woodland. The base of the nest is a roughly cup-shaped platform of sticks, anchored in place with mud, and within this a more delicate open cup structure is built and lined with small twigs and roots. The clutch usually comprises four or five eggs. Both sexes incubate, and after 18 days the eggs hatch. The chicks take about 21 days to reach fledging age, and after leaving the nest they continue to rely on their parents for several more weeks.

Jays in the British Isles appear to be quite sedentary. A single individual is known to have travelled overseas, though whether it was a British-born Jay is not known for certain. This bird was ringed as an adult at Dungeness in south-east Kent in autumn 1955, and then found dead the following year in Zeeland, the Netherlands. Its journey of 218km has been bested by several Jays that made lengthy journeys within the British Isles – one bird ringed as an adult in County Tyrone, Ireland, reached Lincolnshire, 432km away, during the four years and four months that elapsed between ringing and recovery. Another youngster travelled from Surrey to Cornwall, travelling 285km in its first winter.

Ornithologists have long suspected that Jays from northern and north-eastern Europe do move south-westwards in some autumns, particularly when the acorn crop is poor. In 2012, birdwatchers in east Kent noted significant numbers arriving from the sea through late September, with more than 100 counted each day at some locations. There was also a well-documented influx in 1983. However, no foreign-ringed Jay has yet been found in Britain (though the Dungeness-ringed bird mentioned above could have originated in mainland Europe).

That this apparently irruptive behaviour is not borne out by ringing recoveries may suggest that these Jays are not arriving from abroad but are local birds making local movements. However, Jays rarely fall into ringers' hands – their nests are difficult to find, and adults on the move are too large to be caught easily in mist-nets. It is therefore quite possible, perhaps even probable, that the ringing record for this species is still too sparse to give the true picture of the species' wandering tendencies.

The longevity record for a British-ringed Jay is 16 years and nine months, a figure just beaten by a Swedish Jay that lived 16 years and 11 months.

IN THE GARDEN

The arrival of a Jay in the garden is always exciting, given the bird's beautiful appearance. If your garden has some mature trees or is close to deciduous woodland, you stand a good chance of seeing this most colourful crow.

Watching Jays is difficult, even from inside your house, as they are usually extremely alert and sensitive to movement and, what's more, their shrieks of alarm when they spot you and fly into cover will often panic all of the other birds around as well. However, if you are patient, they may grow accustomed to you and allow you to observe them at length. They will feed on all manner of kitchen scraps and will also take nuts and seeds from feeders and bird tables. If you collect up some acorns and scatter them in full view on your lawn, you may be rewarded by the sight of several Jays patiently collecting them and carrying them away.

Jays may attack other birds' nests in the garden. Help counter this by providing alternative food sources for your visiting Jays, and by providing safer nesting sites for the other birds. Thick, prickly shrubs are much easier for 'little birds' to move through than for larger birds like Jays, and nests in such locations are much more likely to be safe than those in sparser and smaller shrubs.

Most large birds struggle to access a vertical bird feeder, but it's no problem for the agile Jay.

Woodpeckers and other tree-climbers

In this section, I cover three unrelated woodland birds that make their living climbing the trunks and branches of trees. As such, they are naturally adept at using bird feeders – both the Great Spotted Woodpecker (family Picidae) and the Nuthatch (family Sittidae) regularly do so. The Treecreeper (family Certhidae) usually shuns bird feeders, but it still often visits gardens.

Great Spotted Woodpecker

| 22cm | |
| 85g | |

GREEN

Dendrocopos major

The arrival of this woodpecker at the bird feeder causes alarm among the smaller birds, and excitement for the birdwatcher. By far the likeliest woodpecker species to be seen in most UK gardens, the Great Spotted is strikingly marked, bold and agile, but it tends to be very shy and flighty so must be observed with care if you don't want to scare it away. Great Spotted Woodpeckers are increasing in Britain and have recently begun to colonise Ireland – hitherto a woodpecker-less island.

INTRODUCTION

This bird is about the size of a Starling but rather slimmer and longer-necked, with a strong dagger-like bill. It is usually seen in classic upright woodpecker stance, clinging to a branch or tree trunk with its pointed tail pressed against the wood as a brace. The plumage is whitish on the underside and face, and black on the upperside, with long white ovals on the back, white patches on the neck-sides, a white outer tail and white barring on the flight feathers. The white cheeks are outlined with black, and the crown is also black. The undertail area is bright red, and males also have a red patch on the back of the neck (females lack this). Juveniles have red crowns (this is limited to the front of the crown in young females but more extensive in males) and a pinkish undertail rather than the bright red of adults. The bill and legs are dark grey. In flight, the bird looks broad-winged with a torpedo-shaped body, and has a bounding flight style.

Its undulating flight path, striking pattern and loud, sharp calls make this woodpecker noticeable and easily recognisable in flight.

RARELY SPOTTED

Very occasionally, the Lesser Spotted Woodpecker (now a very rare bird in Britain) turns up on garden bird feeders. Much more frequently, though, juvenile Great Spotteds are mistaken for Lessers. Male Lessers have a red crown, as do juvenile Greats, but there the similarity ends. The Lesser Spotted Woodpecker is only about the size of a Great Tit, and is compact rather than lanky, with a small bill. It lacks the big white ovals on the back that the Great has; instead, its back has ladder-like white barring, like its wings. Probably the easiest feature to check is the undertail, which is pink in young Greats but white (with some blackish streaking) in Lessers.

The usual call of this woodpecker is a sharp, ringing *kik*. In springtime courtship chases, the participants call repeatedly in quick succession, the notes running together as a sort of chatter. In spring, territory-holding birds also 'drum', striking their bills very rapidly on a resonant branch for a second or so. The resultant sound is a far-carrying creaking tone, as the blows are too close together to be heard individually.

DISTRIBUTION, POPULATION AND HABITAT

The Great Spotted Woodpecker occurs throughout England and Wales, including on some larger islands, and much of lowland Scotland, though not on the northern Scottish isles. The UK population is about 140,000 pairs. The species is also now present on the eastern side of Ireland, and is spreading rapidly. The British population is of the subspecies *D. m. pinetorum*, which is also present in western, central and southern mainland Europe. About 13 other subspecies occur elsewhere in Eurasia and North Africa.

Great Spotted Woodpeckers occur over a large swathe of Eurasia, east as far as Japan and south-east into Myanmar and Laos. They are also present in north-west Africa. The total world population is in the region of 73 million to 111 million individuals and its population is growing across most of its range. In the UK, it increased by an incredible 378 per cent between 1967 and 2016, most steeply between 1995 and 2008. However, since 2010 there has been a slight decline (6 per cent between 2011 and 2016). Its increase may be related to the decline of Starlings, which are competitors for nesting holes, and also the increased rates of garden bird feeding.

This bird can be found in deciduous, mixed and coniferous woodland, and also habitats with more scattered trees, such as parkland and farmland with copses. It is a frequent visitor to gardens with trees.

BEHAVIOUR

Great Spotted Woodpeckers feed mainly on invertebrates in spring and summer, and switch to a more plant-based diet of nuts, pine seeds and similar fare in winter. They are regular raiders of other birds' nests, taking both eggs and chicks, will occasionally feed on carrion, and will access tree sap by drilling holes in the bark in a ring around the trunk.

They find most of their food on and in the trunks and branches of trees, exploring fissures in the bark and looking for places where hibernating insects hide. Beetle larvae that live deep within the wood form a key component of their diet – the woodpecker attacks soft parts of the wood with powerful, splintering blows to reach the tunnels bored by the larvae, up to 10cm deep. It then uses its long bristly tongue, coated with sticky saliva, to

A drumming Great Spotted Woodpecker strikes the wood up to 40 times per second.

RETURN TO IRELAND

Ireland was connected to Britain some 8,000 years ago, and there is evidence that Great Spotted Woodpeckers were once inhabitants there – bones found in cave systems in County Clare have been carbon-dated to the Bronze Age. However, Ireland suffered very extensive deforestation in the 17th and 18th centuries, and there have been no woodpeckers breeding there since then.

Occasional sightings of Great Spotted Woodpeckers did occur in eastern Ireland – on average, about one every five years. However, from 2005 the number began to increase, with three records in that year, and six in 2006, primarily in County Wicklow. The first strong evidence of breeding came in 2008, when a newly fledged juvenile was seen in July, and in 2009 the first active nest was found. The population in Ireland is now growing fast, with 25 confirmed nests in 2013. DNA testing shows that the Irish birds originated from both England and Wales, and probably represent dispersal from areas in western Britain where the local population has reached saturation point.

Both parents continue to feed their fledged young regularly outside the nest for at least a week.

winkle the larvae out. It will also attack the access holes of bird nest boxes to enlarge them enough to reach inside, and will break into the mud nests of House Martins. To get into nuts and pine cones, it uses a firm supporting stump or flat part of a branch as an anvil and then hammers at the item to break it.

Male Great Spotted Woodpeckers hold territory all year, and use their drumming as a form of song, to warn off other males and to attract a mate, which may or may not be the same partner as the year before. When a female joins a territory-holding male, he performs a fluttering display flight with much loud calling. She follows and he shows her possible nest-site locations.

Both birds work on the nest-hole, and can take as long as four weeks to complete it, digging out a cavity up to 35cm deep and leaving plenty of woodchips at the base of the tree (as well as plenty more inside the cavity – they serve as the only nest lining). The female lays four to six white eggs and both sexes incubate them for about 12 days. The chicks grow rapidly, and as they approach three weeks old they may be seen peeping out of the entrance hole. They fledge at about 22 days old, and the parents then split the brood, each feeding a couple of chicks until the young birds become independent about 10 days later. You may see an adult and juvenile at a bird feeder together, the parent extracting food and passing it to the waiting youngster.

This is a distinctly unadventurous species, with only three overseas journeys known from ringing recoveries. These involved a young female that crossed from Kent to Belgium in 1962 (travelling 257km), and two birds from Norway that reached Shetland, in 2003 and 2005 (travelling 424km and 352km, respectively). Populations in northern Europe and Asia are prone to irruptive movements in very cold winters or in response to food shortages. It is also known, through DNA studies, that Great Spotted Woodpeckers have moved from Wales and England to Ireland, and this is probably in response to a shortage of available territories.

Within Britain, a few ringed birds have travelled more than 100km. The longest journey was a female that moved from Kent to Wiltshire (194km).

The oldest British-ringed Great Spotted Woodpecker was ringed as a first-year in Treswell Wood, Nottinghamshire, in 2005, and then re-caught by ringers in the same wood almost every subsequent year up until June 2017, 11 years and 10 months after it was originally ringed. A ringed Swedish bird was re-caught 12 years and eight months after it was first ringed.

IN THE GARDEN

Most garden bird enthusiasts will want to attract this beautiful bird, and may well succeed provided there are some mature trees in the garden or nearby. With their clinging and climbing skills, Great Spotted Woodpeckers excel at using hanging feeders, and will visit them to feed on peanuts, sunflower seeds and all kinds of suet-based bird foods. They also enjoy 'bird pastry' (see Introduction, page 13) pressed into tree bark. Woodpiles will provide them with a place to forage for more natural food.

Great Spotted Woodpeckers drill their nest-holes up to 8m up the vertical trunk of a living or dead tree. They choose a place where the outer (sap) wood is hard, to prevent predators trying to enlarge the hole, but the inner (heart) wood is soft and easy to excavate.

PERPLEXING THE PECKER

One of the drawbacks to having Great Spotted Woodpeckers in the garden is their habit of attacking nest boxes that are being used by tits or other small birds. They will usually target the entrance hole and chip away at its edges to make it bigger – they are also very patient and may work on the box over several days.

Any ordinary plywood nest box is vulnerable to woodpecker attack. One solution is a box made of Woodcrete, a tough material that incorporates woodchips and concrete. However, such boxes are expensive. Fixing a metal plate around the entrance hole will protect it, though it does not prevent the woodpeckers from breaking into the side of the box. Another possibility is to tack some fine-grade chicken wire fairly loosely to the box sides and front. As long as the wire is not too near the nest-hole, it will not get in the way of the box's rightful occupants but should make it difficult for a woodpecker to land.

Nuthatch
Sitta europaea

14cm
24g
GREEN

Watching a Nuthatch scramble confidently down a tree trunk to approach a bird feeder is always a treat, even if the other small birds steer clear of it and its rather intimidating dagger of a bill. Unique among British birds in appearance and character, the Nuthatch has become increasingly familiar to garden birdwatchers as its population has grown and its distribution has expanded over the last few decades.

INTRODUCTION

The Nuthatch is a stocky, short-tailed and big-headed bird with a long, rather sturdy bill. Its upperside is unmarked light blue-grey, darkest on the wing-tips and edges, and on the underside it is pale with a light peachy tint. This shade is almost absent on the cheeks but becomes stronger on the breast and belly, and most intense on the hind flanks and under the tail (where it is marked with some white spotting). In some males the coloration on the flanks and undertail is bright orange or even brick red, while females' flanks are paler. There is a broad blackish stripe running from the upper bill base through the eye and down the neck-sides. The bill is dark and the very strong, sturdy legs and toes are light pinkish, with strong and very curved 'grappling-hook' claws. Juvenile Nuthatches are a little

Grappling-hook claws and long hind toes help a Nuthatch to grip confidently as it climbs downwards head first.

THE RETURN OF TREES

In its ancient history, after the last Ice Age, most of England was covered by natural woodland. This 'wildwood' was famously home to fabulous wildlife that is now lost to us, such as Brown Bears *Ursus arctos*, Wolves *Canis lupus* and Elks *Alces alces*. Through Neolithic times, people spread through the countryside and cleared woodland to create space for farming fields and, in due course, habitation. The pace picked up through the 19th and early 20th centuries, and by the 1940s our forest cover was down to about 5 per cent, with the Brown Bears, Wolves and Elks just distant memories. Other woodland wildlife, including birds like Nuthatches, were running out of living space.

Since then, things have gradually turned the other way. Tree planting, for commercial and conservation reasons, has restored many areas of woodland and today we have about 13 per cent forest cover. Not all of these forests are ideal for wildlife, and woodlands do take centuries to mature and realise their full potential as habitats, but this trend has undoubtedly played a part in the Nuthatch's population boom.

drabber and paler than adults, but it is still often possible to tell young males from females by the more strongly orange-tinted flanks on the former.

When climbing on a tree, the Nuthatch differs from woodpeckers in that it does not use its tail as a brace, and in its ability to climb head downwards.

The calls of the Nuthatch include a loud, bright, ringing *huit*, a more clipped *tuit* and a more drawn-out *hweeet*. Its song is a fast series of similar-toned notes. It is very vocal throughout most of the year but especially in early spring.

DISTRIBUTION, POPULATION AND HABITAT

This species is common and widespread in England and Wales. It is absent only from the flat open fenlands of eastern England and the highest bare uplands of north-west England. Its range is pushing northwards and it is now present over parts of southern Scotland, but it does not occur in Ireland. There are about 220,000 pairs in the UK, following one of the most dramatic population increases of any British bird (a rise of 254 per cent between 1967 and 2015). The increase was steepest between 1990 and 2010 but may now be stabilising.

In Britain, we have the subspecies *S. e. caesia*. There are in the region of 20 other forms present across the species' world range, which encompasses almost all of Europe except the far north, through parts of the Middle East and North Africa, and eastwards across northern and central Asia to the Far East, including Sakhalin, Japan and Korea, and south into Thailand. Its world population is between 10 million and 50 million individuals, and in Europe at least it is generally increasing.

Woodlands of all kinds provide habitat for Nuthatches, but in Britain the birds are most likely to be found in deciduous woodland with a reasonable proportion of mature trees. They can be common in parkland and are frequent in gardens, especially more rural ones but also in towns provided there are some mature trees about.

It takes a combination of skill and brute force to break into larger, hard-shelled nuts and seeds.

BEHAVIOUR

Like many smaller non-migratory birds, the Nuthatch tends to switch from an animal-based diet in the warmer months to more vegetarian options in winter. It preys on all kinds of invertebrates, particularly those that live on or in tree bark. Unlike woodpeckers, it does not drill holes, but it is very capable of chiselling out pieces of loose bark or damaged soft wood to reach beetle larvae, spiders and other prey. It will also catch flies in mid-air, and will chase prey on the ground. There have been observations of it feeding on carrion, and bird table fare in the form of nuts, seeds and suet products is readily taken.

Come autumn, beechmast forms an important part of the diet, as do Hazel nuts and other tree seeds. It will take smaller seeds as well. In areas where beechmast is particularly prevalent in the diet, a poor mast crop results in very low juvenile survival rates, and the same goes where Hazel nuts are a key food. Adults seem better able to adapt when a primary food is in short supply, being more successful at monopolising whatever food is available.

A Nuthatch breaks into hard items by wedging them into a bark crack and then striking hard with the bill. The loud, regular tapping gives away the bird's presence and can be mistaken for the sounds made by a woodpecker as it chisels into wood.

Nuthatches are not sociable birds, even in winter, and you will rarely see more than one at a time, though they may loosely associate with feeding flocks of other birds, such as tits.

Nuthatch pairs stay together all year round, with both birds defending the breeding territory. In spring, they spend more time together, with both birds performing courtship display flights in which they glide in a circle, and courtship feeding also occurs. Despite their enduring pair-bond, extra-pair matings are not uncommon and about 10 per cent of chicks are fathered by a different male to the female's regular mate.

The preferred nest site is a large, deep cavity within a tree trunk, often an old woodpecker nest. Because larger hollows tend to have larger entrances, Nuthatches have developed the habit of modifying the entrance size by plastering mud to the walls around it, sometimes in very large quantities. This helps keep the nest safe from predators, and also from usurping Starlings, which often try to oust nesting Nuthatches. The work of plastering falls mostly to the female and can take her up to four weeks. The inside of the cavity is lined with nothing more than bark and wood chips.

The female lays a clutch of six to nine eggs, and incubates alone for 13–18 days. Both parents feed the chicks until they fledge at about 24 days. Juveniles usually disperse only a short distance from their parents' territory, but may be forced to move further if there is no unoccupied habitat nearby. In areas with sparser populations, established pairs have larger territories and their fledged young may remain within the parental territory for longer.

This bird is not a great traveller and no British-ringed individual has ever been found abroad, nor has any bird ringed overseas been recovered here. The longest movement recorded was made by an

WINTER RATIONS

Nuthatches store a considerable amount of food for later consumption, pushing seeds into bark cracks or hiding them on the ground under a piece of lichen or other debris. Depending on general food availability, birds may not visit their caches for weeks or even months.

Nuthatches in Siberia store many months' worth of food during autumn – even up to a year's worth. Their preferred food source is the Siberian Stone Pine *Pinus sibirica,* and this tree's crop is, in most years, generous enough that there is no need for the Nuthatches to wander away from their home territories. This is rather unusual – many Eurasian songbird species that are entirely sedentary in western Europe are obliged to be at least partially migratory in northern and eastern Asia, moving south to escape the severity of the winters and lack of food.

adult female that was ringed in Staffordshire in December 2005, and then re-caught in Tyne and Wear the following month. She had travelled 260km, perhaps in response to local food shortages. Whatever the reason, she decided to stay put, as she was re-caught at the same site again nearly a year later. There are a handful of other records of birds moving more than 100km, but on average recovered birds have travelled less than 1km from the site where they were ringed. The species is not generally migratory in the rest of its range either, though in north-east Asia it will disperse irruptively southwards and westwards if its main foodplant, the Siberian Stone Pine, suffers a poor season.

The oldest British-ringed Nuthatch was at least 12 years of age and may still be alive at the time of writing – the male bird was ringed as an adult in Leicestershire in 2005 and has been re-caught at the same site in most subsequent winters up to 2017. This is also the European longevity record.

The clamour of hungry chicks when a parent arrives reveals the location of a discreet Nuthatch nest.

IN THE GARDEN

As long as there are some mature trees around, most larger gardens (and a fair few smaller ones) will attract the local Nuthatch. Hanging feeders filled with peanuts, sunflower hearts or suet nibbles will appeal to these birds, and they will also visit bird tables for similar fare. They are rather aggressive to other birds and may temporarily see off tits and finches, so it is a good idea to place two or more feeders a good distance apart if space allows. Nuthatches are confident birds and with patience may come and feed from the hand.

Nuthatches will use hole-fronted nest boxes mounted on tree trunks. They prefer a relatively large entrance to the box – a hole diameter of about 35mm is suitable, and the birds will use mud plastered on the inner side to reduce the entrance size to their preference. If you have Nuthatches in the garden showing an interest in a nest box, make sure that there are some muddy patches close by for them to use.

161

Treecreeper
Certhia familiaris

12cm
10g
GREEN

This little bird is one of the most unobtrusive garden visitors of all, but if you keep an eye on your trees, you stand a good chance of spotting a Treecreeper quietly climbing skywards in a spiral around a tree trunk. It is a relative of the Wren and a somewhat more distant relative of the Nuthatch, and shares traits with both. In common with the Nuthatch, it relies on trees, which means that gardens that attract one species will often also have the other. Treecreepers are, however, much more difficult to tempt to the bird table.

INTRODUCTION

The forked tip of the Treecreeper's tail is rarely apparent as it is usually pressed against the tree trunk as the bird climbs.

This is a small, slight bird with short wings and a long, narrow tail, which it uses as a brace when climbing up a tree. It also has a long bill, which is fine and downcurved. The upperside plumage is mid-brown, marked with paler and darker speckling and marbling, giving camouflage against tree bark. It has a dark eye-stripe and pale eyebrow. The underside, from chin to undertail, is pure white. Juvenile Treecreepers look the same as adults, though they have slightly shorter bills and tails when freshly out of the nest.

The typical contact call is a very thin, high-pitched single note, similar to that of the Goldcrest. The song is a short, rapid trill of similarly high-pitched notes.

TRACKING THE CLIMBER

Treecreepers are not assertive birds at all, but they are quite unafraid of people. If you are watching one at close range and it feels you are too near, it is likely to scramble round to the far side of the tree trunk rather than fly away. Keep watching and you will probably see it reappear on your side of the trunk, but higher up. It will continue to make its way up to and along one of the main branches, but will usually fly down to the base of a different tree before reaching the twig tips. Treecreepers never climb down head first in the manner of a Nuthatch.

DISTRIBUTION, POPULATION AND HABITAT

Treecreepers occur throughout Britain and Ireland, wherever there are enough trees for them. Lack of tree cover explains the gaps in their distribution in the East Anglian fens, the most open upland parts of northern England and the Scottish Highlands, and some coastal regions of Ireland. They are also missing from many offshore islands. The UK population is about 200,000 pairs. Numbers rose quite sharply in the early 1970s but then declined again, and have remained generally stable since the 1980s. An overall 19 per cent population increase was recorded between 1967 and 2015. The British and Irish subspecies, *C. f. britannica*, occurs nowhere else in the world. Occasionally, birds of the paler northern Continental subspecies *C. f. familiaris* turn up on the east coast of Britain in autumn.

Across the species' extensive world range, another nine subspecies occur, and its population totals somewhere between 40 million and 80 million individuals. It has a rather patchy distribution in south-western and southern Europe, but occurs broadly through northern and central Europe and in a broad swathe across central and eastern Asia to Japan.

Treecreepers' dependence on trees dictates their habitat choices. They are most common in deciduous woodland, but can be quite common in pine forest, too, particularly the native Scots Pine *Pinus sylvestris* woodland found in northern Scotland. Areas with more sparse tree cover will also hold some Treecreepers – they are common in more rural gardens, and often present in town parks, provided there are some mature trees around.

A lichen-crusted branch offers lots of hiding places for invertebrates, and is a happy hunting ground for a Treecreeper.

BEHAVIOUR

This species is almost exclusively insectivorous, feeding on all kinds of insects and also spiders, millipedes and other small invertebrates that occur on tree bark. It will occasionally take conifer seeds.

The feeding method of the Treecreeper is limited but effective. It scales tree trunks, sometimes slowly and sometimes in fast jumps, and pauses to check bark cracks and crevices for hiding invertebrates, probing with its long, delicate bill. It does not peck away or chisel at wood but may prise off small bark flakes to access prey beneath. Once it is near the end of a branch, it flies down to begin searching another tree, often landing just above ground level, and starts to climb up, sometimes in a straight line and sometimes in a spiral.

You may also see Treecreepers searching walls in a similar manner, and they will forage on the ground at times, even occasionally picking up seed and nut fragments underneath bird feeders and tables. However, they rarely visit hanging feeders, despite being adept at clambering up vertical surfaces.

Treecreepers are not generally social with their own kind. However, they often associate loosely with feeding flocks of tits, Goldcrests and other small woodland birds, benefitting from their vigilance

From the moment they leave the nest, Treecreeper chicks begin their life of almost non-stop tree-climbing.

against predators. They will also sometimes form collective roosts in the coldest weather – a favourite site for such roosts is in spaces within the soft bark of Giant Redwoods *Sequoiadendron giganteum*.

This is a sedentary and territorial bird species, which will pair with the same partner year-on-year if they both survive winter. The male will sing from early spring and may chase his intended mate between the trees, as well as engaging in courtship feeding. The pair selects a nest site behind a flake of loose bark, or in a crevice within the wood itself. The nest is made from small twigs,

A TOE-TIP IN BRITAIN

There are two species of treecreeper in Europe. The Short-toed Treecreeper *C. brachydactyla* replaces the Treecreeper over most of south-western and southern Europe, and there are many areas further east in Europe where both species occur. However, despite occurring in France and the Low Countries at its closest points to Britain, the Short-toed Treecreeper has only made it to our shores a handful of times (30 records between 1950 and 2015) – like its close relative, it is not keen on making long flights.

Telling the two treecreepers apart is extremely difficult. Their songs are distinct, but lost migrant birds seldom sing. The Short-toed has slightly brownish flanks and a subtle difference in wing pattern, but the slight variation in claw length is very hard to see. The most likely places to find a Short-toed Treecreeper are coastal areas in Kent and East Anglia, but because of its extreme similarity to our own Treecreepers, it seems very likely that not all those that turn up here are noticed by birdwatchers.

ANT AGONIES

Treecreepers aren't the only hunters that seek their prey on the bark of trees. Spend some time in a deciduous woodland in summer, and pay attention to the tree trunks. The chances are that, sooner or later, you'll find some Wood Ants *Formica rufa* marching up and down, investigating cracks and crevices. They are powerful killers for their size and certainly capable of taking any prey that a Treecreeper might also target.

It's apparent that in the case of Wood Ants and Treecreepers, competition for food could be considerable despite the two species being so different. Studies have shown that this is indeed the case – Treecreepers avoid trees with ants on them, and spend less time feeding on trees that have had recent ant activity.

grasses, fragments of bark and perhaps pine needles, with a lining of feathers, moss and cobwebs. Nests are well hidden but are still often attacked by squirrels, Stoats *Mustela erminea* and Great Spotted Woodpeckers, especially those in trees at woodland edges, rather than within a larger stand of trees.

The female lays a clutch of usually five or six eggs, and incubates them without the help of her mate for about 15 days. She also broods the young chicks for the first few days as well as at night, but later on, both parents spend the daytime fetching food for the brood. The young are fully feathered and leave the nest at about 14 days old, but will return at night for a few more days. A small proportion of birds in the south will have a second brood.

It is rare for a Treecreeper to wander any significant distance from where it was hatched, though some juveniles are forced to disperse further than adults in their search for a territory of their own. The longest journey, of 200km, was made by a bird ringed at Spurn Point in autumn 1983, which was then found dead on the other side of the country, in Liverpool, just a couple of weeks later. The timing of its capture, and its location, suggest it could have been an immigrant from mainland Europe rather than a home-grown bird. However, no such uncertainty exists with the second-place traveller – this bird was ringed as a chick in Wiltshire and found dead two years later in Stoke-on-Trent, a distance of 199km. Only three other ringed birds have travelled more than 100km, and the only 'overseas' recovery was a bird ringed as an adult in Norfolk and found days later on a vessel 12km offshore in the North Sea.

The oldest ringed Treecreeper in Britain was ringed as an adult in 2008 at a site in Surrey, and with the exception of 2015 was re-caught at the same site every year since then, up until 2017, making it at least eight years and eight months old. This record has not been exceeded within mainland Europe to date.

IN THE GARDEN

Unless you have trees around, you are unlikely to encounter this species in the garden, but this is a prime example of how gardens can connect up to form a wider ecosystem. Treecreepers don't mind whether the trees they use are all in the same garden or several different ones. A few gardens that each have a mature tree or two can be, from a Treecreeper's point of view, as good as any other small patch of woodland as a feeding or breeding territory.

These birds rarely visit feeding stations but will do so on occasion – try hanging a cage-type feeder against a tree trunk. Suet foods that contain insects are the most likely to appeal to them. You can also buy nest boxes especially designed for Treecreepers, which can be fixed to a tree trunk – they have a triangular profile with a wide top and narrow bottom, to simulate a piece of loose bark, and a side entrance that sits against the trunk. If you have large old trees in the garden, Treecreepers may find a natural nest site in their bark, and they do on occasion use cracks and holes in wooden poles or posts. In winter, they will also roost communally in such sites.

Pigeons
and doves

Plump and waddling, with crooning voices, the pigeons and doves are conspicuous residents of gardens large and small. They are sociable and largely peaceable, mainly preferring to feed on the ground, and unlike most smaller seed-eaters will enthusiastically hoover up the wheat and maize that's added to some birdseed mixes. They belong to the family Columbidae.

Woodpigeon
Columba palumbus

41cm
450g

GREEN

This pretty pigeon is one of our most common and noticeable wild birds in both town and country, and will show up in most gardens where accessible food and water are on offer. In the 2019 RSPB Big Garden Birdwatch, it was the fifth most commonly seen species, and it consistently appears in the top 10. With its crooning voice and generally gentle disposition, it is usually welcome in the garden, though it is quite gregarious and large numbers can overwhelm a bird table.

INTRODUCTION

This is the largest British pigeon species. It has a rather rangy shape, with a long neck and small head, while other species are more compact. The tail is longish and the legs short, giving a waddling gait. Adult Woodpigeons are blue-grey, with a strong pink tint on the breast and a brown wash on the wings and back. The flight feathers and tail-tip are blackish, and there are no dark wing-bars. There is an iridescent greenish patch on the back of the neck and white patches on the neck-sides. The leading edge of the wing also bears a white marking, most obvious in flight, when it appears as a broad crescent. At rest, the wing edge looks narrowly white, but this can be obscured depending on how the body plumage is lying. The legs are dark pink, the bill is pink with a yellowish tip, and the eyes are whitish.

Young Woodpigeons have duskier eyes than adults, and have generally more muted plumage coloration. They lack the white neck marking, though they still show the white wing marking.

The 'song' of this bird is a series of emphatic, slightly throaty cooing notes, usually given in a phrase of five distinct notes with the stress on the second or third, and the last notes shorter. When it takes off from a perch to perform its rising-and-falling display flight, it claps its wings loudly for a few strokes.

Like all pigeons, Woodpigeons have short legs, which makes them a little wobbly when on a narrow perch.

PUBLIC ENEMY

The Woodpigeon's tendency to gather on winter-sown crop fields and eat the shoots makes it *persona non grata* with farmers. Many thousands are shot each year to protect crops, under the General Licence, which permits landowners to kill the birds without needing to apply for a special licence first. Only a handful of bird species can be controlled under this General Licence, and landowners are expected to try to scare the birds away by other means before resorting to shooting.

Although they are not a quarry species in the way that Pheasants and some wildfowl are, Woodpigeons that are shot for pest control reasons can be sold as food all year round. In some other European countries, Woodpigeons are shot for food in very large numbers.

DISTRIBUTION, POPULATION AND HABITAT

This very common and widespread bird occurs throughout Britain and Ireland, including most islands, but is absent from the treeless uplands of northern Scotland. About 5.4 million pairs breed in the UK – nowhere else in the world has such a dense population of the species. The world population, which is in the region of 51 million to 73 million birds, is distributed across western and southern Europe and North Africa, where it is a sedentary species, and also in central and north-eastern Europe and north-western Asia, where it is a summer visitor only. It occurs patchily further east through central Asia. The subspecies *C. p. palumbus* is present over most of its range, including the British Isles.

Since the mid-1970s, the UK Woodpigeon population has risen steadily (a 160 per cent increase between 1967 and 2016), but more recently there has been a small decline (a 4 per cent fall between 2010 and 2015). The Woodpigeon's increase is connected to winter-sown wheat and Oilseed Rape *Brassica napus* subspecies *napus*, the cultivation of which increased dramatically over the 1970s and 1980s. Most seed-eating birds cannot consume the green shoots of these crops but Woodpigeons can, and they have benefited greatly from an extra food resource in the winter months.

Although Woodpigeons usually nest in trees, they are not otherwise particularly tied to woodland habitats. The largest numbers can be found in areas with a lot of arable farmland and some stands of trees, but they are also common in towns and villages, including city-centre parklands, and occur in other habitats such as marshland, heath and moor.

Woodpigeons feed in large flocks in the open countryside during the winter months, roaming from field to field.

BEHAVIOUR

Like other pigeons and doves, the Woodpigeon is mainly a vegetarian. Within that remit it is adaptable and takes a very varied diet, including nuts, seeds and grains of all kinds, young plant shoots and tree flower buds, and berries and the leaves of fleshy plants. It may also consume a few invertebrates that it finds while feeding on the ground.

You will often see Woodpigeons walking about quite slowly on grass or bare ground, dipping their heads to peck up seeds or seedlings from time to time. However, they also feed in trees and bushes, and can be surprisingly athletic in their bid to reach fresh buds or berries. This kind of feeding activity is usually quite noisy and obvious.

Woodpigeons are social birds and will feed in small groups in most gardens – in the wider countryside their feeding flocks in winter can be hundreds or even thousands strong. They will associate with other pigeons and doves while feeding, and also with other birds such as sparrows and Jackdaws.

FLIGHT SHOW

The Woodpigeon's genus name, *Columba*, comes from the Greek word *kolumbos*, meaning 'a diver'. It refers to the male bird's display flight, in which it takes off and rises very steeply with strong wing-clapping flaps, and then glides downwards with stiffly spread wings and tail. So the shape of the bird as it moves through its courtship flight looks like a graceful rising and falling wave like one that might be made by a surfacing dolphin or other swimming animal.

Many birds perform stylised flights like this, as part of courtship or a show of territorial ownership (or both). As a visual show, it works alongside the bird's song to reinforce its presence to rivals.

Male Woodpigeons establish their territories in late winter, and proclaim them through repetition of their rather monotonous crooning song, and also by eye-catching display flights. These take place mostly in the mornings, and territorial activity continues through spring and summer, dwindling in autumn. Rivals occasionally fight fiercely. The breeding season is long in this species, and pairs occasionally even produce young in winter.

When a female is attracted to the territory, the male approaches her and displays through deep bows while softly cooing. A bonded pair may be seen sitting close together, preening each other's neck plumage. Other males entering the territory, though, will be chased away. Occasionally a rival stands his ground and then some quite fierce fighting can erupt, the combatants jumping at one another and trying to strike with wings, feet and bill.

The pair builds a rather flimsy stick nest, usually in a tree but occasionally on a building. As in other pigeons, the clutch is always of two eggs,

Like other pigeons, Woodpigeons demonstrate tender courtship rituals, including sessions of mutual preening.

which both parents incubate, taking turns so that the off-duty bird can go and feed. The eggs hatch after 17 days, and both parents feed the nestlings, initially on 'pigeon milk' (a rich secretion produced within the birds' crops), and later on soft regurgitated seed and other food. The chicks fledge at about 34 days old. The pair may then produce a second brood.

In the east of their world range, Woodpigeons are migratory, moving south in winter. In the UK they appear to be mostly sedentary, with relatively few overseas recoveries of British-ringed birds, and even fewer in Britain of birds ringed overseas. More than 50 Woodpigeons ringed in Britain have been found in France, but the only other British-ringed birds found abroad were one from Northumberland that reached the Netherlands (547km away), and another ringed in Shetland that reached Germany (796km away). A bird ringed in Denmark as a chick in 1925 was recovered in Ireland eight years later, having travelled 1,129km. Other birds have reached us from the Netherlands, Norway, Germany and Belgium. However, the vast majority (some 4,000) of British and Irish ringed Woodpigeons made much

Pigeons drink differently to other birds, sucking in water rather than tilting back their heads to swallow each mouthful.

shorter journeys, with only one individual topping 500km – a bird ringed as an adult in Orkney that travelled 850km to Gloucestershire.

Coincidentally, the oldest known British Woodpigeon was also from Orkney, but this bird had moved only 2km between its being ringed as a chick in May 1981, and being caught by another ringer in February 1999, 17 years and eight months later. This bird is also the European record-holder for longevity.

IN THE GARDEN

Woodpigeons will be attracted to any seed placed out on the lawn or patio, and will also visit an open bird table. Their attempts to use hanging bird feeders are inept and clumsy, but they do succeed to a limited extent (and will knock down any feeder that's not securely attached to something).

They will eat everything contained within any commercial birdseed mix, as well as some kitchen scraps. If you are keen to attract smaller ground-feeding birds but have regularly visiting Woodpigeons, use a 'guardian' cage-type ground feeder to keep the latter out, as they will otherwise hoover up all the food in short order.

These birds enjoy bathing and also drink frequently, so a safe water source is a must for them. Their manner of drinking is to suck water directly into their throats, unlike most other birds, which take a mouthful and then tilt back their heads so it flows down the throat. You may spot them 'showering' as well as bathing – in rainfall they will sit in the open and adopt a tilted-over posture with one wing held skywards, to allow the rain to reach all of their body plumage. They may also do this on a water feature with falling water.

MIGRATION MYSTERY

Although ringing recoveries indicate that our home-grown Woodpigeons do not usually travel far, and that those from other countries very rarely turn up here, many birdwatchers observe large numbers of Woodpigeons on the move in late autumn. In November 2015, counts of flocks estimated to be up to 150,000 strong were logged by birdwatchers in the south and south-west.

The birds in these flocks behave like migrants rather than local birds seeking a food source – they travel at high altitude and are all heading in the same direction. We would certainly expect to have some evidence from ringing recoveries if movements on such large scales did involve birds from overseas. The origin and destination of these Woodpigeons remain unknown for now, proving that even the most common and familiar garden birds still hold a mystery or two for us.

Collared Dove
Streptopelia decaocto

`32cm` `200g` **GREEN**

This elegant pinkish-grey dove is very common in Britain and Ireland, which is why it comes as a surprise to many people that the Collared Dove has been here for less than 100 years. Changes in farming practices across western Europe enabled it to spread from its original geographical range in the Middle East, and it finds itself very much at home in towns and villages where food and nest sites can be found in abundance.

INTRODUCTION

This pretty dove is easily identified by its softly toned, mostly unmarked plumage, neat neck-collar and dainty proportions.

Collared Doves are markedly smaller than any of the pigeon species that visit our gardens, and have a proportionately longer, tapering tail. The plumage is light beige-grey, with a pinkish tint on the underside. The back and wings are washed brownish and the flight feathers are a little darker still. There is a narrow black half-collar around the back of the neck, bordered whitish. In flight, the Collared Dove shows dark wing-tips and white tail corners from above. From below, the tail is contrastingly two-tone with a black base and white outer parts. The legs are dark pinkish, the bill is blackish and the eye is dark red-brown. The juvenile has no white collar, and a skinnier appearance.

The song of the Collared Dove is a monotonous, soporific three-note *coo*, with the stress on the second note. It is tonally rather similar to the Woodpigeon's song but has a different rhythm. In flight, it gives an emphatic single rolling *croon* or *coo*.

DISTRIBUTION, POPULATION AND HABITAT

Collared Doves can be found throughout lowland Britain and Ireland, including on many island groups. They are missing only from open upland areas in central Wales, north-western England, and central and northern Scotland. The population is estimated at 990,000 breeding pairs.

In the UK, Collared Doves have increased quickly and steadily since their arrival in the 1950s (a 311 per cent increase between 1972 and 2015), with numbers peaking in about 2005. Since then, there has been a shallow decline (a 15 per cent fall between 2005 and 2015).

The world population is probably in the region of 8 million individuals. The natural range covers most of Europe and western Asia, parts of North Africa and the Middle East, and a broad swathe of southern and South East Asia, including the Indian subcontinent and reaching east to Korea and north-east China. The species is also present in Japan, probably the result of introduction rather than natural spread.

Collared Doves occur commonly in villages and towns, but are rarer in large cities. They also avoid dense woodland, though can be found in parkland and wetlands with some trees and bushes. They often occur on arable farmland, especially areas where grain is grown and stored, and will feed in stubble fields and around areas where livestock is fed.

BEHAVIOUR

This species takes a typical pigeon diet of mainly seed, with a little other plant matter in the form of berries, buds and shoots. It can eat grains such as wheat and barley, and also maize, but in general prefers smaller seeds than are taken by Woodpigeons and Feral Pigeons. It will also take small invertebrates on occasion.

It mainly forages on the ground, walking in a slow waddle and pecking up food. It is quite sociable and will often be seen feeding in small groups, or with Woodpigeons and Feral Pigeons.

Male Collared Doves sing constantly to attract a mate, choosing an elevated perch from which to coo. After a phase of calling, a male will often then perform his display flight, which involves flying steeply upwards with wing-clapping beats, then gliding down with wings and tail spread, often in a wide circle, to land on another high song perch and sing again.

Once paired up, the male and female display typically tender pigeon bonding behaviour with mutual preening sessions, and the male shows the female some of the suitable nest sites in his territory. These are usually in trees, on a sturdy base formed by a branch fork, but not infrequently on buildings, though usually at least 3m above ground level. Once the female has selected a site, she and her mate build the nest together, with him bringing most of the material and her arranging the basic stick platform that forms the outer structure of the nest. Some lining is added in the form of feathers and other soft material.

The female lays a clutch of two eggs, and both parents share incubation until the eggs hatch after about 16 or 17 days. The chicks, when small, feed exclusively on the crop milk secreted by their parents, and as they mature, the parents feed them on regurgitated seed. They clamour to be fed with squeaking calls and, as they grow older and stronger, vigorous wing-flapping. They leave the nest at about 17–19 days old.

EIGHTEEN

The Collared Dove's species name, *decaocto* (from 'eighteen' in Greek), is imitative of the bird's song. A Greek myth tells that Decaocto was a servant girl who complained constantly about her low rate of pay, despondently repeating 'eighteen' as this was the number of coins she received each year for her toil. The gods transformed her into a dove to free her from her work, but she continued her mournful refrain in her new life.

The Collared Dove's nest is notoriously flimsy, and the bird often chooses to nest on a building rather than in a tree.

Collared Doves are unusually prolific. The pair begins a new brood in the same nest, and can continue to breed through summer and autumn, often having three broods in quick succession and on occasion even more – up to six broods in a year.

Although this species has crossed the entire continent of Europe over the last 90 years, spreading at an almost unprecedented rate, on an individual level it is rather sedentary, or at least it is in Britain today. On average, recovered UK-ringed birds have not travelled further than 1km, and only 14 birds ringed here have travelled overseas, most of them to France. A few more have reached us from abroad – 33 Belgian-ringed birds have been found in the UK, 14 from the Netherlands, four from Germany and one from France. This pattern does reflect the species' historical spread through Europe, as the first British colonists came to us from those countries. The longest journey was made by one of the

AMERICAN INVASION

The Collared Dove's spread across Europe was remarkable, but was also natural, the birds moving under their own steam to exploit new suitable habitat. However, there are now also Collared Doves spreading through North America, and this is due to an accidental introduction. The population originated in the Bahamas, where in 1974 a group of some 50 birds escaped from captivity. From there, they reached Florida and spread through the USA, as well as Mexico and some parts of the Caribbean. They fare best in suburban areas and those with less intensive agriculture.

The population in North America is today estimated to be about 400,000 birds. The spread has been more rapid than in Europe (about 100km a year, compared with 45km a year in Europe). As yet, no obvious negative impact on native wildlife has come to light – the Collared Dove even appears to live alongside its close native relative the Mourning Dove *S. decipiens* without aggressive competition for resources. However, any non-native species that spreads so quickly and so comprehensively has the potential to cause problems.

FOLLOWING THE FARM

The very first breeding report of Collared Doves in Britain came in 1955, when birds were found nesting in Norfolk. Birdwatchers of the day travelled many miles to see them, as has long been the habit when a rarity reaches our shores. Breeding records from neighbouring counties followed over the next couple of years, and sightings came in from much further afield, including Ireland by 1957. By 1970, up to 25,000 pairs were breeding in Britain and Ireland, and by 1996 this figure had risen to more than 125,000.

The colonisation of the British Isles came after Collared Doves had already swept across mainland Europe, from a starting point in southern Asia in 1930. As agricultural methods changed and evolved in western Asia and Europe, so more food became available and the landscape opened up. This enabled the species to spread north and westwards at a comparatively rapid rate. Other factors may have been at play too. The suppression of predator populations in Europe due to overzealous gamekeeping and pesticide use, increased adaptability when it comes to nest-site selection and an increased tendency for juvenile birds to disperse more widely after fledging may all have aided the spread of the Collared Dove population. In Britain today, the species has gone from an exciting rarity to a ubiquitous garden bird in a few short decades, and it's easy to forget that this mild-mannered and unobtrusive bird has such a dramatic history.

German-ringed birds, which travelled 982km to reach Cornwall. The second-longest journey made by a UK-ringed Collared Dove was of 923km and concerned a bird that travelled from Orkney to Kent between 1979 and 1981.

The oldest UK-ringed bird was ringed as an adult in 1997 in the Scottish Highlands, and found dead after striking a window in Orkney in 2015, 18 years and two days after it was ringed. This is also the European longevity record.

IN THE GARDEN

If you put out seed in your garden you are likely to have visiting Collared Doves – the species was the 11th most commonly seen bird in the 2019 RSPB Big Garden Birdwatch. These birds will feed from the ground and from bird tables, and while they are not skilled at accessing hanging bird feeders, they will patrol the ground below and eat fallen seeds. They often visit gardens in small groups, and rooftops are popular song-perches for territory-holding males. In autumn, keep an eye out within Collared Dove flocks for Turtle Doves *S. turtur* – these much rarer, more strongly patterned doves are summer visitors and sometimes join Collared Dove flocks to feed prior to beginning their southwards migration.

Collared Doves are also regular and enthusiastic drinkers and bathers, and will make full use of a bird bath or a shallow garden pond. In common with other pigeons, they like to 'shower' under falling water.

You don't necessarily need trees to attract nesting Collared Doves. They often nest on buildings, finding sheltered (though sometimes highly impractical) spots on ledges and sills, or even on top of light fittings or satellite dishes. They will not use conventional nest boxes but may make use of an open wooden platform positioned in a secure high spot.

Like all members of the pigeon family, Collared Doves are keen bathers, and will also 'shower' by sitting in the rain with their wings open.

Feral Pigeon
Columba livia

32cm
300g
GREEN

The 'street pigeons' of our towns and cities are, technically, Rock Doves – a wild species found on remote sea cliffs. However, street pigeons descend from domesticated Rock Doves rather than wild ones. Their ancestors are escapee racing pigeons, fantails, tumblers and the like, all 'created' from wild Rock Doves through selective breeding. Because of their domestic ancestry, street pigeons are known as Feral Pigeons.

INTRODUCTION

Feral Pigeons are smaller and more compact than Woodpigeons, and usually have reddish eyes and dark bills. In flight, their underwing is usually bright white. Their plumage is otherwise extremely variable. Most are darker grey on the body with lighter grey wings, marked with a double black bar and often some dark chequering. However, solid black, pure white, white-blotched and orange-red variants are all very common. The legs are dark pinkish, but birds with extensive white plumage often have white rather than black claws, and may also have pink rather than blackish bills. There is usually some iridescent green and violet on the neck, and a dark band at the tail-tip. Young birds have duller eyes and less clearly marked plumage.

Territorial males give a single long, low *coo* as a form of song. During the courtship dance, the male makes a similar call but precedes it with a brief clucking phrase.

DISTRIBUTION, POPULATION AND HABITAT

Feral Pigeons occur over most of Britain and Ireland, except inland upland areas. They are on most islands and around most coasts – on northern and western coasts, they mix with wild Rock Doves.

The orange eyes of the Feral Pigeon distinguish it from the Stock Dove (dark eyes) and Woodpigeon (yellowish-white eyes).

COLOURFUL GENES

Domestic pigeons, like other domestic animals, have been selectively bred over the centuries into an array of forms that often bear little resemblance to their wild ancestral species. The Rock Dove has been domesticated for more than 5,000 years, and various breeds have been developed for food, for their flight skills or for their exotic appearance. While racing pigeons, bred for speed and stamina, don't look so very different to wild Rock Doves, the many fancy breeds are often quite bizarre, with frilly headdresses, feathered feet and distorted body shapes.

Let loose into the wild, most of these aberrations will not thrive – only their more conventionally shaped cousins will survive to pass on their genes. So you'll rarely see a Feral Pigeon with extra-feathery ornamentations or a strange physique. However, the range of colours found among domestic birds does still persist in Feral Pigeons. The most unusually coloured individuals stand out in a flock and are more likely to be targeted by predators, but as fewer predators are found in towns and cities, a wide range of colours is maintained in many Feral Pigeon breeding populations.

About 500,000 pairs breed in the UK, the majority in towns and cities. The population has shown a slight downward trend since 1995.

Native Rock Doves occur over southern Europe and Asia as far as the Indian subcontinent, and in much of North Africa. Feral Pigeons occur through northern Europe and Asia, South East Asia, southern and eastern Africa, Australia, New Zealand, North America and much of South America. With an estimated 17 million to 28 million birds in Europe alone, the world population is extremely large and difficult to quantify.

In the UK, Feral Pigeons are most common in towns and cities and most likely to nest on buildings, but they will commute into surrounding countryside to feed. They are also common on sea cliffs.

BEHAVIOUR

Feral Pigeons are seed-eaters and mainly forage on the ground. They will also take other plant material such as young shoots, flower buds and soft leaves, and the odd invertebrate. They eat all kinds of discarded food waste as well. They are gregarious when foraging and will often feed alongside Woodpigeons and Collared Doves, as well as other birds such as sparrows and corvids.

Feral Pigeons form lifelong pair-bonds. Courtship rituals, in which the male struts around a female, bowing and cooing, are a common sight within flocks. Later, the bonded pair show mutual preening and courtship feeding.

Racing pigeons sometimes turn up, exhausted, in gardens. Offer them food, and if they still hang around, you may be able to trace the owner by the ring number.

Pairs may nest in close proximity, each defending just a small territory around the nest, which is an untidy pile of sticks, grasses and other material. The female lays two eggs and both birds incubate. The eggs hatch after about 17 days, and both adults feed the young on crop milk for the first few days, switching to soft regurgitated food thereafter. The chicks leave the nest at about 35 days old, and begin to learn to feed themselves.

Only about 100 UK-ringed wild Rock Doves have ever been recovered, none of which left the UK, and Feral Pigeons are not routinely ringed, so the migratory potential of this species is not known. The same goes for its longevity – the record among wild birds is just seven years and eight months, but domestic pigeons are known to be capable of living into their 20s.

IN THE GARDEN

Feral Pigeons will take any seed on offer in the garden, on the ground or on bird tables. They will also visit bird baths.

Birds of prey

Birds that prey on vertebrates, including other birds, are not always popular in our gardens, but their presence as top predators is a great sign of a healthy local ecosystem and they should be welcomed. Sparrowhawks (family Accipitridae) and Tawny Owls (family Strigidae) are quite regular garden visitors, though they are sometimes hard to see; the Kestrel (family Falconidae) is more conspicuous but scarcer.

Sparrowhawk
Accipiter nisus

28–40cm
150–260g
GREEN

When the little birds at your feeding station scatter in a sudden panic, that's a sign there's a Sparrowhawk around. This stealthy hawk is the bird of prey most likely to be seen in the vast majority of British and Irish gardens. Its recovery from devastating population crashes in the mid- to late 20th century means it is now a frequent sight, and its presence indicates that your local populations of smaller birds are in good shape.

INTRODUCTION

This is a short-winged, long-tailed and small-headed hawk. Sparrowhawks show marked size differences between the sexes. Males are rather small and dainty, while females are much heavier and sturdier. Adult male plumage is blue-grey on the upperside with rusty-red barring below, and reddish cheeks. Adult females are a duller shade of grey-brown, and have greyish barring on the undersides, often with a little pinkish red on the cheeks and flanks. Juveniles of both sexes are solid mid-brown on the upperside and pale with brown barring on the underside – sexing a juvenile is really only possible by assessing its size and build. All Sparrowhawks have broad darker bands on the tail, all often show white patches on the back, and all have yellow eyes except for older adult males, whose eyes are orange or reddish.

In flight, Sparrowhawks look round-winged, and the strong barring on the wing underside is obvious. The flight is fast, with short glides interspersed with powerful flaps – they will also soar on spread wings. The call is a high-pitched, down-slurred single whistling or wailing note, but they rarely call except near their nests.

Male Sparrowhawks become increasingly rusty coloured on the underside with age, and their eyes also become more orange.

BOY OR GIRL?

The adult male Sparrowhawk is easy to recognise, with extensive brick-red coloration on his underside. However, adult females are a similar colour to younger males, and juvenile males and females are indistinguishable on plumage colour. Field guides stress that females are browner than males, but in truth, adult females are nearly as grey-toned as adult males. Pure brown Sparrowhawks are always juveniles, and because male Sparrowhawks are more frequent in gardens than females, most brown-plumaged Sparrowhawks visiting the garden will be young males, yet to complete their first moult (which occurs at close to a year old).

So, how do you sex your juvenile or adolescent Sparrowhawk? The average female weighs half as much again as the average male, but size can be hard to judge. Pay attention to body proportions and the general look. Males are skinny-legged, with small, delicate bills and 'cute' heads with surprised-looking eyes. Females look distinctly more predatory, with thicker, stronger legs, a more projecting bill, and an expression that is more fierce than startled.

DISTRIBUTION, POPULATION AND HABITAT

You will find Sparrowhawks throughout Britain and Ireland except in the high treeless uplands of Scotland and on some Scottish islands. There are about 35,000 breeding pairs in Britain. Worldwide, the total population of some 2.2 million to 3.3 million birds occupies a vast Eurasian range that stretches across all of Europe and much of northern and central Asia. The species is migratory in northern and eastern Asia (mainly subspecies *A. n. nisosimilis*), wintering in Africa and southern and South East Asia. Over most of the rest of its range, including Britain, subspecies *A. n. nisus* occurs, with four other forms found in more southerly regions.

From a very low ebb through the 1950s to 1970s, the Sparrowhawk's population grew through the late 20th century, stabilising in the late 1990s. An overall increase of 108 per cent in England between 1975 and 2015, however, masked a definite decline in more recent years – between 2005 and 2015, numbers fell again by 24 per cent.

The majority of British Sparrowhawks live in wooded areas, most often deciduous woodland, but they can also do well in areas with more patchy tree cover, such as mixed farmland, marshland, parks, and towns with some good-sized gardens. There is some disparity between the sexes' preferred hunting grounds, with males doing better in woodland and females in more open countryside.

BEHAVIOUR

This hawk preys almost exclusively on other birds. It is a powerful hunter for its size and can tackle prey close to its own weight or even a little heavier. In general, males take prey from small songbird size up to Collared Dove size, while females rarely take sparrow-sized or smaller prey, but regularly take Collared Doves and Woodpigeons, and sometimes even formidable fighters like Jays, Magpies and Jackdaws.

Sparrowhawks are solitary surprise hunters, using cover to get close to unsuspecting prey before making the final dash. They will fly just below the top of a hedge or wall, and will also sit in waiting in a hidden position for prey to get close. If necessary, they will chase prey on foot. When they attack, they seize the prey in their feet and squeeze hard with their long toes, which usually drives the

This hawk is more than capable of catching birds as heavy or heavier than itself, such as Red-legged Partridges *Alectoris rufa*.

181

BESET ON ALL SIDES

Several different factors contributed to the Sparrowhawk's devastating decline in Britain through the 19th and early 20th centuries. Extensive woodland clearance robbed it of habitat, while more and better guns in gamekeepers' hands spelled death and destruction for Sparrowhawks and all other predatory birds and mammals. By the time the law was changed to protect birds of prey from deliberate killing, in 1961, a new threat was in the offing – DDT and other persistent pesticides, which lingered in the bodies of prey animals and affected all the predators that ate them. Many birds of prey died from direct poisoning, while others became unable to breed successfully, laying soft-shelled eggs that could not support chick development.

Many people today grew up in a time when Sparrowhawks were very rare, and it's easy to get the impression that the species has experienced a terrific population boom. But in truth, numbers were just returning to something approaching 'natural' levels, and are now showing signs of a new decline, for as yet unknown reasons.

The extreme size difference seen in male (left) and female (right) Sparrowhawks means that between them they can hunt birds of all sizes and avoid competition with each other – demonstrating what biologists call 'niche separation'.

talons in deep enough to kill, but large prey may not succumb immediately, and the hawk is then forced to wrestle with its struggling catch while trying to pluck and eat it.

Sparrowhawks pair up in winter, and on calm, sunny days late in the season you will often see adults of both sexes soaring high and performing swooping aerobatics, sometimes alone and sometimes together. At this time they are often mobbed by corvids, which try to drive them away.

The nest is usually built in a tall conifer, well hidden and close to the trunk. It is a bulky structure of sticks and twigs, sometimes made on the remains of an old Woodpigeon nest, and lined with smaller and softer twigs and bark fragments. In the nest, the female lays four to five eggs and incubates them alone for 33 days while the male brings prey for her. While the fledglings are small, their mother stays with them, as she is a more effective defender of the nest than her partner, but soon both adults need to hunt to keep the growing young fed. The chicks fledge at about 29 days old and are fed outside the nest for another 30 days or so.

Ringing recoveries show that Sparrowhawks from mainland Europe – mainly north-east of us – do regularly reach the British Isles and vice versa, though most birds are sedentary. Sparrowhawks from northern Scandinavia, where the species is partly migratory, have reached Britain from time to time. They include 29 birds that came here from Norway, and there are also 11 records of British-ringed Sparrowhawks turning up in Norway.

The longest recorded journeys top 1,000km; they include a male ringed as a chick in Finland, which was found dead in Suffolk four months later, having travelled 2,179km. Another epic migration was made by a young female that travelled 1,617km from the Yorkshire coast to Sweden. These migrations can be achieved with impressive speed – for example, one bird ringed in Orkney in April 1990 was caught by another ringer in Germany, 853km away, just one week later.

It will be a while before any small birds return to a feeding station after a Sparrowhawk visit.

For all their accident-prone ways (see box, below), Sparrowhawks have the potential to live a long life. The oldest British-ringed bird was a female ringed in the nest in 1982 and found dead 17 years and one month later, just 49km away. A bird in Denmark lived at least 20 years and three months.

IN THE GARDEN

The subject of Sparrowhawks in the garden can be a sensitive one. Nobody who puts food out for their garden birds wants to see them suffer a violent end, but there is no denying that concentrations of smaller birds can attract Sparrowhawks. If you see a Sparrowhawk in your garden, the chances are that it is there to hunt.

Predators can keep prey populations in check, but they can thrive only where prey numbers are healthy, so the presence of a Sparrowhawk is a good sign for your local ecosystem. Nevertheless, you may well want to give your garden birds a fighting chance against the hawks. The best way to do this is to make sure your feeders are positioned away from fences or walls that Sparrowhawks could use as cover to make their approach, but close to some dense prickly bushes or other safe retreats. Even then, the less wary birds may be picked off. There is, however, evidence that the presence of Sparrowhawks can improve the fitness of the songbird population as a whole, making them better able to withstand the other dangers that life in the wild can bring.

DAREDEVILS

When chasing prey, Sparrowhawks are single-minded and determined to the point where they can place themselves in danger. From engaging in desperate pitched battles with birds as powerful as themselves to colliding with obstacles, they are very prone to injuring or killing themselves in the pursuit of a meal. This underscores the importance of every chase and every kill, and how tough a predator's life can be.

If you find an injured Sparrowhawk in your garden, remove it from danger if you need to but handle carefully, using a towel to protect your hands from its talons. Birds that have stunned themselves by striking a window will often recover quickly, but any that are badly hurt will need care from a wildlife rescue and rehabilitation facility.

Kestrel
Falco tinnunculus

34cm
200g

AMBER

Until recently, this beautiful little falcon was the most numerous bird of prey in the British Isles. Today, that mantle has been taken by the Buzzard, but the Sparrowhawk is far more likely than either Buzzards or Kestrels to occur in gardens. If you live in the countryside, though, you are likely to have Kestrels living and hunting nearby. In some areas, Kestrels have adapted to a more urban lifestyle and may turn up even in small gardens.

INTRODUCTION

The grey crown and rather sparse streaking on the underside identifies this bird as an adult male Kestrel.

This is a slim, relatively big-headed, large-eyed, long-winged and long-tailed falcon. The adult male has a light grey-brown head and tail, and a rich chestnut back and wings with some black chequering. The tail has a broad blackish band at the tip, and the flight feathers are also blackish. The underside is pale, marked with fine darker streaks. Females and juveniles are a less rich tone of warm brown, and have brown rather than grey heads and tails. They have heavier and more extensive dark markings all over, including fine dark bands across the full length of the tail, with a broader band at the tip. The eyes are dark brown; the legs, eye-ring and skin at the base of the bill are yellow; and the bill itself is dark grey, smallish and hooked.

In flight, the Kestrel looks slim and rakish with pointed wings (though these look broader when it soars). It has a fast flight and when hunting it habitually hovers with fast wingbeats and fanned tail, holding position for several seconds at a time – no other British bird of prey does this. The call is a loud, shrill *kee kee kee*.

DISTRIBUTION, POPULATION AND HABITAT

Kestrels are common over most of the British Isles, including on the majority of island groups. They are rare or absent in the highest, barest upland areas of northern Scotland, north Wales and Northern Ireland. In the UK, there are about 46,000 pairs. The population has fluctuated but generally fallen over the last few decades. The Kestrel was badly affected by widespread DDT use through the 1950s, but by 1975 its numbers had recovered well. However, there was another steep fall through the later 1970s and early 1980s, probably related to farmland management changes. A couple of decades of fluctuation followed, with the population dipping to pre-1970 levels around 2010. Overall, it declined by 15 per cent between 1967 and 2016, but by 24 per cent between 1991 and 2016. It is Amber-listed because of this general downward trend.

The Kestrel is extremely widespread through Europe, Asia and Africa. It is a resident species throughout Europe and southern Asia, and in northern and sub-Saharan Africa. It occurs only as a summer visitor over northern and central Asia, these populations moving to southern Asia and Africa in winter. There are 12 subspecies, of which *F. t. tinnunculus* occurs in Britain and extensively through Europe and northern Asia. The total world population is somewhere between 4 million and 6.5 million individuals.

In Britain, Kestrels are most closely associated with open lowland habitats with grassland and scattered trees. They do well on mixed farmland, with some arable fields and some pasture, but can also be found in light woodland, marshland, moor and heath, in parks and, in some areas, in town and city centres, including as visitors to gardens. They often hunt along motorway and railway verges, where the narrow but relatively natural strips of grassland can hold plenty of prey species, such as Field Voles *Microtus agrestis*.

BEHAVIOUR

This falcon is a predator with a strong preference for small rodent prey (especially Field Voles, which can be incredibly numerous in grassland). Its visual range includes part of the ultraviolet spectrum, and vole urine is visible under ultraviolet light. This means that it can see where voles

The Field Vole, favourite prey of Kestrels, is incredibly abundant in Britain, with a population of about 75 million.

URBAN KESTRELS

Spot a medium-sized bird flying between tower blocks in central London, and it'll probably be a Feral Pigeon. However, it might also be a Kestrel. The much bigger Peregrine Falcon *F. peregrinus* is well known for nesting on city buildings, and fares very well in the cityscape, preying on the abundant Feral Pigeons. However, in London and some other cities, the Kestrel is more widespread.

To survive in the city, Kestrels have to change their ways – much more so than their bigger relatives, which find a skyscraper a very acceptable alternative to a sea-cliff. By nature, Kestrels prefer to hunt small rodents in grassland, but neither voles nor meadows are available in the urban sprawl, so most city Kestrels have switched to eating mainly birds. They have also learned to nest on ledges on buildings, rather than in the tree holes they usually prefer.

WINDHOVER

Hovering flight is one of the most energy-expensive kinds of animal movement. The most adept avian hoverers, the hummingbirds, have stupendously high metabolic rates to fuel their 80 beats-per-second wingstrokes and 500 beats-per-minute heart rate.

Kestrels use hovering flight to hunt because it enables them to scan for traces of prey from a static position, but they do not have hummingbird-level metabolism. They are able to keep down the energy costs of the hover by hanging against the wind, using its uplift to help them maintain their position. Studies have shown that this makes the energy cost of hovering about the same as for normal directional flapping flight. On days where the wind speed is not high enough, or too high, Kestrels will not use hovering flight but instead will watch for prey from a perch.

Although falcons resemble hawks, buzzards, eagles and other birds of prey, their DNA shows that they are not part of this group, nor even closely related to it. Their similarities are down to convergent evolution (both are adapted to be hunters), but the falcons' closest genetic relatives are, in fact, parrots!

have marked their runs through the grasses, and so target areas with recent activity. Its diet also includes small birds, reptiles, amphibians, and a great variety of insects and other invertebrates.

Hunting Kestrels are most often seen hovering, holding position with remarkable accuracy thanks to six wingbeats a second and constant small adjustments of the fanned tail. They will often drop to lower levels in stages before making the final feet-first pounce (or flying on to a new spot). The prey is caught with the feet and killed with a powerful bite from the bill, which has a projection (called the tomial tooth) on the upper cutting edge, for just this purpose.

Kestrels will also sit on perches and watch the ground below for prey – you'll often spot them perched on overhead street lights or telegraph poles by roadsides. They can also catch insects and small birds in flight, and will chase insects on foot. They may store some food to eat later.

Kestrel pairs take ownership of their nest sites (usually tree holes or ledges) in late winter, and defend a territory around it from other Kestrels. The nest has very little or no nesting material, being essentially a scratched-out scrape. The female incubates her four or five eggs alone for 28–29 days, during which time her mate brings her food; this continues while the chicks are small. As they grow, both parents hunt for them. The young fledge at about 35 days old and stay together nearby for several more days while the parents continue to care for them.

Many Kestrels are ringed in Britain and abroad as chicks, as their nest sites are often easily found and accessed. Nearly 7,000 British-ringed birds have been recovered to date. Most have travelled short distances, but this species is partially migratory, with a few British breeding birds (especially those breeding in Scotland) moving south into Europe or even North Africa in autumn, and some birds from further north and east heading to our shores in winter.

Of the 269 British-ringed Kestrels found abroad, the majority (182) were in France, mainly on the western side, with 21 reaching Spain. There are also several records from the Netherlands, Belgium, Germany and Portugal. The 275 foreign-ringed birds found in Britain have mostly come from Scandinavia (62 from Sweden, 56 from Finland and 40 from Norway) and the Low Countries (61 from the Netherlands and 32 from Belgium).

The longest recorded journey was undertaken by a Scottish-ringed chick that travelled 2,590km to reach Morocco; another three British-ringed birds have been recovered in Morocco after journeys of more than 2,000km. The only other Kestrel to travel a similar distance was ringed in Spain and recovered in the Scottish Highlands, having covered 2,392km.

The oldest British-ringed Kestrel was ringed as a chick in Northamptonshire in 1987, and found dead in 2003 in Rutland, having moved just 7km from its birthplace in its 15 years and 11 months of life. A bird in Germany lived for at least 20 years and five months, and another in Denmark reached an age of 16 years and five months.

IN THE GARDEN

A small raptor in the garden is most likely to be a Sparrowhawk, but if you live in the countryside you may well have Kestrels visiting, or at least pausing on your roof from time to time. They will nest in large tree holes, but also use large open-fronted or hole-fronted nest boxes, though may have to compete for these against various other species, including Barn Owls, Stock Doves, Jackdaws and Little Owls *Athene noctua*.

IDENTIFYING SMALL RAPTORS

Looking out at your lawn to see a bird of prey hunched over a smaller bird it has caught is now a common experience, and the raptor in question is usually a Sparrowhawk. However, it might be a Kestrel, and at a glance the two are rather similar. Check the following points to work out which you have.

Upperside plumage coloration The upperside is entirely blue-grey, brownish grey or dark brown in the case of the Sparrowhawk (depending on age and sex), but a distinctly brighter, lighter chestnut brown in the Kestrel (with a grey head and tail in the adult male), with obvious blackish markings.

Eye colour Sparrowhawks have piercing yellow (or orange-red in older males) eyes, while Kestrels have very dark brown eyes.

Tail pattern The Sparrowhawk's tail has a few evenly spaced, even-width, broad dark bands. The Kestrel always has one broad band at the tip only, with many narrower bands above (except in adult males, which lack extra bands).

Underside pattern Sparrowhawks have heavy horizontal barring on their underside, while Kestrels have vertical streaking.

Kestrel

Sparrowhawk

Tawny Owl
Strix aluco

38cm
420–520g
AMBER

This is the largest and most well known of our owl species, though we are much more likely to hear its lovely trembling call than to see it, at least as any more than a dark shape against a moonlit sky. Tawny Owls are quite common in towns, villages and even some cities, though you'll need to stay up late or get up early to have a chance of seeing them.

Their short, broad wings give Tawny Owls a slow but very agile flight, perfect for negotiating woodland interiors.

INTRODUCTION

This is a large, round-headed owl with a short tail and wings. The plumage is rich red-brown at a glance, but a close view reveals that it is exquisitely patterned in shades of brown, black and cream. A minority of birds have a much greyer colour palette (these are known as grey morphs). In general, adults are barred on the upperside and streaked on the underside, and in flight the underside of the wings and tail show extensive dark barring on a pale backdrop. The broad, squarish head has a clearly outlined facial disc, which is brownish with cream around the inner edges of the large blackish eyes. The bill is yellowish, and the legs and toes are covered in fine grey feathers.

There are four other species of owls living wild in the British Isles, but the birds are also rather popular as pets and for falconry. Because a tame owl is likely to seek out human contact, the owls that turn up in gardens are often escapees, of species not native to Britain.

The most popular owls in captivity are various species of eagle owls. These birds are large or very large, and have conspicuous feathery ear-tufts, as well as (usually) yellow or orange eyes. If you encounter a big and oddly fearless owl with 'ears' in the garden, check its legs for any metal rings or jesses (leather straps used in falconry). Escapee birds of prey can be reported at the Independent Bird Register (see page 220) – it's also worth posting on local Facebook groups.

Young Tawny Owls leave the nest well before they have adult-like plumage, and are clad in soft grey 'mesoptile' plumage, which is intermediate between fluffy down and true feathers. The first proper juvenile plumage is coloured and patterned like the adult's, and there are no sex differences in plumage either, though females are distinctly larger than males (as is the case with nearly all birds of prey).

The male's territorial call is a drawn-out, tremulous and fluting hoot. Females also hoot, though rarely, and theirs is higher-pitched and has a more throbbing quality. Both sexes also have a sharp yelping *ke-vick* contact call; the female often answers her mate's hoot with this call.

DISTRIBUTION, POPULATION AND HABITAT

Tawny Owls are widespread in mainland Britain but are absent from Ireland and most Scottish islands, a reflection of their reluctance to disperse very far from their natal site and to cross open water. They are also rare or absent in the open uplands of northern and western Scotland. About 50,000 pairs breed in the UK. They are of the subspecies *S. a. sylvatica*, which is also present in western France and Spain. In the UK, the species declined by 19 per cent between 1967 and 2016, with the fall steepest between 1995 and 2005 but continuing today (there was a fall of 10 per cent between 2005 and 2016). The reasons for this decline are not yet fully understood.

The world range includes all of Europe except the far north of Scandinavia, and north-west Africa, northern parts of the Middle East, and into central western Asia as far south and east as northern India. Besides *S. a. sylvatica* there are another seven subspecies, mainly separated from one another by various Eurasian mountain ranges.

Tawny Owls occur in woodland and at woodland edges, and can live in areas that are more open provided there are at least some large trees around with holes for nesting and places to roost safely. This includes town parkland and some garden environments. Availability of nest sites is a key factor that limits their numbers.

Owls swallow most of their meals whole, producing pellets of the bones and other indigestible bits some time later.

BEHAVIOUR

The classic image of an owl pouncing on a mouse is just a small part of the Tawny Owl's ecological role as a predator. It has an extremely varied diet – any living thing that it can subdue is fair game. It preys on all kinds of mammals up to the size of juvenile Rabbits *Oryctolagus cuniculus*, birds up

CLINAL VARIATION

Sometimes it is (relatively) easy to recognise a subspecies – it's a population within a species that is separated geographically from other populations, and consistently shows its own distinctive traits. The Tawny Owls in North Africa are separated from all other Tawnies by sea, and their DNA and plumage shows them to be clearly different to their nearest neighbours in Spain and Portugal.

However, there is often also geographical variation within a subspecies. In the case of the Tawny Owl, there is a definite tendency for the proportion of grey morphs to increase in areas further north, where the habitat is dominated by spruces and other coniferous trees rather than broadleafs. Good camouflage is vital for Tawnies to keep them hidden when they hunt and when they roost. The colder tones of conifer bark and foliage are a better camouflage backdrop for greyer birds, so they are more likely to survive and breed, while more rufous birds do better in broadleaved woodland where the colour palette is richer and redder.

to its own size (including other owls), reptiles, amphibians, fish, earthworms and insects, and it will also take carrion. As a highly territorial predator, it needs to be very adaptable in diet terms, as no single prey type can be relied upon all the time, and travelling out of its territory to hunt would be very risky, as it would come into conflict with neighbouring Tawnies.

The usual hunting method Tawnies use is 'sit and wait'. They sit on a preferred perch and scan the ground below, using hearing as much as sight – if not more so – to locate prey moving around. They attack their quarry with a silent pounce, manoeuvring with great agility between branches, and kill with the talons and bill. Most prey items are swallowed whole, with bones and fur regurgitated in pellets later. Tawnies will also fly along hedgerows to flush out roosting birds, wade to catch fish and frogs, and search on the ground for worms. Over the years they build a very in-depth familiarity with their territory, and learn the best places to look for different kinds of prey.

Tawny Owl adults that are paired up will share their territory through winter without having much to do with one another. By late winter, males are hooting more often, and females are also more vocal, as they step up their campaign to warn off interlopers and to prepare for mating and nesting.

A Tawny Owl chick is ready to venture out of its nest and climb into nearby branches at just three weeks old.

Like many owls, Tawnies prefer to nest in tree holes, but cavities large enough to accommodate these large owls are thin on the ground. A good nest site is key to a good territory, and nest sites are used year after year, even when both original birds have died and been replaced. Often they are hollows left by decay when a branch has fallen. Tawnies will also use nest boxes. Less favoured sites include animal burrows on the ground, and the old nests of other birds such as crows. The female sits very tight while her mate provisions her with food, and the two or three eggs hatch after about 30 days of incubation. Because incubation begins as soon as the first egg is laid, and there may be an interval of two days between laying, the oldest chick is several days ahead of its youngest siblings and much more likely to survive if there is a food shortage.

Chicks leave the nest at about three weeks old but are still small and downy, albeit able to climb strongly. They hide in branches near the nest and beg for food when a parent comes to the tree. They can fly at about 37 days old.

This owl is exceptionally sedentary in Britain. Juveniles have to move away from their parents' territory to find a place of their own, and this is a very high-risk time for them. Those that survive and find a productive patch will stay put for life if they possibly can, and this is usually within 10km of their birthplace. One juvenile ringed in the Scottish Highlands as a chick was found six months later in Carmarthenshire, Wales, a distance of 668km. This individual is very much the outlier within ringing recovery data for the species, though a couple of others have travelled beyond 200km. No British-ringed Tawny has ever been found abroad, or vice versa.

The oldest British-ringed bird was ringed as a chick in Aberdeenshire, and found dead just 4km away, 23 years and five months later. There are a couple of records from Europe of birds living to at least 22 years and five months – one from the Czech Republic and the other from Finland.

IN THE GARDEN

Listen on a calm night and you may well hear your local male Tawny Owl hooting, especially early on in the breeding season. The female, if the male is paired up, may well reply with a *ke-vick* call. The chances of seeing either bird are not great, but on a bright night you might see them in flight or perched on a rooftop or fence.

Tawny Owls readily use nest boxes, and nest boxes purpose-built for Tawnies are widely available. It's unwise to erect a box anywhere near your house, though, as parent Tawnies are fiercely protective and will dive and strike at people who come too close to the nest. Erecting a nest box for Tawny Owls is therefore an option only for those with large and quiet gardens; however, if you have space, you would be doing a lot to help this declining species.

HUNTING THE HUNTERS

In Ireland, where there are no Tawny Owls, the Long-eared Owl *Asio otus* is common in all kinds of woodlands. However, in Britain the Long-eared is a rare breeding bird, and mostly occurs in pine plantations and other suboptimal habitats. This is because it is kept out of the best habitats by the bigger, stronger Tawny Owl.

The Tawny is the 'top owl' in Britain, and it will hunt and kill other owls if they intrude on its territory. This is 'intraguild predation' – the tendency of predators to target smaller predators, to eliminate competition as well as to prey on them. For the Tawny Owl, with its exceptional dependence on a productive territory, the tactic is particularly important. Most birds of prey are somewhat more mobile, at least outside the breeding season, so are less committed to eliminating their competitors.

Aerial feeders

The aerial 'plankton' of tiny flying insects and baby spiders drifting on their silk parachutes is food for a special cohort of birds that make their living on the wing. The Swallow and House Martin (family Hirundinidae), along with the Swift (family Apodidae), all belong to this group and often hunt over gardens – they also like to nest on and in buildings.

Swallow
Hirundo rustica

18cm
19g
GREEN

A much-loved harbinger of summer, the Swallow is an energetic little bird that graces villages and farms through the warmer months. Most of those in Britain nest inside open buildings and can be seen hunting over and around gardens as well as the wider countryside.

INTRODUCTION

The Swallow is a small but long-tailed bird, with long wings and elongated outer-tail feathers – in adult males, the latter look particularly fine and needle-like. The upperside is dark, looking blackish in poor light but showing a strong violet-blue sheen in sunlight. There is also a blackish breast-band, and the throat and a small patch at the front of the forehead are dark orange-red. The underside is creamy white, and the tail underside reveals a band of pale 'windows' halfway up each feather when the tail is fanned out.

The tiny bill is blackish, as are the small legs and feet, and the eyes. The sexes are alike except for the male's longer tail, evident when a pair is perched together. Juvenile Swallows are a little drabber in plumage, with pale buff rather than rich orange foreheads and throats, and while their tails

Its cheerful voice and exuberant flight makes the Swallow our most beloved avian harbinger of summer.

are still forked, the outermost feathers are not disproportionately elongated. The flight is fast, agile and flickering.

The male's song is a bright, varied twittering. Its most commonly heard call is a sharp *vit*, which attains a grating, metallic quality when given in alarm.

DISTRIBUTION, POPULATION AND HABITAT

From late March or April to October, Swallows are widespread throughout the British Isles, occurring across the mainland and on all islands and island groups. However, they do not breed in the highest parts of northern Scotland. As winter approaches, virtually all Swallows leave our shores, but occasionally one or two will linger in winter in the far south-west of England. About 860,000 pairs breed in the UK.

Swallow numbers have fluctuated considerably in Britain over the last few decades. The net change between 1967 and 2016 was a slight increase (4 per cent); more recently, numbers have fallen, with a 21 per cent decline between 2011 and 2016. The factors driving population change in Swallows are diverse. The radical changes in farmland use and management over recent years will no doubt have affected this open-country insect-eating bird, as will changes in nest-site availability – today there are fewer derelict barns and other buildings where Swallows can nest. But this is a long-distance migrant that spends half the year in other parts of the world – conditions on the migration route and wintering grounds will also affect its survival rates.

The Swallow is a very widespread bird. In summer it breeds right across Europe and most of Asia, and also throughout North America except the far north. In winter these populations migrate south, so you will then find Swallows across sub-Saharan Africa, southern and South East Asia, and Australasia. Over its range there are about eight recognised subspecies, of which the one found in Britain and most of Eurasia is *H. r. rustica*. The world population is estimated at between 290 million and 500 million individuals.

Swallows in the British Isles are most often found on farmland, since this offers the combination of open country that suits their hunting style and nest sites in the form of open and accessible buildings. However, they can also commonly be found in marshy and wetland areas, coastal areas, around villages, on heathland and moorland, and in larger parks. On migration, they could be seen anywhere.

BEHAVIOUR

This bird is an insectivore and feeds almost exclusively on prey it catches in flight, with a focus on smaller items that can be engulfed in its wide mouth without any need to struggle with the item. The rictal bristles – short, stiff feathers that line its mouth-edges – help to keep prey from escaping, and parent birds collecting food for their brood can carry several squashed insects in the bill at a time.

Preferred prey includes small swarming flies such as midges and mosquitoes, and also 'ballooning' baby spiders, dispersing on silk threads. Birds may also take non-flying invertebrates climbing in long grass.

Hunting Swallows often fly very close to ground level over fields, darting between grazing livestock. They skim very low over open water, but will fly at higher levels too. Their method for hunting insects is also used to collect nest-lining material – they often 'catch' feathers and straw in flight. However, they land on the ground to collect mud, and may also land to catch insects resting on surfaces, especially in cooler weather. You may see several feeding over the same field or lake, or resting in groups on overhead wires.

Swallows are famous for returning to the place of their birth after their first (and each subsequent) migration. Here they will try to reclaim their previous year's nest site, or find one nearby if this is their first year of breeding. Males return first and claim territory, and court females as they return with song and a display flight. Females choose the best partners in terms of physical condition, and with the best nest site. Pairs that bred together in previous years may re-form but often do not.

The males (and females, once paired up) defend a small territory around the nest, but Swallows do not establish a feeding territory as they have to range so widely to find enough food. Nests can be placed quite close together, within a few metres of one another in some cases.

TOP TAILS

As with most birds, when Swallows come to pairing up, it is the male that advertises and the female that chooses. Among other factors, females prefer males with the longest tail-streamers, as this is an 'honest' indication of physical health and fitness. Studies have shown that males with long tail-streamers instantly become much less popular if their tail feather tips are trimmed shorter, even though they continue to sing and display more strongly than their naturally shorter-tailed counterparts.

Such is their aerial skill that adult Swallows can post food into their chicks' open mouths without needing to land.

Although females select a partner to help them raise a family, they are also on the lookout for mating opportunities with other males nesting nearby, which may be genetically 'better' than their regular partner. Males will take these opportunities readily, but they also want to prevent their own mate from having any sneaky liaisons, so they don't waste their time rearing another male's offspring. Therefore, they guard their mates fiercely, as much as they can. If they do spot their mate about to copulate with another male, they may try to disrupt proceedings by giving 'false' alarm calls, as if a predator is nearby.

Swallows build untidy nests from mud pellets, straw, feathers and other materials, both members of the pair working together. The nest is usually partly fixed to a vertical surface but supported from below as well – beams against walls inside barns are perfect nest sites. The previous year's nest may be repaired and reused if it is still in reasonable condition. The female lays a clutch of four or five eggs, and does most of the incubation for the 18 days it takes for them to hatch. Both parents feed the young, which fledge at about 21 days old. The chicks tend to stay together for some days after fledging, sitting huddled together and waiting for a parent to feed them. Gradually their flight and hunting skills improve.

Swallows usually have two broods. Post-breeding, adults and juveniles form large gatherings as they prepare to begin their migration, and often roost communally in reed beds, sometimes with martins (both House and Sand).

Swallows are summer visitors to the British Isles. The first sightings are usually in mid-March, with the main rush of arrivals taking place through the first couple of weeks of April. After breeding, our Swallows make a return southward migration, mostly leaving through early October. Nearly 15,000 Swallows have been ringed in Britain and Ireland, and out of those, 1,442 have been recovered abroad, 454 of them in South Africa. The general pattern of recoveries suggests that British-ringed Swallows mostly bear west to fly through Spain and cross Gibraltar to reach Africa. Then they must cross the Sahara before tracking south along the western side of the southern half of the continent. The wintering grounds are open savannah and wetland areas, similar to their European breeding habitat. Many British-ringed Swallows travel in excess of 9,000km.

The oldest Swallow ringed in Britain lived to be 11 years and one month old – this is also the record from Europe. A handful of others have just reached double figures, including one ringed in Yorkshire as a chick and found in South Africa 10 years and six months later, 9,903km from 'home'. With two migrations of this distance each year, the oldest Swallows rack up something in the region of 200,000km of transcontinental flight through their lives.

IN THE GARDEN

Locally nesting Swallows may rest on your rooftop, on overhead wires or even in trees, and will fly overhead on their way to or from their nests. They will nest in outbuildings that are permanently accessible, even if this is only via a small opening (such as a single broken window pane), which you may consider a good or a bad thing, depending on the circumstances! Swallows will also use purpose-built nest boxes placed in openly accessible but sheltered places, such as inside a porch.

Migration holds many dangers, but it enables Swallows and other insect-eaters to breed successfully in temperate regions.

SOLVING THE MIGRATION MYSTERY

Naturalists have long wondered where Swallows go in winter. One 19th-century notion was that they spent the colder months hibernating in riverside mud, a theory that developed through observations of pre-migration flocks diving into reed beds to roost. As our knowledge of bird life around the world improved, the idea of long-distance migration became more widely accepted, but it was not proved until December 1912.

Ringing wild birds to track their movements was first practised in Britain in 1909, and the idea caught the imagination of a number of amateur naturalists. In May 1911, a Staffordshire man called John Masefield ringed a brood of Swallow chicks in the nest in his porch. Each ring was marked with his address and a unique identifying number. On 23 December 1912, the Swallow bearing ring B830 was caught inside a building near Utrecht in South Africa, and the finder wrote to Masefield to let him know. This was the first ever concrete evidence that a small songbird could make a journey of more than 9,000km, and it sparked a surge of interest in migration studies that continues to this day. As GPS tracking technology improves, we are getting close to a time when we can follow the exact migratory routes individual Swallows take. This data will help us work out what serious hazards the birds face on their migration, and how best we can protect them as they travel.

House Martin
Delichon urbicum

12cm
19g
AMBER

The common name of this species shows how closely linked to people it has become over the last few centuries. Although it originally nested on cliff faces (and, in a few areas, still does), the House Martin is mainly a bird of towns and villages in Britain. However, its cup-shaped mud nests, glued under eaves of buildings, are becoming a rarer sight today, and fewer of us now have the pleasure of seeing and hearing this bird around our homes every summer.

INTRODUCTION

This is a small bird with crisply marked black-and-white plumage, the black head and body feathers showing a dark blue sheen in strong light. Its upperside is black except for the rump, which bears a prominent squarish white patch. The underside, from chin to undertail, is entirely white. It has a small dark bill and dark eyes, and its pinkish legs and toes are covered with tiny, fine white feathers. In flight, it shows rather broad-based, pointed triangular wings and a medium-length tail with a pronounced fork. Juveniles have the same pattern as adults but their dark plumage parts are drabber and their pale cheeks slightly dusky looking.

The flight call, commonly heard around the nest, is a rather dry, rolling *chirp*. The male's song extends this note into a slightly more tuneful twitter.

DISTRIBUTION, POPULATION AND HABITAT

House Martins are present almost throughout the British Isles in the summer months, mainly between late March and October. They do not breed in the highest parts of northern and north-western Scotland – they are also scarce on the most northerly Scottish islands. The UK population is about 750,000 pairs.

House Martin numbers in the UK and particularly in England have fallen considerably over the last few decades, with an especially marked decline between the early 1980s and 1990s. The downward

The House Martin can be told from other similar species by its pure white underside, from chin to undertail.

FEATHERY FEET

Nearly all birds have bare feet and toes – the grouse and the owls are the main exceptions. The House Martin is our only songbird to have a feather covering on its feet. It seems baffling, when you see House Martins gathering on the ground at puddle edges, that these birds evolved to have fluffy white feet when the only time they land on the ground is to collect mud. Apparently, any extra time spent keeping their feet clean is worthwhile for the benefit the foot feathers bring, but we don't yet know exactly what this benefit is. The best guess so far is that the feathers help keep the bird's feet warm when it is roosting on the wing at high altitudes – the fact that Swifts (which also roost in flight) have feathered feet too would seem to support this hypothesis.

trend has since continued, albeit more gradually. Overall, there was a decline of 70 per cent between 1967 and 2016 in England. For the UK as a whole, numbers fell by 22 per cent between 1995 and 2016. The species is faring considerably better in Scotland (with a 128 per cent rise between 1995 and 2016) and Northern Ireland (a 47 per cent rise between 1995 and 2016) – however, England holds about two-thirds of the whole UK House Martin population.

The world breeding range includes the whole of Europe, as well as north-western Africa and across through northern and central Asia, reaching western China. Most of these birds winter in Africa, south of the Sahara. There are two subspecies – *D. u. urbicum* in northern parts of the breeding range and *D. u. meridionale* in southern Europe, North Africa and west-central Asia (wintering in southern Asia). In total, the world population is some 10 million to 50 million individuals.

Most British House Martins nest on buildings, almost invariably below the eaves and preferring more open settings than Swallows. Single nests may be found but groups of two to 10 are more usual. Colonies are most often found in villages but also in some towns – however, this species is rare in large cities. There are also a few colonies on coastal cliffs. They hunt over lakes and marshland, farmland and other open areas, and their autumn roosts are often in trees, rather than in reed beds as is the case with Swallows.

Each of the 'pellets' that make up a nest is a mouthful of mud, carried there and stuck in place by one of the pair.

BEHAVIOUR

An aerial-hunting insectivore, the House Martin feeds mainly on small flies, but will capture all kinds of winged insects that are small enough to be trapped in its wide gape. It hunts over water and open countryside, pursuing prey on the wing. It will skim very low over water to take mosquitoes and other flies as they emerge, but does not hunt low over grassland as frequently as Swallows.

The birds are quite gregarious and you will frequently see several hunting together; they also often keep company with Swallows and Sand Martins *Riparia riparia*.

A CHANGING WORLD

It is very noticeable when we lose House Martin breeding colonies because these little birds are so closely linked to human habitation, and their nests are very prominent. Not everyone welcomes the martins, and deliberate destruction of nests is undoubtedly a problem for this species. Another problem is the widespread use of new plastic building materials that aren't suitable for nest-building. However, there are also wider influences on House Martin populations.

Over the last 50 years, the average arrival date for House Martins in spring has moved back and they now show up 16 days earlier than they did in the 1960s. This may be due to climate change making the winter habitat less hospitable than it used to be as the austral autumn approaches. However, an early arrival on the breeding grounds could make it more difficult for the birds to find enough food, and expose them to bad weather and cold nights. The Sahara Desert's gradual expansion could also be making migration more challenging, and the wholesale decline in insect life in Europe will affect breeding success. Solving the House Martin's problems will require a range of investigations and changes across many countries, but there is still a lot that UK householders can do to help.

House Martin nests can be vulnerable. House Sparrows may appropriate them, and hungry Great Spotted Woodpeckers sometimes drill into them. Also, Sparrowhawks can learn to ambush the adult birds as they visit their nests.

House Martins complete their northbound spring migration much more quickly than their southbound autumn journey, and return to the site of their birth (or where they bred the previous year, if different). They will reuse the same nest if they can, repairing it as necessary, or rebuild close to the original spot. Nests may be built very close together, with neighbouring pairs showing little or no aggression.

Both sexes build the nest, sticking together lumps of mud to form a cup with a small entrance at the top. The female lays four or five eggs, and both sexes incubate the clutch for 13–19 days. The chicks take about 22 days to reach fledging age. House Martins have two broods in a year, and sometimes three (although late broods may be abandoned).

House Martins are summer visitors, arriving in April and departing in October. They are usually back with us a week or so later than Swallows, and linger a little longer into autumn. Ringing recoveries of this species have mainly been from south-west Europe and North Africa, with a single recovery from Nigeria (5,133km from the ringing site). This bird was ringed as a juvenile in Hertfordshire and found five months later.

The oldest British House Martin on record is a bird ringed as a juvenile in Bedfordshire, and re-caught at the same site seven years and one month later. This is completely eclipsed by a record from Sweden of a bird re-caught by a ringer 15 years after it was initially ringed, and another in Germany that reached 14 years and six months of age.

IN THE GARDEN

While House Martins are not garden visitors, how you treat your garden could have a significant effect on them. They feed on flying insects, which are becoming more and more scarce in Britain. Maintaining a wildlife-friendly garden with native plants and some overgrown natural areas will help boost insect numbers, as will establishing a garden pond.

If House Martins nest on your house already, or are nesting nearby, you may be able to help them by providing some wet patches of ground where they can collect the mud they need for nest-building, particularly if it is a very dry spring. They will only be tempted to come down to spots in the open with good all-round visibility. Artificial House Martin nests can help your colony to grow, or perhaps encourage local birds to begin to nest. It is best to put up more than one, close together, to appeal to these colonial-nesting birds. They should be positioned under the eaves.

If you have nesting martins and are having problems with the mess they leave behind, you can fit a platform below the nest to catch droppings. It is illegal to tamper with any active nest, so if any changes need to be made, this is best done during the winter, ready for the next breeding season.

Stone walls and wooden beams are ideal for House Martin nests, but the birds find it more difficult to stick their mud pellets to modern eaves and fascias made of uPCV. Putting up nest boxes can help.

WINTER SECRETS

To date, ringing recoveries have not taught us very much about where our House Martins go in winter, and how they get there. There are observations of House Martins in winter across parts of sub-Saharan Africa, and this presumably includes British breeding birds, but definitive data are lacking. It is possible the birds spend these months foraging above canopy-height in rainforest habitats, rather than using open savannah as do Swallows. The truth will be revealed once satellite-tracking technology advances a little further – at present, trackers are either too large or their battery life is too short for GPS tracking to be workable for migrating House Martins.

Swift

Apus apus

16cm

44g

AMBER

Swifts are the fighter pilots of the bird world, screaming in squadrons at roof height along our streets at breakneck pace. They resemble Swallows and martins but are not related to them – in fact, hummingbirds are their closest relatives. They are highly specialised to a life in the air, even sleeping in flight. Their decline in Britain is worrying, but there is much that householders can do to improve their fortunes.

INTRODUCTION

The Swift resembles a Swallow or martin in its shape and manner of flight, but it is not closely related to these birds. Its plumage is brownish black on both the upperside and underside, with a variable but always small whitish patch on the chin. In most light conditions it simply looks black. Its outline is distinctive, with long, narrow, sickle-shaped wings, a streamlined neck-less body, and a relatively short but deeply forked tail. Juveniles are paler than adults and, with a very close view, show pale fringing to some body feathers, especially on the belly, giving a vaguely scaly impression. The bill is very small and dark, the head is flattish, and the eyes are dark under a slightly raised brow ridge, which, together with a very black patch in front of the eye, creates a frowning impression. The legs and feet are finely feathered and very weak and small, but the claws are strong. The feet are not usually visible in flying birds as they are concealed under the feathers.

The call is a harsh, drawn-out, shrill scream, which can be heard both from birds in flight and those in their nesting cavities; away from nest sites, the Swift is usually quiet.

The Swift's screaming call is a classic summer sound in towns and villages, however, the species is now in serious decline.

IDENTIFYING SWIFTS AND HIRUNDINES

Telling apart the Swallow, House Martin and Swift can be tricky if you don't know what to look for, as they are all similar in shape and behaviour, and are all also very fast moving. Luckily, all three have a different arrangement of dark and pale on their undersides – so as long as the bird flies overhead, you will be able to identify it easily. The Swift (right) has an entirely dark underside, except for a small pale throat-patch that is difficult to see. The Swallow (centre) has a pale belly but dark throat and upper breast.

The House Martin (left) is entirely white on its underside, from chin to undertail.

In the wider countryside, there is one more aerial feeder to worry about – the Sand Martin. This small brown-and-white martin also has a distinctive underside pattern – it is white below but with a dark band across its breast. All four species also differ in tail shape, colour tone and call, but underside pattern is probably the easiest 'go-to' characteristic to check.

DISTRIBUTION, POPULATION AND HABITAT

Swifts are very short-staying summer visitors to the British Isles. They are widespread throughout England and Wales, and eastern and central Scotland, but are rare or absent in the Scottish uplands, especially in the north and west. They are also rather scarce on the western side of Ireland. About 87,000 pairs breed in the UK, with non-breeding birds boosting numbers later in the season. This species' population has declined steadily since counts began in 1995 – a fall of 53 per cent was recorded in the UK between 1995 and 2016, through the BTO's Breeding Birds Survey. The decline has been most pronounced in Wales. The fall in Swift numbers could have many causes, of which a lack of nest sites is certainly likely to be one, along with reduced populations of flying insects.

Swifts breed across nearly all of Europe and in north-west Africa. They also have a very extensive breeding range in Asia, reaching the far eastern coast and the northern Middle East, though are absent from north-east Asia. They winter in Africa, south of the Sahara. The world population is in the region of 95 million to 165 million individuals. There are two subspecies: *A. a. apus* occurs in the west of the range and winters in southern Africa, while *A. a. pekinensis* occupies most of the Asian range and winters in eastern and southern Africa.

In Britain, Swifts mainly breed in towns and villages. They are extremely wide-ranging and may be seen flying over any habitat type, but are most likely over open fresh water (coastal and inland) and open pasture and marshland. Weather patterns greatly influence where they go to forage.

BEHAVIOUR

Swifts are insect-eaters, and catch all their prey on the wing. As well as flying insects, they take baby spiders that use silk threads to 'balloon' through the air, sometimes to great heights. The most important food sources for them are swarms of mosquitoes, gnats and other flies that emerge from water.

CITIZEN SCIENCE

The Common Birds Census, which ran from 1962 to 2000, provided us with valuable data on bird population trends over its active years. However, its methods didn't work well for all bird species, including Swifts. The breeding and foraging behaviour of Swifts is such that it is difficult to locate active nests unless you spend considerable time in an area, as the breeding birds may travel hundreds of kilometres away from home on their foraging flights.

Because most British Swifts nest in buildings, and usually buildings that have human occupants too, the general public is often better placed to monitor their nesting activity than ornithologists working 'in the field'. Accordingly, each summer the RSPB runs its annual Swift Survey, asking the public for their observations of Swift breeding behaviour. This data will help build a clearer picture of where Swifts are and are not breeding in the UK.

Swift chicks can fast for a day or more if they have to, an adaptation to a highly unreliable food supply.

Swifts fly with great agility, and although they are capable of travelling very fast they can also manoeuvre at low speed to capture prey. They will hunt from barely above ground level over grassland and water, to 1,000m up or even higher, depending where prey can be found and on weather conditions. Because Swifts are capable of remaining in flight almost indefinitely, they fly ahead of or around weather fronts rather than resting them out, and can cover more than 800km in a day.

Swifts are long-lived birds, and are slow to mature, not breeding until they are four years old. Many of the Swifts we see around our towns are youngsters, not making a serious nesting attempt but forming pair-bonds and exploring possible nest sites. Remarkably, birds that pair up at one year old will stay paired through the next three years until they are ready to nest, despite being separated for eight months each year. Pair-bonds persist for life, and matings outside of the pairing are rare. Swifts copulate in flight, an act that must be made a little easier over years of practice with the same partner!

Finding an unoccupied nest site is difficult. Prospecting birds fly fast and close past entrances of possible nest holes, touching the entrance with their wings while screaming. If the site is occupied, the resident Swift comes to the entrance and screams in reply. The intruder may not take no for an answer, though, and sometimes Swifts invade others' nests and fight for possession.

Once a pair has a nest site, a little lining is added in the form of feathers, straw and other bits of lightweight material that the birds catch in the air. The female lays two or three curiously elongated eggs, and both birds incubate for 19–25 days. The eggs can withstand being left for some time, which allows the parents to continue to feed even if they need to make very long flights to get away from bad weather. The chicks are similarly resistant to being left, though going without food for a day or more slows their growth. This is why the fledging period is so variable – anything from 37 to 56 days. Once mature, the chicks leave the nest and must learn to catch flies immediately as their parents will not feed them in the air. They will not touch land again for at least eight more months.

Swifts are summer visitors to the UK. Their stay is very short – most arrive in late April and early May, and leave their breeding grounds as early as mid-July, with their chicks following a little later. Sightings dwindle fast through autumn. Many of the latest autumn sightings involve the European Pallid Swift *A. pallidus*, a very similar species.

Ringing recoveries and tracking studies show that our Swifts winter in Africa, well south of the Sahara, and get there via France, Spain, Morocco and the western side of the African continent. The

In midsummer you will often encounter groups of Swifts hunting over lakes and reservoirs, working hard to keep their chicks fed.

longest journey undertaken was by a bird that was ringed as an adult in Norfolk and found in South Africa, 9,366km away. Ringing recoveries also show that Scandinavian-born Swifts pass through Britain on their way south.

The oldest ringed British Swift was at least 18 years old. In Europe, a Swedish bird and a Swiss bird both reached at least 21 years old.

IN THE GARDEN

The spectacle of groups of Swifts racing over the garden is a wonderful highlight of summer. These birds will never fly down into your garden for food, but the more wildlife-friendly gardens there are in your neighbourhood, the better this will be for Swifts. Garden ponds in particular help increase the supply of flying insects.

Swifts rely on accessible spaces in buildings to use as nest sites. Because they cannot perch in the conventional way, only cling, they usually use spaces directly accessible in a vertical wall. These kinds of cracks and crevices tend to come about through wear and tear, and get plugged up when a house is renovated, whether they are problematic or not. However, it is not difficult to provide an alternative option. Swift nest boxes are available from many retailers and are also quite easy to make. They should be fixed high on a sheltered wall. Modern housing can include nest sites for Swifts within the brickwork, in the form of hollow 'Swift bricks'. These have a concave nest-chamber inside, spaces behind and in front for ventilation and drainage, and a small, inconspicuous hole for entry. You can purchase recordings of screaming Swifts to encourage passing birds to stop and check out the accommodation on offer.

Swifts cannot usually take off from the ground. If you find a grounded Swift, adult or juvenile, 'relaunch' it by holding it high on a flat hand, so it can catch the air under its wings. If this fails, the bird may be unwell and in need of care – contact a local wildlife rescue centre.

TAKING SWIFT ACTION

The RSPB has been involved with several other Swift projects besides coordinating an annual population survey, including providing advice to construction companies and helping to establish Swift-friendly zones in city centres. It also works with conservation groups such as Swift Conservation and Action for Swifts to help protect and support vulnerable Swift populations.

Other garden birds

The final section of this book is concerned with the more unusual garden visitors. Some will be regularly seen by a few lucky garden owners, while others are unpredictable but, under the right conditions, could potentially call in at almost any garden.

MALLARD
Anas platyrhynchos

This familiar dabbling duck is a common breeding and wintering bird throughout the British Isles, wherever there is suitable open water for it to feed and nest. Males are easily told from other duck species, and in the case of females, note the large size, brown rather than white belly, and iridescent deep blue wing-bar. The Mallard's presence on the Amber list of species of conservation concern is because numbers overwintering here have fallen significantly since the 1980s, but our breeding population increased through the late 20th century and has been stable since the turn of the century.

Even a smallish pond can attract visiting Mallards.

The Mallard is ancestor to most domestic duck breeds, and the wild Mallard flocks living naturally in Britain are often joined by garden escapees. Domestic-type Mallards are highly variable in appearance, including size and shape, but males always retain the distinctive curled central tail feathers.

Breeding usually begins in mid-spring. Females incubate the eight to 14 eggs and care for the ducklings alone, while males form 'bachelor' groups. In late summer, both sexes moult, and males temporarily develop a female-like eclipse plumage, to provide camouflage while they replace their flight feathers.

Pheasants are shy for good reason, but those regularly visiting gardens soon lose their fear of people.

Mallards may be resident in your garden if you are lucky enough to have a very large pond. They may turn up in other gardens too, especially if there is some kind of water feature, but they also appreciate an area of lush lawn. They will eat grain and birdseed, often loitering under hanging bird feeders to clear up spillages; if you have regularly visiting or resident Mallards, you could buy some specialist wildfowl food for them.

PHEASANT
Phasianus colchicus

This handsome bird occurs everywhere in the British Isles except far north-western Scotland and on some islands. However, it is not a native British species, but was brought over here from Asia sometime before the 18th century, to provide sport for shooters. Today, our free-living population of more than 3 million birds is vastly inflated every autumn, as shooting estates release some 38 million more young birds. Our Pheasants originate from many parts of Asia and represent several different subspecies, hence the rather varied appearance of males in particular. White and melanistic Pheasants are also quite common.

Pheasants that evade the guns through autumn and winter will breed the following spring. The female goes it alone after mating with the male of her choice, and makes a nest in a well-hidden place on the ground. She lays 10–14 well-camouflaged eggs and incubates them for about 25 days. The chicks can run around and feed themselves within an hour or so of hatching, and follow their mother away from the nest area. They can fly at about two weeks old, though it takes several more weeks for them to attain adult size and for the young males to begin to develop colourful adult plumage.

Rural gardens near woodland, with birdseed on offer, will attract Pheasants. They prefer to feed on the ground but will visit bird tables too. They tend to be shy and wary by nature but will quickly become confiding when they learn they are in no danger.

GREY HERON
Ardea cinerea

94cm 1,500g GREEN

The arrival of a Grey Heron in the garden could be bad news for the goldfish in your pond, but seeing this spectacular bird is always exciting, and there are ways to protect the fish from its attentions. There are about 13,000 pairs of Grey Herons breeding in the UK, and that number can double in winter as visitors from mainland Europe arrive. They occur almost everywhere in the British Isles and are not limited to wetland areas, though they certainly prefer to hunt around water.

Grey Herons nest in colonies (heronries) in trees, often overlooking water. The large stick nests are augmented each year, and new pairs will try to find a space on the outskirts of the colony. The parents incubate their three or four eggs for about four weeks, and the chicks take another eight weeks or so to leave the nest, making their first flights in midsummer. Juveniles can be recognised by their grey crowns, and lack the black eyebrow markings of the adults.

Any garden with a pond may attract this handsome and imposing visitor.

The birds prey mainly on fish but also on other aquatic life, and will hunt on dry land for reptiles and small mammals. A hunting Grey Heron either stands stock-still, waiting for an opportunity to strike, or stalks its prey slowly, but it may also occasionally run after fish in shallow water. To protect your garden fish, use a chicken-wire cover for your pond. Avoid plastic mesh as this can entangle birds. Make sure you provide another water source where birds can drink – ideally a wildlife-friendly pond without ornamental fish.

MOORHEN
Gallinula chloropus

34cm 350g GREEN

This charming chicken-sized bird is a fairly regular visitor to rural gardens and those that adjoin rivers and other open water. It is distinctive both on land and in water owing to its constantly bobbing head and tail. Although a good swimmer, it also spends much time walking on dry land and even scrambling

Long-legged and big-footed, Moorhens are as happy on land as in water.

in trees, and you don't necessarily need to have a pond in your garden to attract it. About 270,000 pairs breed in the UK. Moorhens are very widespread in lowlands, though absent from open uplands and areas without any still or slow-flowing fresh water.

Moorhens nest on the ground, often near water, and lead their chicks to water after the six or so eggs hatch. Both parents incubate the eggs (for three weeks) and care for the young until they are independent (at about eight weeks old). The chicks can swim well from birth but need to be fed by their parents in their early weeks. Juveniles of the first brood remain in their parents' territory and often help feed and care for the chicks in the second brood – an unusual example of cooperative breeding. Juvenile Moorhens are rather nondescript grey-brown birds, but are easily identified if you have a clear view of the white flank-stripe and undertail.

In the garden, Moorhens will feed on natural foods, including all manner of small invertebrates as well as vegetation. They will hoover up any scraps that fall from the bird table, and if you have a pond they will probably explore it.

209

WOODCOCK
Scolopax rusticola

34cm	
280g	RED

When severe winter weather strikes, birds of the wider countryside often seek refuge in gardens, and the Woodcock is a typical example. Like its close relative the Snipe, this is a medium-sized bird of the sandpiper family, with well-camouflaged plumage and a very long bill that it uses to probe soft ground in search of worms and other soil invertebrates. Both species can turn up in gardens – most often in the countryside but occasionally also in towns.

Woodcocks breed in Britain, preferring damp, quiet woodland with ample hiding places on the ground for them to nest. If you head for such woodlands on a warm summer night, you may find males 'roding' – patrolling their territory in high, linear flight, and advertising their presence with sporadic grunting or squeaking calls.

About 78,000 male Woodcocks hold territory in the UK in summer. The species is much more numerous in winter, when nearly 1.5 million birds migrate here from mainland Europe. Autumn migrants often become disorientated and turn up in unexpected places, but it is in freezing and snowy winter weather that you are most likely to find a Woodcock (or a Snipe) visiting the garden. The more severe the weather, the more fearless these birds will be. If possible, keep some patches of soil dug over to help them find food.

The odd eye position gives Woodcocks a near-360-degree field of view.

The Snipe and Woodcock look quite similar, but can be told apart by their head pattern (horizontal stripes in Woodcock, vertical barring in Snipe), and the fact that the Woodcock is bigger and heftier with a proportionately shorter bill.

HERRING GULL
Larus argentatus

60cm	
950–1,200g	RED

If you live in a seaside town, you probably know this bird well – it is the archetypal rooftop-nesting, chip-stealing 'seagull'. It is also increasingly establishing colonies inland. There are about 130,000 pairs nesting in the UK, all around our coastline, but its numbers have fallen dramatically and alarmingly, particularly on the remote clifftops that are its original and natural habitat. The numbers overwintering here from Europe have also fallen.

Herring Gulls build their seaside 'towns' on the rooftops of ours.

Herring Gulls are loosely colonial, though they defend the area around their nest from other pairs, which means that you will probably only ever have one pair nesting on your rooftop. Many adults stay near their breeding site all year, but birds younger than four years old are not ready to breed and lead a more nomadic life, especially in winter. They often roost on inland reservoirs, and by day visit farmland and rubbish dumps to forage.

Many people are not great fans of gulls, and find Herring Gulls in particular to be rather intimidating as well as noisy and messy. Where people regularly throw food for them, Herring Gulls can become quite fearless, and they may also dive-bomb people near their nests. If you can overcome these problems, though, Herring Gulls are fascinating birds to watch, with intelligent and inventive natures to rival any crow or Magpie. In the garden, they will come down to eat almost anything, and will readily snap up any household scraps. Use caged guardian-type feeders to keep them away from food meant for smaller garden visitors.

BLACK-HEADED GULL
Chroicocephalus ridibundus

36cm
250–330g
AMBER

This small gull is the most frequently met member of its family inland, and indeed has no particularly strong ties to the sea. It mainly breeds in marshland, though also on shingle banks and islands in coastal lagoons, as well as on some low-lying offshore islands. It is very widespread in the lowlands of the British Isles, particularly in winter, and in the UK as a whole there are some 140,000 breeding pairs. Numbers shoot up in winter as visitors arrive from further north and west, bringing our population to more than 2 million individuals.

Breeding-plumaged Black-headed Gulls are easy to identify. In winter plumage, the dark brown 'hood' that gives the species its (rather inaccurate) English name is replaced with white, with just a small dusky spot behind the eye, but the bird's size and pronounced white leading edge and black trailing edge to the outer part of the wing make identification easy.

Black-headed Gulls are very common in urban parkland with lakes during winter, and also on open playing fields. They are less frequent in gardens but will often rest on rooftops. They are not comfortable in smaller spaces at ground level, but they will come down for food on larger lawns and may also visit bird tables. They will take all kinds of kitchen scraps. The rarer (and again, rather inaccurately named) Common Gull *Larus canus* often associates with Black-headed Gulls and may occasionally turn up in gardens too. It resembles a smaller, dainty, darkish and long-winged Herring Gull.

The distinctive Black-headed Gull is a regular winter visitor to some gardens.

STOCK DOVE
Columba oenas

33cm
300g
AMBER

This pretty dove is easily overlooked, due to its resemblance to both the Woodpigeon and some colour forms of Feral Pigeon. It is not very common as a garden bird but can be a regular visitor in more rural areas. It is best identified by its smallish size, large black eyes, pinkish bill, and rather plain grey plumage that lacks white patches and has only a faint darker wing-bar.

In the UK there are about 260,000 pairs of Stock Doves. They are found throughout England and Wales, being commonest in the lowlands. They are scarcer in Scotland and Ireland, where they are mainly confined to central and eastern Scotland, and to the south and east of Ireland. They feed on farmland but need tree holes in which to nest, so are rarely encountered far from woodland or copses. Parkland with large mature trees is good Stock Dove habitat. They compete with the likes of Jackdaws, Ring-necked Parakeets and Kestrels for nest sites, and rarely come off best. They were badly affected by pesticide poisoning in the mid-20th century, but their numbers are rising at present (there was a 22 per cent increase in the UK between 1995 and 2015) and if this continues they are likely to be changed from Amber to Green in the UK list of species of conservation concern.

Stock Doves will feed on seed and grain in gardens, both on the ground and on bird tables. They are usually rather timid, but with patience will become confident enough for a closer approach. They may use a large, hole-fronted nest box mounted high on a large tree.

Stock Doves are most frequent in larger, rural gardens but do occur in towns and cities too.

Barn Owls heading out to hunt may fly over local houses and gardens.

BARN OWL
Tyto alba

34cm
300g
GREEN

The beautiful Barn Owl is one of our most easily recognised and most beloved wild birds, even though it is not particularly easy to see. Only householders in the quietest and most rural spots are likely to see Barn Owls in or near the garden, but this bird does have a particular tie to human habitation, usually preferring to nest in buildings. As the species' population continues to recover strongly from the devastating effects of DDT poisoning through the 1950s and 1960s, the chance of an encounter continues to grow. There are about 4,000 pairs in the UK at present, following a spectacular 238 per cent increase between 1995 and 2015.

Barn Owls prey almost exclusively on small rodents and especially on the Field Vole, which is very common in rough grassland, pasture and farmland. They usually hunt at night, but may be active from as early as mid-afternoon when feeding well-grown owlets or if inclement weather curtailed their hunting activities the night before. If your home overlooks farmland, marsh or heath, or other suitable open countryside, look out for Barn Owls at dusk.

If you spot owls active locally, you can try to encourage them to nest by putting up a nest box. Suitable boxes can be purchased or built quite easily, or you can make your own – the Barn Owl Trust offers guidance on this, as well as how to pick the best spot (see Further reading, page 220). Using the correct dimensions is very important to ensure the safety of the growing owlets.

KINGFISHER
Alcedo atthis

16cm
40g
AMBER

The most startlingly colourful British bird, this species is a surprisingly frequent visitor to gardens. Kingfishers are unmistakable with their iridescent blue and green upperparts, orange underside and squat, big-headed and long-billed outline. They are highly specialised feeders, capturing their prey by plunge-diving into water. A diving Kingfisher immerses itself completely and must then fight free of the water while holding its still struggling catch. The prey is usually a small fish but Kingfishers also catch dragonfly larvae and other aquatic invertebrates. They dive either from a perch or from hovering.

Amber-listed because of a steep population decline in the late 1970s and early 1980s, Kingfishers are now faring better, with a 29 per cent increase between 2011 and 2016. Today's population is probably more than 5,000 pairs, and this species can potentially produce three broods of five or six young in a season. Improved water conditions in many streams and rivers in the UK have helped the Kingfisher considerably, but it suffers serious population declines when there is a prolonged winter freeze, as occurred in 2009.

Kingfisher numbers are rising, and garden sightings of this stunning bird are on the increase.

You may have a Kingfisher visit your garden at any time of year if you have a pond or stream. The most likely times, though, are in late summer, when juveniles are dispersing, and in winter when frozen ponds force birds to wander in search of places to feed. Kingfishers seem particularly prone to window strikes, and are also vulnerable to getting tangled in obstacles around water – this is why fishpond guards should be made of chicken wire rather than flexible plastic mesh.

GREEN WOODPECKER
Picus viridis

32cm
190g

GREEN

This striking bird is our largest woodpecker and the only one with green plumage, making it very easily identified. It is usually timid and quick to flee, so the typical view is of a fast-disappearing yellow-green rump and pointed tail. However, if you are lucky enough to have one (or more) visiting the garden, you should have better views. It can be found throughout lowland England and Wales, and sparingly in southern and eastern Scotland, but is not present in Ireland or on most British islands. Some 52,000 pairs breed in the UK.

Unlike the 'pied' woodpeckers, this bird feeds mainly on the ground, where it hops about like an oddly shaped thrush in search of ants' nests. It uses its strong bill to dig into the ground, and its long, sticky tongue to sweep up mouthfuls of ants. Its preferred habitat is grassland with many anthills and large mature trees nearby where it can nest. It excavates a large nesting hole in soft wood, in which it rears one brood of five or so chicks. The juveniles are drabber and streakier than adults until their first moult, in late summer or autumn.

This woodpecker is not a habitual visitor to bird-feeding stations – its preference for feeding on the ground means that it doesn't tend to investigate hanging feeders in the way that Great Spotted Woodpeckers do. You are most likely to have it in the garden if you have a large expanse of lawn, and it may then eat suet pellets or mealworms scattered on the grass.

A shy and well-camouflaged bird, the Green Woodpecker gives itself away with its laughing call.

LESSER SPOTTED WOODPECKER
Dryobates minor

14cm
21g

RED

This tiny woodpecker is, sadly, one of the most threatened British birds, with a population decline of 73 per cent between 1974 and 1999, after which it became too scarce to be effectively monitored through the BTO's Common Bird Census. It appears to have continued to decline since then, and today our breeding population is estimated at just 1,000–2,000 pairs – it's not known why its numbers have fallen so precipitously. It is present in England and Wales but its distribution is very patchy. It occurs mainly in deciduous woodland and prefers to feed high in the trees. In winter, it may join wandering flocks of tits and other small birds.

Like other woodpeckers, these birds drill out their own nest-hole in soft wood (living or dead), and during the breeding season the male proclaims his territory by drumming (more softly and in longer bursts than the Great Spotted Woodpecker) as well as calling (a high, weak *kee kee kee*). Because this is now such an uncommon breeding bird, it's very important to keep well away from its nest site, but if you are lucky enough to have a local pair, they may visit your garden in winter.

Try offering peanuts or suet blocks in hanging cage-style feeders suspended against tree trunks, quite high in the tree and perhaps with some surrounding cover. Beware confusion with juvenile Great Spotted Woodpeckers, which have red crowns like male Lesser Spotteds, but are much larger, with pink rather than white undertails and large white shoulder-patches.

The 'ladder' pattern on the back helps separate this bird from Great Spotted Woodpeckers.

The crest gives this little bird a unique and instantly recognisable silhouette.

CRESTED TIT
Lophophanes cristatus

Birdwatchers visiting the Caledonian pine forests of north-east Scotland will be eager to see the Crested Tit, one of the bird species found there and nowhere else in Britain. If you happen to live in this area, you may well have these delightful little birds visiting your garden. They are very distinctive, with their prominent pointed crests and black-and-white-striped faces – they also have an easily recognised purring call.

Although it is common and widespread on mainland Europe, the Crested Tit has a very small range in Britain, occurring only in pine forest in the Spey valley and surrounding area. It has a breeding population of just 1,500 or so pairs, but its population is probably stable and it is not of any conservation concern. Projects to re-establish more forest in the region could allow it to spread.

In the garden, the Crested Tit is easy to attract and behaves much like other tits, though in its range it is always greatly outnumbered by Coal Tits. It will come to hanging bird feeders of all kinds and also feeds from bird tables and on the ground. Red Squirrels also visit bird feeders and will scare off the small birds. You could address this by putting up a specialised box-type squirrel feeder, to divert their attention. At several nature reserves and woodland parks in the area, feeding stations placed in the forest itself offer visiting birdwatchers a great chance of 'connecting' with Crested Tits, especially in winter.

The Skylark's facial pattern gives the impression that it is wearing spectacles.

SKYLARK
Alauda arvensis

When prolonged freezing weather strikes, this can drive a variety of bird species more usually found in the wider countryside to take shelter in gardens. One of those species is the Skylark, and its arrival in gardens often causes confusion because we are most used to seeing it in its towering songflight over an expanse of pasture, not hunkered down on a snowy lawn.

The Skylark is quite large for a songbird, with a proportionately small head that bears an inconspicuous (in winter) crest. Its plumage is light brown with bold darker streaking. It is easily confused with the Meadow Pipit, another potential cold-winter visitor, but is bulkier with a thicker bill, and its underside streaking is less extensive.

Skylarks are farmland birds, often nesting in arable crop fields as well as in rough grazing pasture. Some modern farming methods, including planting wheat in winter rather than spring, are detrimental to its breeding success, hence its population crash of 63 per cent in England between 1967 and 2016. Its numbers seem now to be stabilising (albeit at a much lower level than a few decades ago) and conservationists have identified several simple ways to support breeding populations on farmland.

If you live near open farmland, look out for Skylarks in winter. They eat insects as well as plant matter, but in winter mainly take seed – scatter some in bare patches near the lawn and you could attract them, along with other seed-eaters like sparrows and buntings.

WAXWING
Bombycilla garrulus

18cm
63g
GREEN

With its outrageous punky crest, beautifully soft-looking pink and peachy-orange plumage with accents of bright yellow and scarlet, and its tendency to arrive in large and fearless flocks, the Waxwing is a very special winter visitor. Its fondness for the ripe berries of Rowan trees, pyracantha shrubs and the like mean that it is also a frequent garden visitor in the years when it arrives in abundance.

Sadly (for birdwatchers at least), most winters do not see a large influx of Waxwings. The species' movements are dictated by food supplies. Two factors apply – a good breeding season in their native Russia and Scandinavia, followed by a poor berry crop that autumn. This means lots of hungry Waxwings and not much food. The result is an 'irruptive' movement, with thousands of birds heading south and west, and arriving on our east coast from late autumn. At the time of writing, the last really big year was winter 2010/11, but even in the 'worst' years a few hundred Waxwings will arrive. They flock around berry-bearing shrubs and trees, strip all the booty and then move on, typically breaking into smaller groups as winter progresses.

You are more likely to see Waxwings if you live in the north and east. The first arrivals in autumn are often in Shetland, and eastern Scottish towns like Aberdeen are perfectly placed to receive them. In big years, though, they will spread right across the British Isles. They are nearly impossible to miss when they do appear, and in addition to berries will feed avidly on apples and other fruits.

In a 'big' year, almost any garden with fruiting bushes or trees could attract Waxwings.

The simple, rather slow-paced two-note song of the Chiffchaff can be heard from mid-March.

CHIFFCHAFF
Phylloscopus collybita

10cm
9g
GREEN

This little bird is a summer visitor that has, over the last few decades, become increasingly common in winter as well. Most British Chiffchaffs (some 1.2 million pairs) do migrate south to Iberia and North Africa, but at least some of the 500–1,000 or so that are here in winter appear to be local breeders. Others probably join us from further north-east.

The Chiffchaff is a 'leaf warbler', one of a group of small, slender, insect-eating birds with greenish plumage that forage mainly in trees. Wintering Chiffchaffs often join groups of other small birds such as Goldcrests and rove around trees and bushes, searching dead leaves and bark fissures for small hibernating insects. Their fine bill allows them to access small spaces that thicker-billed, more generalist feeders like the tits cannot reach. With their very small bodies, they are extremely vulnerable to cold and so are most common in areas where the mean temperature stays a little higher than average, such as in towns and around industrial sites, as well as gardens (including in town centres).

It is possible that you could see Chiffchaffs in the garden at other times too. From mid-March, listen for the male's repetitive two-note song, which is rather like that of the Great Tit but slower-paced. In autumn, migrating Chiffchaffs may pass through your garden, and you could also see migrant Willow Warblers *Phylloscopus trochilus*. These are very similar, but longer-winged, and the young birds are a distinctively rich yellow on their undersides (Chiffchaffs look drabber).

Spotted Flycatchers have an alert look, and appear big-headed with very long wings.

SPOTTED FLYCATCHER
Muscicapa striata

14cm 17g RED

In the mid-20th century, it was not unusual for even quite small town gardens to have a breeding pair of Spotted Flycatchers. However, this species underwent an 87 per cent decline in the UK between 1967 and 2016, placing it decisively on the Red list of species of conservation concern and making its presence in most gardens nothing but a memory. The fall is thought to be related to habitat changes in its African wintering grounds, but it is also affected by the wholesale decline of larger flying insects in Britain and elsewhere.

Spotted Flycatchers are sleek, long-winged songbirds, which fly out from favourite perches to seize flies, moths, damselflies and other winged insects, their broad-based bills closing on their victim with an audible snap. They visit us in summer and are among the last species to arrive, usually not appearing until the second or third week of May. Even so, they usually manage to fit in two broods before heading south again in autumn.

They prefer woodland edges with sunny spots, as well as large parks, churchyards and rural gardens. As hole-nesters, they prefer areas with some mature trees that will have suitable cavities. Although they will not take any bird-table fare, they will use open-fronted nest boxes – it's well worth placing a box or two in sheltered high places in the garden if you ever see the birds locally. A wildlife-friendly garden with plenty of insect-attracting flowers will help nesting Spotted Flycatchers to breed successfully.

Coloration aside, the Black Redstart has a definite similarity to the Robin in its shape and stance.

BLACK REDSTART
Phoenicurus ochruros

14cm 16g RED

Any book about garden birds in mainland western Europe will mention the Black Redstart, a mountain bird that has adapted to the urban environment. However, although this species commonly delivers its strangely gravelly song from rooftops in villages, towns and cities over much of France, it is a real rarity in Britain, with a breeding population of only 30 or so pairs. Most of these occur around large, often derelict buildings in city outskirts – east London is a stronghold.

In spring and autumn, migrating Black Redstarts turn up along our coasts and may linger for a while – about 400 individuals will stay with us through the whole winter. These birds come to us from Europe, and are most frequent along eastern, southern and south-western coasts. They often gravitate towards urban areas and will turn up in seaside gardens.

At first glance, the Black Redstart looks rather like a Robin, with the same upright posture, hopping gait and general body proportions. Both sexes have the shivering red tail that distinguishes redstarts as a group, and older adult males are unmistakable with their black body plumage, but young males and females are smoky grey-brown. They could be confused with females of Redstart *P. phoenicurus*, but that species is much warmer brown and is not with us in winter. If you are lucky enough to find this bird in your garden, try offering dried or live mealworms – it will also take suet foods, from bird tables or the ground.

GREY WAGTAIL
Motacilla cinerea

 18cm
 18g
RED

With its strikingly long tail, bright plumage and bold, strutting manner, this is an eye-catching little bird and a very welcome, though uncommon, garden visitor. Grey Wagtails are quite widespread in the British Isles and mainly breed around fast-flowing streams and rivers, hunting in the shallows as well as catching flies over the water. In winter, many Grey Wagtails move away to lowland areas and can be found exploring lake shores, weirs, flat roofs and other areas with standing or flowing water. If your garden has a large pond that includes some kind of flowing water feature, you may attract this bird in winter, and over time it can become delightfully confiding.

The species is strictly insectivorous, and its historical population decline (a sharp fall between 1970 and 1985) may be related to river pollution, reducing the number of stoneflies, mayflies and other insects with aquatic early life stages. The population trend since 1990 has fluctuated, but there was another short, sharp drop around 2010, when very severe winters took their toll (as was the case with many other insect-eating species).

Although its plumage varies with age and sex, the Grey Wagtail always has a bright yellow lower belly and undertail, making it easily distinguishable from the Pied Wagtail. It is also more likely to stay close to water, while Pied Wagtails often forage on the lawn. Offer mealworms (dried or fresh) to tempt your Grey Wagtail to stay – some individuals will hang around the same garden for weeks on end, especially in cold spells.

The vivid yellow undertail makes the Grey Wagtail eye-catching, even in its grey plumage.

With its spotted breast, the Meadow Pipit recalls a miniature thrush.

MEADOW PIPIT
Anthus pratensis

14cm
19g
AMBER

This very widespread species is the archetypal 'little brown job', with its rather nondescript streaky plumage. It is found in open countryside of all kinds, from farmland, marshland and heathland to high, bleak moor, and with a population of nearly 2 million pairs it is one of our most common songbirds. However, it is enduring a prolonged period of gradual decline, with a fall of 46 per cent in England between 1967 and 2016, and of 7 per cent in the UK between 1995 and 2016. More recently, it has shown a small increase, especially in Scotland (a 21 per cent rise between 2011 and 2016).

Meadow Pipits are not typically garden visitors but, like Skylarks, will come into gardens, especially in open rural areas, in very cold weather. They forage inconspicuously in the grass, searching for insects and small seeds, and when disturbed fly up steeply with a loud, plaintive *weet weet* call. They often roam in small flocks in winter.

If you have a large garden with areas of lawn or meadow, look out for this bird in winter and try offering dry or live mealworms if you see it. The largest, most rural gardens may even attract the birds to breed, though as ground-nesters they are at very high risk of losing their brood to marauding cats. The presence of Meadow Pipits in the local area significantly increases the chance of you seeing a Cuckoo, as they are among the Cuckoo's favourite hosts (along with Dunnocks and Reed Warblers).

The Hawfinch has subtle but pleasing coloration, and a unique silhouette.

HAWFINCH
Coccothraustes coccothraustes

18cm
58g
RED

As a group, finches are quite reliable garden visitors. The Hawfinch, however, is not, because of its rarity and very shy nature. About 500–1,000 pairs breed in the UK, and up to 15,000 more arrive in winter from mainland Europe – occasionally a lot more. In late autumn 2017, the reporting rate was 12 times higher than average, and these exceptional numbers allowed many birdwatchers throughout the UK to see the species for the first time.

This is our biggest and heaviest finch by far. Even if you only see it silhouetted in a high treetop (regrettably, this is a typical view!), its large head and extremely hefty bill make it readily identifiable. Seen close at hand, its plumage is distinctive and very beautiful, with shades of orange, chestnut, blue-black and dove grey, but it is a lucky UK householder who ever sees a Hawfinch in the garden, even though in northern Europe it can be a regular bird-table attendant.

This species' distribution is very patchy. Most of its breeding strongholds are in England, but in winter it is very unpredictable. It has a fondness for Hornbeam *Carpinus betulus*, Beech and cherry trees, feeding on their seeds, and will eat all kinds of other seeds. If you live close to deciduous woodland and have a large, quiet garden with trees, you may be lucky enough to see this magnificent finch on the bird table – but there is more chance you'll spot it perched in a high treetop, warily surveying the scene.

LINNET
Linaria cannabina

14cm
19g
RED

Although this finch is quite common and not particularly shy, it remains curiously scarce as a garden visitor. Many reported sightings of Linnets visiting gardens are actually misidentified redpolls, which are superficially similar – Linnets are larger, though, and lack the redpolls' distinctive dark patch in front of the eye.

Linnets occur in farmland, marshland and other open countryside with some scrub and bushes. They often nest in hedgerows, the pink-breasted male singing sweetly from a high perch while the female builds a beautifully crafted and well-hidden nest deep in a thorny shrub or tucked away on the ground. Come autumn, adult and young Linnets join forces to form sometimes huge flocks, which roam in search of weedy clumps, stubble-fields and other feeding grounds. The flocks are often augmented by Goldfinches.

Like many farmland birds, Linnets underwent a serious decline in the UK between 1970 and the late 1980s, in response to changes in farming practices that reduced their food supply and nesting habitat. Since 1990, numbers have been stable overall, though a more detailed look reveals that the species is continuing to decline in most eastern areas, while increasing slightly in the west.

If your garden does attract Linnets, they will feed on all kinds of smaller seeds, especially sunflower hearts and nyjer, from hanging feeders and on bird tables. You are most likely to attract them if your garden is rural, close to farmland or undisturbed coastal marshland, and has some native bushes. A meadow area with native wildflowers will provide a source of natural food for them in the form of seeds.

Though it is numerous in Britain, the Linnet is an open-country finch and is rare in gardens.

Further Reading

RSPB (rspb.org.uk)

The RSPB is the leading body for conservation of birds and other wildlife in Britain. Its website offers advice on a number of activities, including how to build a garden pond, large or small,(rspb.org.uk/birds-and-wildlife/advice/gardening-for-wildlife/water-for-wildlife/making-a-pond), and how to grow a wildflower meadow in your garden (rspb.org.uk/get-involved/activities/give-nature-a-home-in-your-garden/garden-activities/startawildflowermeadow/).

The RSPB also runs the world's largest garden wildlife survey – the Big Garden Birdwatch. (Further details can be found here rspb.org.uk/get-involved/activities/birdwatch.)

British Trust for Ornithology (bto.org)

The British Trust for Ornithology (BTO) is a charity devoted to understanding the population and distribution of birds in Britain, with a particular focus on how and why bird populations are changing. It operates a number of nationwide surveys to which all birdwatchers and volunteers can contribute.

The Garden BirdWatch survey, first started in 1994, asks volunteers to become 'citizen scientists' by keeping a record of the number of birds seen in their garden all year round. If you would like to participate in this project, or indeed any of the other garden-based projects organised by the BTO, further information can be found here bto.org/volunteer-surveys/gbw/about.

You can log sightings of birds at any time using the BTO's BirdTrack website (bto.org/volunteer-surveys/birdtrack/about) or app.

The BTO also offers detailed guides on things you can do to help and support our garden birds, including how to make a nest box (bto.org/how-you-can-help/nnbw/make-a-nest-box).

Rare Breeding Birds Panel (rbbp.org.uk)

The Rare Breeding Birds Panel (RBBP) collects data on very rare bird species breeding in the UK and publishes its reports online (rbbp.org.uk). If you have Willow Tits nesting in your garden, or if you see any evidence of breeding behaviour, you should inform the RBBP.

Independent Bird Register (independentbirdregister.co.uk)

The Independent Bird Register was established in 1994 to help ensure that lost and found birds could be reunited with their keepers. If you encounter an escapee bird of prey, it can be reported using the contact information available on their website.

iRecord (brc.ac.uk/irecord)

You can log your bird, and other wildlife, sightings any time using the iRecord website or app. Recording this information can help support research, and make a real contribution to science and conservation.

Brambling Numbers

If you are interested in how many Bramblings are arriving on our coasts as autumn progresses, you can use bird reports from north-east coastal areas, including bird observatories on Fair Isle (fairislebirdobs.co.uk), Filey (fbog.co.uk), Flamborough (fbo.org.uk), Holme (noa.org.uk) and Landguard (lbo.org.uk).

The Barn Owl Trust (barnowltrust.org.uk)

The Barn Owl Trust is a charity dedicated to conserving the Barn Owl. If you notice owls that are active locally, you can encourage them to nest by putting up a nest box. The Barn Owl Trust offers guidance on how to build your own nest box, as well as how to pick the best spot (barnowltrust.org.uk/barn-owl-nestbox/barn-owl-nestboxes).

Acknowledgements

I would like to thank Julie Bailey at Bloomsbury for commissioning this book, and Jenny Campbell for applying her editorial and managerial skills to see the project through to completion. My thanks are also due to the copy-editor, Lucy Beevor, the page designer, Lee-May Lim, and the proofreader, Susi Bailey, who worked on the text and layout as they have developed. I am also grateful to the many photographers whose lovely images grace these pages. The RSPB's advice and guidance throughout the research and writing process has been invaluable, and I have also benefited from the expertise and experience of many 'bird people', friends and colleagues – from field ornithologists to amateur (but passionate) garden birdwatchers – in expanding my own knowledge and appreciation of Britain's wonderful garden birdlife.

Although I've not always been lucky enough to have a home with a garden, I've always had unfettered access to some wonderful and wildlife-rich gardens in both town and country, thanks to friends and family. I'm grateful to all of them for this generosity, and for the many moments of wildlife-watching that we have shared.

Photographic credits

Bloomsbury Publishing would like to thank the following for providing photographs and for permission to reproduce copyright material within this book. While every effort has been made to trace and acknowledge all copyright holders, we would like to apologise for any errors or omissions and invite readers to inform us so that we can make corrections at future editions.

Key: t = top; tl = top left; tr = top right; c = centre; b = bottom; bl = bottom left; br = bottom right, l = left, r = right.
AL = Alamy; GI = Getty Images; IS = iStock; NPL = Nature Picture Library; RS = RSPB Images; SS = Shutterstock.

Front cover Laurie Campbell/RS; **back cover** Stephan Rech/GI; **1** Ben Hall/RS; **2** Paul Sawer/RS; **6** Nigel Blake/RS; **8** Richard P Long/SS; **9** David Tipling/birdphoto.co.uk; **11** David Tipling/birdphoto.co.uk; **12** David Tipling/birdphoto.co.uk; **14** Will Howe/SS; **15** Mark Richardson Imaging; **17** Andy Hay/RS; **18** Peter Turner Photography/SS; **19** Ray Kennedy/RS; **20** Ian McGlasham/SS; **22** Gary Chalker/GI; **24** David Tipling/birdphoto.co.uk; **25** David Tipling/birdphoto.co.uk; **26–27** Ben Hall/2020 VISION/NPL; **28–29** David Tipling/birdphoto.co.uk; **30** David Tipling/birdphoto.co.uk; **33** Kletr/SS; **34** David Tipling/birdphoto.co.uk; **35** Mart R Porter/AL; **36** David Tipling/birdphoto.co.uk; **37** David Tipling/birdphoto.co.uk; **38** David Tipling/birdphoto.co.uk; **39** t NDavid Tipling/birdphoto.co.uk; **41** clarst5/SS; **42** David Tipling/birdphoto.co.uk; **43** t David Tipling/birdphoto.co.uk, b David Tipling/birdphoto.co.uk; **44** Martin Mecnarowski/SS; **45** Ben Hall/RS; **46** David Tipling/birdphoto.co.uk; **47** t Steven R Smith/SS, b H-AB Photography/SS; **48** Wildlife World/SS; **49** tl Erni/SS, tr Coatesy/SS, b TashaBubo/SS; **50–51** Paul Hobson/NPL; **52** Targn Pleiades/SS; **53** David Tipling/birdphoto.co.uk; **55** t Andrew Turner/AL, b Kaleel Zibe/RS; **56** El Coronesta/SS; **57** Mark Sisson/RS; **58** t Carel Fabritius/Public Domain, b David Tipling/birdphoto.co.uk; **59** David Kjaer/RS; **60** Erni/SS; **61** t Ronald Wilfred Jansen/SS, b Ondrej Prosicky/SS; **62** David Tipling/birdphoto.co.uk; **64** Anton MirMar/SS; **65** David Tipling/birdphoto.co.uk; **66** Marianne Taylor; **67** Mark Hamblin/RS; **68** Abi Warner/SS; **69** Marianne Taylor; **70** David Tipling/birdphoto.co.uk; **71** Ernie Janes/RS; **72** SS; **73** Wildscotphotos/AL; **74** David Tipling/birdphoto.co.uk; **75** SanderMeertinsPhotography/SS; **76–77** Andrew Mason/RS; **78** Steve Byland/SS; **79** David Tipling/birdphoto.co.uk; **80** ExclusivePictures/SS; **81** MyImages – Micha/SS; **82** janveber/SS; **84** Heritage Image Partnership Ltd/AL; **85** Drakuliren/SS; **86** David Tipling/birdphoto.co.uk; **87** t IanRedding/SS, b Sandra Standbridge/SS; **88** Marianne Taylor; **89** Piotr Kamionka/SS; **90–91** David Tipling/birdphoto.co.uk; **92** Kerrick/IS; **93** David Tipling/birdphoto.co.uk; **94** David Tipling/birdphoto.co.uk; **95** COULANGES/SS; **96** David Tipling/birdphoto.co.uk; **97** t Sandra Standbridge/SS, b Karel Bartik/SS; **98** t Erni/SS, b M Rose/SS; **100** David Tipling/birdphoto.co.uk; **101** Jan Sevcik/RS; **102** David Tipling/birdphoto.co.uk; **103** t Paolo-manzi/SS, b Oliver Smart/RS; **104** David Tipling/birdphoto.co.uk; **105** Marianne Taylor; **106** Julian Popov/SS; **107** t Wildlife World/SS, b Nick Vorobey/SS; **108–109** Markus Varesvuo/NPL; **110** Jozef Sowa/SS; **111** t Mark Richardson Imaging, b Sandra Standbridge/SS; **112** David Tipling/birdphoto.co.uk; **113** David Norton/RS; **114** Marianne Taylor; **115** Abi Warner/SS; **116** Bob Glover/RS; **117** tony mills/SS; **118** Michal Pesata/SS; **119** Erni/SS; **120** Brent Stephenson/NPL; **121** David Tipling/birdphoto.co.uk; **122** David Tipling/birdphoto.co.uk; **123** Steve Round/RS; **124** Roger Tidman/RS; **125** Erni/SS; **126** David Tipling/birdphoto.co.uk; **127** Steve Round/RS; **128** t Genevieve Vallee/AL, b Robert Orchard/GI; **129** Petr Simon/SS; **130** David Tipling/birdphoto.co.uk; **131** David Tipling/birdphoto.co.uk; **132–133** Nick Upton/NPL; **134** vcaenis/SS; **135** Maciej Olszewski/SS; **136** birdpix/AL; **138** David Tipling/birdphoto.co.uk; **139** t Chris Gomersall/RS, b Abi Warner/SS; **140** David Tipling/birdphoto.co.uk; **141** t AGAMI Photo Agency/AL, b Maslov Dmitry/SS; **142** Karel Bartik/SS; **143** David Tipling/birdphoto.co.uk; **144** David Tipling/birdphoto.co.uk; **145** Marianne Taylor; **146** Hayley Crews/SS; **147** t Ernie Janes/RS, b Frank Hecker/AL; **148** David Tipling/birdphoto.co.uk; **149** rock ptarmigan/SS; **150** Erni/SS; **151** Richard Packwood/RS; **152–153** David Tipling/birdphoto.co.uk; **154** Erni/SS; **155** t Viktor Busel/SS, b David Tipling/birdphoto.co.uk; **156** Sandra Standbridge/SS; **157** MMCez/SS; **158** David Tipling/birdphoto.co.uk; **159** David Tipling/birdphoto.co.uk; **160** Nigel Blake/RS; **161** Erni/SS; **162** Davydele/SS; **163** David Tipling/birdphoto.co.uk; **164** Jenny Hibbert/RS; **166–167** Edwin Giesbers/NPL; **168** Mark Richardson Imaging; **169** Erni/SS; **170** t Marianne Taylor, b Ondrej Chvatal/SS; **171** Tobyphotos/SS; **172** Dennis Jacobsen/SS; **174** Valentin Valkov/SS; **175** David Tipling/birdphoto.co.uk; **176** El Coronesta/SS; **177** stockphoto mania/SS; **178–179** Terry Whittaker/NPL; **180** Mark Medcalf/SS; **181** Ernie Janes/RS; **182** Arco Images GmbH/AL; **183** Erni/SS; **184** David Tipling/birdphoto.co.uk; **185** Christophe Courteau/NPL; **186** t Marianne Taylor, b David Tipling/birdphoto.co.uk; **187** t JohnatAPW/SS, b Somogyi Laszlo/SS; **188** Daniel Dunca/SS; **189** Mark Bridger/SS; **190** Richard Brooks/RS; **191** Helen J Davies/SS; **192–193** Richard Bedford/RS; **194** Borislav Borisov/SS; **195** David Tipling/birdphoto.co.uk; **196** Emil Von Maltitz/GI; **198** David Tipling/birdphoto.co.uk; **199** t flaviano fabrizi/SS, b Paul Broadbent/SS; **200** Victor Suarez Naranjo/SS; **201** Andrew Linscott/SS; **202** Markus Varesvuo/NPL; **203** l David Tipling/birdphoto.co.uk, c Alex Puddephatt/SS, r Asakoulis/SS; **204** WildPictures/AL; **205** Jaro Mikus/SS; **206–207** Kevin Sawford/RS; **208** t David Tipling/birdphoto.co.uk, b David Tipling/birdphoto.co.uk; **209** t SS, b Sandra Standbridge/SS; **210** t Toni Genes/SS, b bearacreative/SS; **211** t Tomasz Kowalski/SS, Erni/SS; **212** t David Tipling/birdphoto.co.uk, b Scott M Ward/SS; **213** t Marcin Perkowski/SS, b David Tipling/birdphoto.co.uk; **214** t David Tipling/birdphoto.co.uk, b Erni/SS; **215** t Rowland Cole/SS, b Sandra Standbridge/SS; **216** t M Rose/SS, b David Tipling/birdphoto.co.uk; **216** t M Rose/SS, b David Tipling/birdphoto.co.uk; **217** Erni/SS; **218** t Marianne Taylor, b Carl Day/SS; **219** David Tipling/birdphoto.co.uk.

Index